DISABILITY AND SOCIAL CHANGE

Private lives and public policies

Sonali Shah and Mark Priestley

First published in Great Britain in 2011 by

The Policy Press
University of Bristol
Fourth Floor
Beacon House
Queen's Road
Bristol BS8 1QU
UK

Tel +44 (0)117 331 4054
Fax +44 (0)117 331 4093
e-mail tpp-info@bristol.ac.uk
www.policypress.co.uk

North American office:
The Policy Press
c/o International Specialized Books Services (ISBS)
920 NE 58th Avenue, Suite 300
Portland, OR 97213-3786, USA
Tel +1 503 287 3093
Fax +1 503 280 8832
e-mail info@isbs.com

© The Policy Press 2010

British Library Cataloguing in Publication Data
A catalogue record for this book is available from the British Library.

Library of Congress Cataloging-in-Publication Data
A catalog record for this book has been requested.

ISBN 978 1 84742 786 1 paperback
ISBN 978 1 84742 787 8 hardcover

The right of Sonali Shah and Mark Priestley to be identified as authors of this work has been asserted by them in accordance with the 1988 Copyright, Designs and Patents Act.

Cover design by The Policy Press
Front cover: image kindly supplied by Getty Images
Printed and bound in Great Britain by TJ International, Padstow
The Policy Press uses environmentally responsible print partners.

FSC
www.fsc.org
MIX
Paper from
responsible sources
FSC® C013056

Contents

Acknowledgements

At the heart of this book are the life stories of many individual people (who, for reasons of confidentiality, appear under self-selected pseudonyms in the text). We are especially grateful to each of them for their generosity in sharing such intimate accounts of their lives.

The research on which the book is based was made possible by the award of a three-year Nuffield New Career Development Fellowship, hosted by the Centre for Disability Studies at the University of Leeds. We are particularly grateful to the Nuffield Foundation for the additional flexibility of support they provided during this project.

We would also like to extend our thanks to the many colleagues, in the School of Sociology and Social Policy and beyond, who informed our thinking, commented on draft material or helped in more practical ways to make the research possible. Particular acknowledgement is due to Nick Ellison, Saul Becker, Bren Neale, Sarah Irwin, Anne Borsay and Dan Goodley.

Introduction

The second half of the 20th century, perhaps more than any other period, produced great changes in how we think about and respond to disability as a public issue in Britain. Not only was there a proliferation of new public policies but also an awakening of political consciousness about disability. But what of those who lived their lives through this period? How do the lives of young disabled people today compare with those who grew up in previous generations? In short, has life changed? This book seeks answers to these questions by using a combination of biographical experiences and historical policy analysis.

The source material came from a three-year empirical research project conducted at the University of Leeds and funded by the Nuffield Foundation. In particular, the biographical narratives used for illustration are drawn from a selection of 50 life history interviews with three generations of women and men (born in the 1940s, 1960s and 1980s) who grew up in England. Each of these generational cohorts grew up in changing times. The oldest generation were born during, or shortly after, the Second World War and grew up with attempts to more systematically address disability in British social policy (and the emergence of the post-war welfare state). The second generation, born in the 1960s, experienced childhood and early adulthood at a time when assumptions about the social exclusion of disabled people were coming under scrutiny (for example, in critiques of segregated care and special schools, and in the rise of the early disabled people's movement). The youngest cohort, born in the 1980s, are the first generation to reach early adulthood in an era of non-discrimination and human rights legislation affecting all aspects of their lives.

The book focuses on the stories of those who were diagnosed or labelled with physical impairments prior to compulsory school age (that is, from birth or infancy) and includes people who grew up in Northern, Southern, urban and rural parts of England (although one participant had attended school in Scotland before moving to England). This selection includes 15 people representing the oldest generation, 19 from the middle generation, and 16 from the youngest generation (a total of 50 out of 60 interviews).

The selection of stories is not statistically representative and the aim was to elicit a diversity of life experiences while balancing age cohorts with gender, and including ethnic minority experiences where possible. Recruitment was largely by voluntary response to project publicity (disseminated through general media, disability magazines, disability organisations, educational institutions, leisure and service providers).

In terms of gender, it proved particularly difficult to recruit men with childhood physical impairments from the oldest generation to share their personal stories, and they were under-represented (there were no difficulties in recruiting men from the middle and youngest cohorts). The generational boundaries were also 'stretched' slightly. For example, it was more important that the oldest cohort completed schooling and entered the adult labour market before the 1970 Chronically Sick and Disabled Persons Act than that they were born precisely within the '1940s' (e.g. the selection includes one man born in 1951 and one woman born in 1938).

The book addresses a variety of themes through these first-hand accounts but, as the title suggests, it focuses on the relationship between changes in public policies and people's private lives. Importantly, it aims to move beyond the individual stories to consider what they can reveal about wider trends and developments over time. The evidence illustrates how policies, institutions, environments and relationships framed the choices available to young disabled people and their families as they negotiated their lives. Public policies and institutions have a powerful influence in shaping life choices and chances. They may have unintended consequences too, beyond their public purpose. For example, policies on health care, education or employment may have dramatic impacts on people's family lives, social relationships and self-identity.

Examining historical change through the connections between private lives and public policies allows for discussion of agency and choice as well as structure and environment. In this way, the book affords an opportunity to understand more about the ways in which people negotiate, resist and subvert the life transitions and expectations that are thrown up by public policies. Indeed, personal accounts underline how people often live their lives in spite of, rather than because of, public support and policy expectations.

This book could be read in different ways. It will no doubt be of interest as an account of change in public policies and institutions affecting disabled people during a particularly significant historical period. It provides testament to the lived experience of growing up with physical impairment and disability in a changing world. It also seeks to contribute to greater understanding of the contingencies of doing qualitative longitudinal research and disability history.

As authors, it has been an intriguing and challenging journey to weave our version of history from the warp and weft of the 'stories' and 'facts'. Our stimulus came from those who so generously shared their life experiences but we wanted to move beyond the 'biographical'. The stories provided many examples that support familiar claims in the disability studies literature but there were also surprises, traces of less well-known policy developments and pointers to less well-rehearsed debates. We have not sought to contest the validity of the accounts people gave us about their own lives but we have located them in a wider social, historical and theoretical context. For this interpretation we take complete responsibility. The writing was completed shortly after the General Election of 2010 but, where possible, we have also noted early changes in government policy.

The book is organised into seven main chapters, followed by a shorter conclusion. The first chapter introduces, briefly, some of the key themes that have framed British disability policy debates in recent decades and takes a closer look at the core sociological challenge of connecting biography with history. In the context of disability this raises important questions about the place of personal experience in public politics and in disability research.

The second chapter moves directly to examine some of the individual stories generated during the research. It provides short summary versions of six life stories, two people from each of the three generations. Each pair of stories raises discussion about the kinds of social contexts and policy changes that have impacted on life choices and chances. The issues raised are then summarised in key points. The remaining chapters are arranged thematically, exploring a range of topics concerned with the connections between private lives and public policies.

Chapter Three examines how public policies and institutions, notably hospitals and schools, impacted on children's opportunities to develop and sustain family life and relationships. It illustrates the importance attached to family and to informal support networks in the biographical accounts (often as sources of agency and resistance against the disabling influence of public policies). Chapter Four then looks, more specifically, at the role of medical institutions and medical authority in the lives of young people with physical impairments. It illustrates change in the influence of health professions over non-medical decisions in people's lives, and change in medical and therapeutic regimes.

Chapter Five focuses on educational provision, particularly on schooling, as influential in shaping life experiences and expectations (including changes in the selection and allocation of pupils to different types of schools and the social implications of segregated schooling). Moving from childhood into adulthood, Chapter Six explores change in employment policies and the impact this has had on young people's life opportunities and career expectations (including entry into the adult labour market, treatment and support at work, and changes in the labour market).

Chapter Seven returns to a more holistic approach, reflecting on the ways in which public policies and institutions have framed young people's attempts to make sense of disability in their private lives. The treatment of disability as a public issue creates both opportunities and barriers in negotiating personal relationships and identities. The discussion here illustrates the personal impact of direct and indirect discrimination, of the social spaces created by public institutions, of changes in access to role models and the emergence of new kinds of social and cultural capital through disability politics and culture.

Overall, the aim of the book is to reveal how life has 'changed' for young disabled people growing up in Britain from the 1940s to the present day. It seeks, somewhat ambitiously, to reveal the interplay between biography and history, between the private and the public, and between the micro and the macro, over time. In so doing, it introduces new biographical data and new ways of approaching it. By using evidence from life stories in critical ways, to reveal and contest historical evidence, it seeks to move beyond the 'biographical turn' in social science and to show how critical policy analysis adds value to stories, and vice versa.

ONE

Policy, history and biography

This chapter sets the scene for the book's main themes, by examining the challenge of linking biography with history in terms of disability policy in 20th-century Britain. As explained in the Introduction, some of the key areas of policy that have affected people's personal lives are explored in more detail in subsequent chapters, including areas such as the provision of public health care, education and employment. The main purpose of this chapter is to provide a context for reading the individual biographical experiences related in Chapter Two.

The chapter begins by briefly outlining some of the key change dimensions in public policy since the 1940s, comparing the current state of the art with past policy developments and policy claims arising from the disabled people's movement. The second part moves to a more detailed discussion of how individual biography can be used to reveal, and raise questions about, these social changes.

Changing policies and claims

The disability studies and policy literature has provided much evidence that people with impairments are disadvantaged in important areas of social life, such as education, employment, family life, political participation, cultural representation; or in access to public goods and services, like transport, housing, access to information, and so on (for example, Topliss, 1975; Barnes, 1991; Prime Minister's Strategy Unit, 2005; Williams et al, 2008). The challenge is to explain how and why this happens but also to gauge the extent to which the situation changes over time and whether changes in public policies have real impacts on people's lives.

Alongside continuing concerns about the considerable inequalities and barriers that face disabled people in Britain there has also been mounting evidence of change in the treatment of disability as a public issue (in public attitudes towards disability; in the emergence of the disabled people's movement; in the shift from welfare-based to rights-based social policies; in technological developments; and in labour market opportunities, for example). While we do not share the unguarded optimism of some policy makers, it is our hypothesis that young disabled people in 21st-century Britain are making life choices in a different opportunity structure from their recent predecessors. To put this into context, it is worth taking a brief tour of the changing policy landscape over the past 70 years.

Developments in the post-war period

The dramatic political and policy innovations of the 1940s were widely credited with ushering in the modern British welfare state (for example, Bruce, 1966) although its origins were already clearly evident before the middle of the 20th century (Roberts, 1960; Fraser, 1973). The foundations for national insurance and health services provision had been laid before the war but publication of the much-vaunted Beveridge Report in 1942 marked a turning point towards more comprehensive social protection and security throughout the life course, 'from the cradle to the grave'. Within this context, the government position on disability was summarised by the then Minister of Health, Henry Willink:

> The question of assisting persons, such as the blind or cripples, who suffer from permanent disablement, whether total or partial, is engaging the attention of the Government in connection with the proposals in the Beveridge Report. The aim of the Government is to rehabilitate them wherever possible. (*Hansard*, 20 January 1944, v396, c374W)

The emphasis on rehabilitation (and prevention) took for granted a leading role for hospital medicine. However, in the broader scheme, 'rehabilitation' was also characterised by social policies that sought greater social inclusion and recognition of rights to greater public participation. Thus, disability was being considered anew in terms of key areas like education, employment and social protection.

Debates on social protection had been coloured by concerns to ensure social justice in the post-war period (by 1942 there were already some 38,000 people receiving forces pensions in the 'total disablement' category at an annual cost of £4.5 million). In the case of employment resettlement (discussed in Chapter Six) public concern had been heightened by the moral cause of those with physical impairments arising from service in the armed forces. Thus, in a debate on the National Insurance (Industrial Injuries) Bill in 1946 Members were urged to ensure 'that such men are in no degree worse treated than are casualties in civilian life' (*Hansard*, 18 February 1946, v419, cc800-917). For example, it was intended that exemption of War Disablement

Pension from income tax should mean that a disabled veteran in work could be 'better off than he [sic.] was before he was disabled' (*Hansard*, 20 July 1943, v391, cc716-864).

Among key legislative Acts, the introduction of Family Allowances in 1945, the 1946 National Insurance Act and the 1948 National Assistance Act all had something to say about disability. The 1948 Act gave local authorities new powers to expand welfare services, although they were not widely exercised until later. This enabling policy framework laid the groundwork for the array of social services and community-based supports that would rapidly expand through the 1970s and 1980s.

The 1944 Disabled Persons (Employment) Act set out an apparently comprehensive package that sought to combine employment guarantees with compensatory 'sheltered' work and targeted individualised interventions to prepare people to enter the labour market. Similarly, the 1944 Education Act established, at least in principle, an expectation that disabled children could be taught alongside their peers although it also strengthened the institutional and administrative segregation of special schools. The historical significance of these post-war developments has been reviewed at some length (notably by Topliss, 1975; Barnes, 1991; Borsay, 2005) yet the ensuing decades saw a growing disillusionment about the fulfilment of ambitious policy goals, fuelled by an increasing evidence base demonstrating continuing exclusion.

Reports in the 1950s (for example, Department of Education and Science, 1956) urged greater support for disabled children and their families at home, while a 1957 Royal Commission on the Law Relating to Mental Illness and Mental Deficiency flagged increasing concerns over the conditions of residential institutions. The Survey of the Handicapped and Impaired in Great Britain was conducted in 1968–69, focusing on living conditions and needs for service provision (see Harris et al, 1971).

Implementation of the 1970 Chronically Sick and Disabled Persons Act is widely heralded as a significant development, although, as Topliss and Gould (1981) argue, many of its enabling provisions built only incrementally on the 1948 National Assistance Act. Local authority social services departments were newly established, following the 1969 Seebohm Report, and sought to provide a unified system of public social work, focused on support for the family. There were moves towards more support for community living and more targeted social security benefits (see Topliss, 1979).

Rights and responsibilities

In a changing political climate, the 1970 Equal Pay Act, 1975 Sex Discrimination Act and 1976 Race Relations Act had begun to respond to equal rights claims from feminist and anti-racist movements. By contrast, parallel claims from disabled people were only beginning to be heard by the mid-1970s (non-discrimination legislation would take two more decades). However, with the growth of health consumerism (Zola, 1972; 1977) and a breakdown of the post-war welfare state consensus (Abel-Smith, 2005) there were increasing opportunities to challenge the authority of public services and their associated professions. Lay challenges to professional knowledge and the creation of alternative policy futures (Barnes and Mercer, 2006) were stimulated by the mobilisation of self-help movements and the sharing of information, for example, through the establishment of the Disablement Information and Advice Line (DIAL) in 1976 (Davis and Mullendar, 1993).

The 1975 United Nations Declaration of the Rights of Disabled Persons had called for states to promote the full integration of disabled people into all aspects of economic and social life. At the same time, the activism of people with physical impairments was beginning to coalesce around distinct policy claims, notably via the Disablement Income Group, the Union of Physically Impaired Against Segregation (UPIAS) and the Disability Alliance. The UN designated 1981 as its International Year of Disabled People and this marked a turning point for the mobilisation of the disabled people's movement too, with the establishment of the British Council of Organisations of Disabled People and Disabled People's International (Driedger, 1989; Hasler, 1993). Building on the activism of UPIAS in the 1970s, the publication of Mike Oliver's *Social work with disabled people* (Oliver, 1983) also benchmarked the concept of a 'social model' of disability, now so widely quoted in the rhetoric of contemporary policy debates (see also Oliver, 1990; 1996).

In terms of public policy, passage of the 1981 Education Act marked a shift towards presumptions of more inclusive schooling. The first attempt to introduce anti-discrimination legislation was made by Jack Ashley, Minister for the Disabled, in 1982 (following establishment of a Parliamentary Committee on Restrictions against Disabled People in 1979). The little-referenced 1981 Disabled Persons Act also sought to address physical access in the built environment.

The 1986 Disabled Persons (Services, Consultation and Representation) Act placed a new duty on local authorities to assess people's individual needs for the support that could be provided (as defined in the 1970 Act). Following the 1988 Griffiths Report, and the 1989 White Paper *Caring for people*, the 1990 NHS and Community Care Act introduced a more direct relationship between users and providers of support services, within a 'mixed economy' of care (Morris, 1993; Priestley, 1998a). Following the success of the Independent Living Fund, established in 1988, the 1996 Community Care (Direct Payments) Act then recognised, for the first time, the right of some disabled people to purchase and manage their own personal support using public funds (Riddell et al, 2005a).

During the 1980s and 1990s, amid a resurgence of New Right politics in Government, policy attention turned increasingly to curbing spiralling welfare expenditure, of which disability-related welfare benefits were identified as a major concern. The election on a New Labour Government in 1997 saw a continuation of this theme and the emergence of a strong 'rights and responsibilities' agenda for disability policy-making. The 1999 Welfare Reform Bill sparked public protest over attempts to cut benefit payments to some disabled people and major initiatives were launched to reduce eligibility for non-working disability benefits such as Incapacity Benefit. Such policy has continued and rapidly intensified, with disability benefits targeted for very substantial cuts in eligibility in the 2010 comprehensive spending review.

As Barnes (1991) catalogues in some detail, the 1980s had witnessed growing political claims for a comprehensive legislative approach to disabled people's social exclusion. The passage of the 1995 Disability Discrimination Act (DDA) was certainly a landmark achievement in establishing rights to non-discrimination across broad areas of policy affecting people's lives. Its implementation was, however, phased over a ten-year period (beginning with a strong focus on discrimination in employment, extended to cover public goods and services in 1999). Considering the focus of this book on children and young people, it is relevant to note that extension of such rights to educational provision did not finally occur until implementation of the 2001 Special Educational Needs and Disability Act.

To enforce the DDA, and promote its aims, an independent Disability Rights Commission (DRC) was established in 1999 to replace the less significant National Disability Council (and mirroring more closely the parallel work of the Commission for Racial Equality and Equal Opportunities Commission). As well as dealing with individual cases of discrimination, the DRC sought to raise awareness and add to the evidence base on disability discrimination, pointing increasingly to its institutionalised character.

In 2006 a new Disability Equality Duty was established, placing a positive duty on all public bodies to promote, as well as ensure, the rights established in the DDA. Following the 2006 Equality Act, the DRC was closed in 2007 and merged into the new Equality and Human Rights Commission. At the same time, policy coordination in Government was strengthened with the establishment of a cross-departmental Office for Disability Issues (ODI). Building on a major report from the Prime Minister's Strategy Unit (2005) on *Improving the life chances of disabled people*, ODI's focus has been to develop a forward strategy to achieve equality for disabled people by 2025, consolidated in a 'Roadmap' based on 14 themes, including a specific focus on outcomes for children. The five-year Independent Living Strategy (launched in 2008) also includes commitments on successful transition to adulthood for young disabled people.

The first decade of the 21st century was thus marked by a continuing rise in the prominence of disability equality rhetoric in public policy making. In this context, the UK's ratification of the United Nations Convention on the Rights of Persons with Disabilities, in June 2009, appeared to mark something of a watershed in public commitment. Its far-reaching provisions establish a comprehensive set of human rights, in all key areas of life, with obligations on states to ensure, protect and promote those rights through a variety of policy actions (Kanter, 2007). However, economic crisis and the election of a Conservative–Liberal Democrat coalition Government in 2010, with its proposals for vast budget cuts in the Comprehensive Spending Review, have revived uncertainty about the capacity of the state to fulfil its obligations.

To meet the challenges of the disability rights agenda we need to learn from the lessons of history, and to learn from the experiences of disabled people in particular. It is no coincidence that the developments described took place alongside the emergence of policy claims from the disabled people's movement, campaigning for equality and full participation in all spheres of social life and human rights. Indeed, the kinds of thinking that have allowed us, as researchers, to reappraise disability as a social issue spring directly from ideas developed within disability activism focused on social change (Campbell and Oliver, 1996).The most significant achievements (both academic and political) have arisen from a 'social interpretation', or 'social model', of disability (UPIAS/Disability Alliance, 1976; Oliver, 1990).This historic shift in thinking about disability as a public issue, rather than just a personal trouble, has allowed both activists and academics to engage in far-reaching critique and to envisage the possibility of more enabling policy responses.

As the preceding whirlwind tour illustrates, the second half of the 20th century was marked by a remarkable acceleration in recognition and response to disability as a public issue. However, the narrative coherence of this account belies a multitude of private stories and real lives. It is, therefore, with the connections between public policy and people's lives that the remainder of this book is concerned. How have ordinary people with physical impairments experienced these turbulent times, and how have policy changes altered their life choices and chances? To what extent have policy developments made a difference? In order to answer such questions it is important to turn to another major challenge that has prompted much debate in critical disability research: how to connect individual experiences with grand accounts of social and historical change.

Connecting the individual and the social

The central theme of this book concerns the complicated interactions between public policies and private lives, a connection that has proved of increasing interest to social scientists and historians (Szreter, 2009). While the preceding section highlighted broad developments in British disability policies the focus now turns to researching real lives. In particular, it focuses on the relationship between biography and history, and its application to understanding disability and social change. The discussion draws on debates about the value and use of biographical narrative in the social sciences, and in critical disability studies in particular. The first section reviews recent debates about the use of life stories in explaining change over time. This is followed by discussion of the use of personal narratives and stories in critical disability studies, including some of the tensions that arise in reconciling individual accounts with social model analysis. The discussion is illustrated with reference to examples from the research literature to demonstrate the potential for use and abuse of life story data. This, in turn, raises questions about the relationship between structure and agency, biography and history.

Lives and times

In his seminal work on the *Sociological imagination* C. Wright Mills identified 'the study of biography, or history, and of the problems of their intersection with social structure' as core concerns (Mills, 1959, p 149). Moreover, in his advice on crafting an intellectual project, he urged:

Know that the human meaning of public issues must be revealed by relating them to personal troubles – and to the problems of the individual life. Know that the problems of social science, when adequately formulated, must include both troubles and issues, both biography and history, and the range of their intricate relations. Within that range the life of the individual and the making of societies occur; and within that range the sociological imagination has its chance to make a difference in the quality of human life in our time. (p 226)

Research on the connections between individual experiences and social relationships has taken many approaches but has consolidated increasingly around life course concepts and methods (including previous work by the authors of this book). Sociological interest in birth cohort studies has a long history (Eisenstadt, 1956; Ryder, 1965) and there has been much interest in the possibility of connecting individual lives with historical times (for example, Riley et al, 1968). Within the mainstream of life course research, Elder (1994, p 5) identified four key concerns – 'the interplay of human lives and historical times, the timing of lives, linked or interdependent lives, and human agency in choice making'. It is to these concerns, in relation to disabled people and disability policy, that our approach is addressed.

First, it is important to remember that people born in different historical times are exposed to different historical worlds and opportunity structures that affect their choices and chances in life. Following Elder, it is important, for example, to ask what effect historical changes have really had on individual lives – such as changes in social roles and attitudes, technologies, laws, policies and the public institutions and professions that implement them.

Second, Elder points out how the relative timing, or 'social timing', of major life events and roles can vary between different generations, cultures or social groups. There is much evidence that significant life transitions (like leaving school, entering work, living independently or becoming a parent) can be delayed or displaced for disabled people when compared to trends in the general population. So, for example, when we read in aggregated social statistics that young adults in Britain are remaining longer in full-time education, living in their parental home and before having children of their own this obscures the specific experience of groups who may be atypical (not only disabled young people, but looked-after children, teenage mothers, and so on).

Understanding the social timing of life transitions among minority groups is therefore of considerable interest.

To identify and explore the connection between personal lives and social change it is necessary to look across and through time (Thomson et al, 2003). There are both quantitative and qualitative approaches to this (for example, through life event histories or narrative life histories). In qualitative longitudinal (QL) research time becomes the primary medium through which data is generated and explored (Saldana, 2003). Time is a multi-dimensional concept operating in at least three distinct ways (Adam, 1998; Hareven, 2000). It may be seen as biographical time (flowing from birth to death); as generational time (linking people with their birth cohort and those of their parents and children); or as historical time (linking people to chronological events and changing social environments). Change over the life course can be understood in many ways but there has been a tendency to construct life experiences as 'individual' histories or projects, which brings us to a third principle.

As much feminist writing has reminded us, people live relational and interdependent lives, producing intertwined and reciprocally constructed biographies that are embedded within an ongoing dialogue of historically-situated family histories (Vierzigmann and Kreher, 1998). Circles and networks of interdependence contribute intimately to the construction and reconstruction of individual biographies – via interactions with parents, peers, partners, carers, colleagues, and so on. Recent attention has thus turned to the potential for researching the relational character of lives longitudinally as they unfold (Neale and Flowerdew, 2003). Disability presents an interesting paradox in this respect. On the one hand, disabled lives have been often represented as more 'dependent' upon other people (almost by definition, in policy terms). On the other hand, they have been often represented as less reciprocal – as though the social relationships experienced by people with significant impairments were more about receiving than giving. Examining real lives and relationships offers an important way to question these kinds of stereotypes and assumptions.

Finally, maintaining an awareness of agency and choice is important because it helps to avoid the risk of social determinism in explaining disability history. The individual model paradigm of disability, particularly in its 'medical model' guise, draws on a powerful discourse of biological determinism, which suggests that impairment is the primary influence on life choices and chances. However, there is a parallel danger in the social model paradigm, if incorrectly applied to assumptions about individual lives – that is, that 'society' is the only determinant influence on people's lives (Crow, 1996). The disabled people's movement presents a strong counter to this, emphasising the potential for social change through collective agency, and arguing forcibly for greater individual choice and control in independent living. Consequently, it is essential to examine not only how social change shapes the opportunity structures within which life choices are made but also to examine the choices that people can and do make within those constraints. In this way, life stories provide important evidence about the ways in which agency, resistance and resilience can change lives in spite of the barriers.

As the preceding application of Elder's principles suggests, contemporary life course research can make biography more sociological by connecting individual lives with historical time and with other people's lives. The aim in this book is to re-connect the 'individual' experience of disability with its 'social' context in post-war Britain. However, using life stories to do this raises some difficult questions. Can research based on intimate personal experiences really be anything more than voyeuristic? Can we really connect individual experiences with wider explanations of macro-social change? Can disabled autobiographers also contribute as critical social historians? Can a history of disability really be known through disabled people's biographical narratives?

Biography and the social model of disability

As Plummer (2001) contends, in a rapidly changing world it would be easy to lose our past, and documented life stories help to ensure that voices are remembered for the future. In the context of disability, French and Swain (2000, p 160) also remind us that 'History is owned and documented by those in power, and invisibility and silence are cornerstones of oppression'. It is therefore particularly important to listen to the life stories of historically under-represented groups of disabled people (Goodley, 1996), not only so that we can inform future generations and remind the wider community of different cultures and practices, but also to 'contribute to a more complete understanding of the issues related to change in people's lives' (Atkinson, 1998, p 19). In this context, there is much merit in preserving the remembrance of disabled people's life stories as historical material. Yet there must also be concerns about the motivations and implications of simply collecting stories for stories' sake.

First, it is important to assert that 'disabled people are not the *subject matter* of the social interpretation of disability' (Finkelstein, 2001, p 1). Rather, the primary purpose is to reveal and challenge the network of social relations, institutions and barriers that inhibit the full participation and equality of disabled people in society. From this perspective, much existing biographical research may appear little more than individualistic. Second, the social interpretation of 'disability' is not directly concerned with embodied experiences of 'impairment' (Hughes, 2007; Priestley, 1998b; Thomas, 1999). Rather, it has focused on understanding how disability is 'imposed on top of our impairments' and how such impositions might be challenged (UPIAS/Disability Alliance, 1976, p 3). However, in people's everyday accounts, experiences of disability and impairment are often undifferentiated, or interwoven, so that establishing a cogent approach to biographical research within the social interpretation, or 'social model', of disability is anything but straightforward.

Despite the established theoretical focus on 'disability' in social model research both academic researchers and activists have retained very considerable emphasis on disabled people's lived experiences. The use of individual accounts in research has been viewed variously as authentic, grounded, ethical, even emancipatory (Goodley, 1996; Smith and Sparkes, 2008), often under the claim of 'nothing about us without us' (Charlton, 1998). The narration of disabled people's first-hand experiences is viewed by many as an essential component of credible and accountable disability studies (and a key foundation for collective political mobilisation). Yet, where disabled people's lives become the sole focus for research there are dangers of de-politicisation, what we might call a kind of ontological drift – a subtle but pervasive shift in assumptions about the nature of disability itself, away from the social towards the individual.

The study 'of' marginalised social groups, including disabled people, may be of historical interest but it can obscure the underlying, less observable, structural forces that produce that marginalisation (such as capitalism, imperialism and patriarchy). To avoid the ontological drift towards research preoccupied only with disabled people, as though their lives were the only objects of scrutiny, it is necessary maintain a focus on disability as an underlying social reality. At the same time, claims for authentic 'nothing about us without us' narratives mean that disabled people's experiences must also play a part in the study of disability.

Two concerns arise from this paradox. By no means are all the life experiences of disabled people also experiences of 'disability' (Thomas, 1999). To read those experiences without a disability focus is to risk a study 'of' disabled people that is perilously voyeuristic and irrelevant to political action for change on social issues. Studying experiences of 'disability' without a coherent idea of what that concept means is likely to produce little more than individualised and apolitical accounts. The challenge for critical disability research has been to maintain an ontological position that acknowledges the commonality of disability as a form of oppression, while valuing the diverse voices of those who experience disability in different ways. This balancing act is assisted by formulating the research problem more precisely.

From a social model perspective, the empirical focus of narrative research needs to shift from the 'life experiences of disabled people' to 'experiences of disability in people's lives'. This subtle linguistic turn is important – responding to Finkelstein's reminder that the subject matter is disability but acknowledging that people's experiences provide unique evidence of the ways in which disability manifests itself. In this way the importance of individual experiences is better understood as an epistemological issue rather than an ontological one. That is, although biographical accounts may not be an end in themselves they do provide a useful empirical lens through which to observe change in disabling societies.

Learning about disability from stories

The 20th century saw a rich vein of auto/biographical writings about disability, not least in Helen Keller's (1905) seminal *The story of my life* and Scott's (1969) *The making of blind men*. However, with subsequent political and theoretical developments such works have come to be viewed as rather outdated in their language and approach. A key turning point in the development of disabled people's biographical writing in Britain came with the publication of Paul Hunt's (1966) book *Stigma: The experience of disability*. As a result of advertisements placed in newspapers, Hunt collected more than 60 personal narratives and published 12 of them in an edited collection (six women and six men, including himself). As Barnes et al (2003, p 77) emphasise, Hunt's stated intention was to move beyond 'sentimental autobiography' by situating experiences of disability in everyday lives not simply in terms of impairment but in relationships with a society dominated by 'normal' people (Hunt, 1966, p 146).

Hunt's approach as editor was primarily to give voice to the unheard stories of ordinary people, rather than interrogate those stories with intensive social or historical critique (although the accounts themselves, especially Hunt's own, are sometimes intensely socially critical). In his introduction, Hunt underlined the diversity and individuality of these 'vivid accounts' as well as the 'valuable insights' they revealed into the social situation of disabled people in Britain in the late 1960s. A similar approach was evident in Jo Campling's (1981) collection *Images of ourselves:Women with disabilities talking*, in which she invited 25 women to 'write whatever they wanted about their situations as women with disabilities'. As a social scientist with an interest in social policies, Campling may well have been tempted to contextualise and reflect on the evidence.Yet, apart from adding 'the briefest of introductions to each piece', she notes in her introduction: 'I have limited the editorial function to the minimum and I have not presumed to make a commentary or interpretation.The contributions speak for themselves; anything else would be superfluous and an intrusion' (pp vii–viii).

Humphries and Gordon's (1992) *Out of sight* made extensive use of first-hand accounts, gathered from disabled people's remembrances of their childhoods, schooling, entry into the labour market and relationships, from 1900 to 1950. In this case, there was more attention to the social and historical context of those experiences.

The emergence of critical disability studies in the 1980s and 1990s led to a proliferation of new writings dealing with diverse aspects of disability as a social problem. Some of this work explicitly linked new ideas about the social model with historical developments in British public policies. For example, Barnes' (1991) *Disabled people in Britain and discrimination* provided a systematic review of policy developments and outcomes to make the case for national anti-discrimination legislation. This kind of critical policy analysis was enormously important in providing the big picture although it did not draw explicitly upon accounts of disabled people's lives in doing so.

The publication of Borsay's (2005) *Disability and social policy in Britain since 1750* also addressed significant changes in the public treatment of disabled people (up to the 1970s) and has stimulated a growing interest in historical research. Borsay's approach also made links between public policy and disabled people's experiences (selecting from previously published examples like those provided by Humphries and Gordon, 1992).

The 'biographical turn' in social sciences has marked much recent work in disability studies and there has been considerable interest in using narrative approaches to analyse experiences of disability (for example, in Goodley et al's 2004 edited collection *Researching life stories* or Booth and Booth's 1998 *Growing up with parents with learning difficulties*).The use of personal narratives as evidence is now widespread and our understanding has been enriched by it. However, such accounts have only been politically meaningful where they have helped to evidence and challenge disabling barriers in society.

Connecting individual biographies with disabling barriers, institutions and relationships is therefore essential.

The research for this book was motivated by the two authors' shared interests in disability and the life course, arising from a number of previous projects. For example, Shah's (2005a) research on *The career success of disabled high fliers* used life history interviews with disabled adults to illustrate the interplay between personal and social factors in professional employment careers. Related themes were addressed in researching the career choices of young disabled people in full-time education (Shah, 2005b; 2008). Here the analysis also related individual biography to specific policy context (for example, policies and good practice for involving young people in planning their own futures). The biographical accounts also revealed career aspirations and desires for future social change, as well as the range of individual and contextual factors that facilitated or constrained their career choices.

Similar interests, in the life experiences and pathways of young disabled people, were evident in Priestley's involvement with the ESRC *Life as a disabled child project* (see Watson et al, 1999) and in a subsequent study of transitions to adulthood for young disabled people leaving care (Priestley et al, 2002). Biographical methods revealed the relational character of young people's lives, and the significant impact of help or hindrance from other people (family, friends, professionals). Both projects revealed much about young people's negotiated construction of disabled identities arising from subjection to processes of labelling, segregation, and surveillance.

Taken together, these various projects provide a number of pointers. For example, thinking longitudinally about 'careers' (for example, through education, social care or employment) helps to trace the choices, relationships, environmental barriers, public policies and social spaces that influence life course pathways, identities and outcomes over time. The accumulation of biographical examples from different projects also pointed to the importance of thinking about collective as well individual biographies (that is, how episodes from personal stories relate to pathways shared with many other disabled people in the same generational cohort).

Priestley's (2001) edited collection *Disability and the life course: Global perspectives* suggested ways of connecting biographical data, from people of different generations, with socio-historical change. In particular, the conclusions highlighted the need to think about lives in terms of time, place, trajectory, turning points and available resources. A theoretical framework for understanding the more structural relationship between

---

disability, generation and the life course in contemporary societies was developed in *Disability: A life course approach* (Priestley, 2003).

Biography and social structure

One of the persistent and justifiable criticisms of life history studies (often conducted from a social constructionist or social psychological perspective) is that they fail to adequately address sociological concepts of structure. As Hubbard (2000, 11.4) notes, 'Life histories have the potential to reveal how people interpret and understand social structures and encourages an exploration of how social structures are perceived by individuals at key turning point moments in their lives'. Yet, narrative and non-narrative life history methods have the capacity to contribute more than this, and to move beyond individual perceptions.

That is not to say that individual agency is not important. As Beck (1992, p 90) points out, 'The individual himself or herself becomes the reproduction unit of the social in the lifeworld' or, as Giddens (1984) suggests, social norms and structures do not exist independently of social actions by human agents, and are shaped by them. For example, significant change occurred during the latter half of the 20th century with the emergence of the disabled people's movement and social model of disability, but this arose from acts of collective and individual agency (French and Swain, 2006). Although many disabled people share common experiences of institutionalised oppression, disabling barriers may be experienced and negotiated in very different ways. Unique intersectionalities of multiple discrimination also play a part in people's relationships with social structures over time. For instance, structural inequalities in education and labour markets may affect individual life choices not only in terms of disability but also in terms of gender, ethnicity, social class or sexuality.

Riley and Riley (1999) offer a reminder of sociology's enduring fascination with the interrelationships between people's lives and social structures. Their work on ageing led them to infer that 'cohort differences in lives must result from some kind of still unknown interplay between a relatively unchanging genetic background and a continually changing society'. However, they also argue that sociology has largely failed to address this problem due to the individualisation of 'life course' research, in which an empirical focus on changing *lives* obscures our understanding of changing social *structures*. Thus, they conclude, 'this approach has become a virtual obsession, in which structural phenomena, if heeded at all, have been largely reduced to "contextual" characteristics of individuals' (Riley and Riley, 1999, p 126).

Addressing a similar problem, Gordon and Longino (2000) identify three levels of connection between biographical ageing and society – demographic structure (in their case an ageing population), institutional structures (such as work, family and welfare institutions), and the regimes of everyday life that represent our encounters with and consumptions of social structure. In this way they demonstrate the importance of taking into account the changing political, moral and cultural economies within which individual lives are lived over time. Such an approach is helpful in thinking about the experience of disability policy in post-war Britain and informs the analysis presented in later chapters.

Viewing disability research from a critical realist perspective is helpful in explaining the approach. Bhaskar (1975; 1997; 1998) argued that positivist and hermeneutic research approaches are limited in their application to social scientific enquiry because of a failure to address the underlying reality of social phenomena beyond individuals or groups of individuals. This tendency to 'social atomism', he argued, arises from the failure of methodological individualism to explain the real social context of individual experiences. Bhaskar identified three levels of reality, differentiating between observable 'empirical' realities, 'actual' events and the 'real' nature of persistent social relations and systems that give rise to them. Drawing on this typology, the social relations of disability (in the social model sense) are very 'real' in their capacity to produce material consequences but they are not directly observable. Disabling barriers, of many different kinds, can, however, be seen as 'actual' manifestations of disability, while people's encounters with them are 'empirical' realities that are yet more clearly observable.

Narrative biographical research does offer a window onto these empirical realities, with the potential to provide 'traces' of deeper social relations and macro-social change (for example, Chamberlayne and Rustin, 1999; Ulrich, 2000; Priestley, 2001). As Thomas (1999, p 8) contends, 'experiential narratives offer a route to understanding the socio-structural'. Establishing the connections between individual biography and disabling barriers is therefore an important task. The characteristics and patterns of barriers help us to model the less observable forces of their creation in society. As Bhaskar notes, the direction of causality travels primarily in one direction (in this case from the social relations of disability to life experiences) while our understanding of it (in this case through empirical life history research) progresses in the opposite direction.

In addition, as Bhaskar rightly points out, 'actual' realties exist in space and time and this is central to the methodological approach in this book. For Oliver (1996, p 33), disability involves 'all the things that impose restrictions on disabled people; ranging from individual prejudice to institutional discrimination, from inaccessible buildings to unusable transport systems, from segregated education to excluding work arrangements, and so on'. Yet these 'actual' manifestations of disability can and do change over time. They can be made and they can be unmade, at least to some extent. Disabling barriers arise and may be removed, policies and institutions come and go, and relationships may be short-lived or develop over time. Although people's pathways through life are often severely constrained, life choices change. The challenge is then to apply this knowledge to better understand how life chances and choices for young disabled people in Britain today have 'changed' compared to the experiences of those in earlier post-war generations. It is therefore essential to read narrative accounts of disabling barriers as temporally situated.

Conclusions

This first chapter has painted a broad picture and raised many questions – about grand narratives of policy development and about the possibility of understanding history through biographical accounts. To summarise, the first part of the chapter highlighted the extraordinary acceleration and diversification of disability policy making that took place in Britain from the Second World War to the end of the 20th century, and into the present century. Although brief, the examples convey a sense of the twists and turns through decades and flag some of the key policy developments that are explored in later chapters. The larger part of the chapter focused on connecting history with biography, connecting 'personal troubles' with public issues. Thus, it unveiled some difficult, but very necessary, debates about using biographical narrative in critical disability research – particularly how to respond to the paradox of including the authentic voices of disabled people while maintaining a focus on the structural character of disabling societies.

The chapter raises some interesting questions. In what ways can the life experiences of young disabled people in Britain today be considered as similar or different to those of previous generations (and what role has social policy played in this)? What are the significant human relationships that facilitate or impede life chances for young disabled people and how have changes in policies, institutions and environments impacted upon these relationships? How successful have past policies been and what more could be done?

The next chapter turns the lens around and views developments from the perspective of individual lives lived through changing times. Rather than simply 'telling' these stories it is important to consider them critically in the context of the bigger picture presented earlier, and to begin the processing of asking how policy makes a difference. In preparation for that task, and drawing on the theoretical discussion, the following principles and techniques are useful in approaching the stories.

It is important to look for evidence of real change (or absence of change) in real lives but also to look for evidence of difference between lives (especially between generations). It is useful to identify significant events in individual life course pathways but also important to look for the 'relational' characteristics of life transitions. It is important to recognise the psycho–emotional implications of these events but to acknowledge that people who tell their own life stories are reflective and critical historians too. It is important to consider individual experiences of disability from a social model perspective and to identify the environments, relationships and institutions/policies that make a difference in people's lives.

Questions for discussion

- What have been the major changes in public policies affecting disabled people's lives since the 1940s?
- What can we hope to learn from the stories of individual disabled people's lives that we cannot learn from looking at the bigger picture?
- What kinds of concerns are raised by disability research that relies heavily on biographical evidence, and how can these concerns be addressed?

TWO

Telling stories

As explained in Chapter One, this book examines how life has changed for young people with physical impairments in England over three generations, and how public policies have affected this. However, as (Priestley, 2001, p 240) points out, 'life can be a complex, often messy, business and people's life experiences do not fit neatly into academic disciplines or theoretical models'. The focus here is on those real lives rather than the constructed boundaries of policy making. The chapter introduces the three generational cohorts of disabled people who contributed their life stories. These are illustrated by six vignettes (summary life stories), which were agreed and validated by those who told their stories at much greater length. After each pair of vignettes (two from each generation) there is discussion of the issues they raise. These are then explored in more detail in the thematic chapters that follow.

The examples provide a flavour of the experiences and remembrances explored in the interviews. It is not the intention here to produce definitive biographies or case studies, or to tell the 'whole story', but to illustrate the range of experiences and to prompt questions about relationships between private lives and public policies. For example, the stories illustrate connections between medical treatment, education, employment, family relationships, self-identity and disability politics.

Children of the 1940s

Those in the oldest generation were born around the time of Second World War or shortly after and grew up with the first attempts to address disability more systematically in British social policy. In particular, they and their families negotiated experiences of disability during the emergence of the post-war welfare state (for example, in relation to radical new legislation on employment, education and health services in the wake of the Beveridge Report, as highlighted in Chapter One).

Florence

Florence was born in the late 1940s, the daughter of a single parent, but when doctors diagnosed that she would never walk, her birth mother left her. At the age of one, she spent a year in a hospital before being placed in a children's home and with foster families. However, they were unable to cope with a child with physical impairments, and Florence was picked on in the children's home, so she was sent back to hospital 'because there was nowhere else'. Although her mother was contacted regularly (for example, when consent was needed for an operation) she maintained her distance and no one from the children's home came to visit Florence in hospital.

When Florence was five years old she was fostered, and eventually adopted, by the family of a woman visiting the ward. Her new family assumed that Florence would cope with obvious physical barriers, like the steps to the front door, 'they just didn't have a clue, although they knew I couldn't walk it just didn't register'. With the physical barriers, no other young children in the house and no lasting contact with other disabled children (other than acquaintances she met on hospital visits) there were few opportunities to develop peer friendships early on.

As time went on, Florence's impairment was less obvious and she would often choose to hide it in social situations but this had implications for developing closer relationships, especially romantically. Added to this, Florence had never really known what caused her impairment, whether it could be inherited, and whether it might affect her chances of having children of her own one day. Although she experienced a few short-term relationships there was nothing serious and over time she decided to remain single: 'I think that I have taken a conscious choice ... not to go down the married route and not to have a child, and I think my biggest choice that way was that if people didn't know what my disability was ...'.

Institutional medical treatment played a big part in childhood, although Florence's impairment was not diagnosed until her mother became concerned that she was not walking. Failing to persuade the doctor, her mother took her to the hospital for more tests. The resulting (incorrect) prognosis that Florence would never 'stand, walk or do anything' led to the prolonged time spent in hospital – a year for treatment and two more because there was nowhere else to go. Florence remembers the Nightingale wards of early 1950s with 'like 20 beds on each side of a ward with the nurses stationed down one end'. Visits were restricted to one hour on two afternoons a week. She spent much of the time lying face down with her wrists tied to her bed. Most days there was physiotherapy, which continued as an outpatient until she could negotiate steps (although she was not issued with any walking aids and her adoptive mother refused to have an 'invalid buggy'). In the holidays there were more operations to break the bones in her legs in an attempt to lengthen them. Later, as an adult, Florence elected to have one leg amputated because of the pain, 'it's been the best thing that's happened'.

Although special school had been discussed, Florence attended mainstream schools throughout the 1950s. When she was six, her mother persuaded the education authority to enrol her in the local infant school. There were some physical barriers to negotiate but they were solved in informal ways, 'when I needed to get up the six steps the teacher just picked me up and carried me up'. There was more of a battle to enrol in primary school, as it was not within Florence's walking distance, and there was no transport provided for disabled pupils. However, she felt accepted by her peers, who also supported her to negotiate the physical environment. This changed somewhat at secondary school, particularly with name calling and teasing, 'You know, like, you can't catch me, you walk silly, spastic'.

There was no provision of individual support or adjustments at school, 'The fact that I couldn't run from one end of the pitch to the other never bothered them. They just shoved you in goals'. For social reasons, Florence would have preferred the special school because she knew other children from the hospital went there but her mother would not have it. Reflecting now, Florence feels there would have been little opportunity to gain career qualifications there and that there might have been 'no way out'. Having said this, she still encountered barriers to her career aspirations from various professionals, who focused on her impairment rather potential adaptations. Although she wanted to be a teacher they advised her to forget the idea and to learn skills for clerical work instead.

Florence left school and entered her first paid job in the mid–1960s as a telephonist and clerk. Her second job was as a typist, which she enjoyed, despite there being no lift and two flights of stairs to her office. Florence chose to identify her impairment on job applications, even though registering as a disabled person was optional, 'whilst you didn't hide the disability you weren't really encouraged to go for it'. Later, Florence moved from clerical work to work with disabled children (in the same special school she might have gone to herself) then, later, into social work training. In her current job Florence notes that she now has an orthopaedic office chair that can be fully adjusted, equipment that was not available to her in earlier jobs. She also drives, but only because she met, by chance, someone who could make adaptations to her car.

Beyond the hospitals, disability identity was rarely acknowledged in Florence's young life, or she passed it off where she could. She felt 'different' at secondary school but her practical needs went largely unrecognised. Within the family, 'my mother wouldn't allow any school photographs to be taken until I was totally seated. .... there is nothing that would suggest disability in a picture'. Because she had been encouraged to 'get away with not registering', it was difficult to claim eligibility for disability benefits or support later in life. Looking back, Florence believes that having disabled friends as a child would have made it easier for her to find a positive disability identity. She has seen big changes in opportunities for educational inclusion during her life and feels there is a greater public awareness now, 'because disabled people are out and about'. Yet, she remains frustrated about the extent of physical barriers that still exist.

Dan

Dan was born in the mid-1940s, the oldest of three brothers. His father worked away but there was an extended family, in a close working-class community, with plenty of opportunities for friendships with neighbourhood children and cousins. The housing was basic, even in its time, with no indoor bathroom or hot running water, and the children would take a bath once a week at the local pub or public baths. Dan's mother died when he was ten and the children lived with their grandmother, with whom Dan had a close relationship, until their father remarried and they moved to another city. In general, however, Dan remembers childhood as both happy and ordinary. He has married twice and has children and grandchildren of his own.

Irrespective of disability, there were strong family expectations of mutual care and support, carried out in the absence of social assistance from public services. Older relatives were cared for by younger family members and the possibility of residential care for his grandmother was strongly resisted. It was, however, common for families like his to receive some charitable help. Dan remembers the trips, food and entertainment they provided for disabled children. He always felt supported by his family, neither over-protected nor constrained by them.

Dan's impairment, caused at birth, was recognised early on and 'the doctor said to my parents that my disability would worsen, you know, as I got older'. When he was seven or eight years old Dan went through orthopaedic surgery but does not remember being told much about the procedure: 'I can't remember a doctor sitting down like they do now, and saying "this is going to happen, this is the result"'. He then spent considerable time as an in-patient to recover, followed by irregular periods of hospital stay later on throughout his childhood.

Dan was enrolled in a mainstream school and, although there was some initial teasing, he made friends and joined in with other children. Having missed out on some of his schooling, due to the time spent in hospital, it was suggested (by the doctors) that he go to a local special school – 'it was a real big old type of building and we used to be taken on a blue single decker bus with the … Council Education Department written on the side'. It was not what he wanted, however, because 'you knew that you was different from anybody else, those outside'. There was little academic challenge and his neighbourhood friends were at ordinary schools. After a year and half he transferred to a mainstream secondary modern school, where it was 'more maths and English, rather than making raffia baskets'.

On leaving school at 16, Dan applied to join the Navy, like other men in his family, but he was rejected because of his impairment, 'the bloke looked at me and he says, "You can't join the Navy". I said "why?" … He said "You won't be able to march".' It was the first time that Dan remembers feeling disabled. He registered for a disabled person's 'green card' with the Labour Exchange, where he was offered a job as a lift attendant in a department store, one of the occupations designated for disabled people at that time. Dan did not want any of the designated jobs and, with the help of a friend, found alternative work. However, the employer fired him, citing concerns about the safety of using machinery with his type of impairment. Fortunately, there were plenty of jobs available at this time and Dan was never out of work in the 1950s and 1960s.

He found himself unemployed for the first time in the 1970s and returned to the job centre, where he was assessed by a Disablement Resettlement Officer and offered a job in a sheltered workshop operated by the local social services department (despite his work experience in the open labour market). He spent five years there on a variety of jobs, 'I did all sorts, I helped make furniture, drove the wagon'. His career interests then took a different turn, towards social care, and he found employment as a residential worker for people with learning difficulties – a role created as a result of the closure of large residential hospitals in the 1980s. He has also worked with older people.

Going to special school changed Dan's childhood perceptions about disability, from something associated with older people to something that affected children like him. However, he did not really identify himself as disabled until he had left school, 'someone disabled was someone who could do a lot less than I could do'. He has seen significant changes in policy during his lifetime, in education, employment and social care. He is enthusiastic about the opportunities offered by developments in support for independent living but feels that, despite legislation, professionals and social services still have control over many disabled people's lives. There have been changes in medical treatments and technologies, and in professional and public attitudes, 'I think we've moved a million miles in that respect'. However, Dan still views Britain as lagging behind the US in terms of awareness, resources and legislation.

Key points and discussion

Florence and Dan's stories raise a number of questions about the experiences of disabled children and young people from the oldest of the three generations. In terms of historical time, their early lives were marked by significant changes in public policies affecting disabled people in Britain. The landslide election of Attlee's Labour Government in 1945, and the embedding of a post-war welfare settlement (noted in Chapter One) were significant historical events and traces can be seen in the stories. But the absence of public intervention is visible too.

Dan's childhood story conveys an everyday ordinariness, embedded in informal networks of support and the mutuality of his extended family and local community. Indeed, when Young and Willmott reported their seminal study on *Family and kinship in East London* (1957) they remarked on the persistence of extended family ties in urbanised working class communities at the time. They also showed how changes in public policy, such as the planning of local authority housing estates, could undermine such ties.

Reading Dan's story in the context of the critical disability literature, and the stories from later generations, provides a useful reminder that the past was not always a place dominated by institutional segregation. Oliver (1990, p 38) cites Ignatieff's (1983) assertion that rise of the asylums and workhouses during 19th-century industrialisation 'met a need among poor families struggling to cope with burdens which for the first time may have been felt to be unbearable' – the implication being that working–class families, in particular, turned to institutional provision. The development of institutional welfare policies in Britain, from the 19th into the 20th century, did impact dramatically on family life for many disabled people but we should keep in mind that the large majority of disabled children, then as now, lived with their families in private households.

The contrast with Florence's story is clear. In the absence of support from family, public provision had little to offer her by way of a 'normal' life. Her experiences of isolation in hospitals and children's homes, simply 'because there was nowhere else to go', raise obvious questions about the extent of public provision at this time. As her story reminds us, up until at least the mid-1970s disabled children were uncommonly placed for foster care, their files often marked as 'unfit for adoption' at birth (Rowe and Lambert, 1973). In Florence's case, the turning point was a chance intervention by another family. Up to this point she had been largely abandoned by the state, as well as her birth mother, on a life course trajectory towards indefinite institutionalisation.

There are also traces of the pervasive presence of medical and therapeutic intervention in Florence's life. Her early years of confinement point to the importance of hospitals, as much as social care institutions, while Dan's story hints at the extension of medical authority into other life-changing decisions like choices between mainstream and special education. In both stories, positive outcomes were largely attributed to the resistance and agency of parents (mothers) or other significant individuals, rather than to public services. Attention is also drawn to feelings of 'difference' created by attending special school and the lack of adjustments or formal support structures at school.

A similar lack of adjustment or protection in the workplace is clear, but the two stories of employment do show more obvious traces of public policy impacting on life chances and choices. Florence's decision not to 'register' as a disabled person and Dan's rejection of a 'designated' occupation reveal conscious encounters between the public and private (explored in Chapter Six). In both stories, there is a sense of career choices made with the support of friends rather than professionals, and in spite of prevailing policy frameworks for employment quotas or occupational rehabilitation. Dan's subsequent experience with the Disablement Resettlement Officer in the 1970s, and the adaptive office furniture provided to Florence, hint at other changes. It is also worth noting that both developed second careers working with other disabled people in the expanding community care field.

It was institutional segregation, in hospital or special school, that first marked out a sense of identity difference for Florence and Dan as children. However, their stories tell of attempts to negotiate growing up without drawing great attention to claims for special entitlement, public support or special rights. Neither of the stories is marked by a particularly strong, or clearly defined, sense of 'disability' in younger life.

Children of the 1960s

The second generation, those born in the 1960s, experienced childhood and young adulthood at a time when assumptions about the social exclusion of disabled people were being increasingly challenged (for example, in widespread critiques of residential institutions and segregated schools, in moves towards greater support for community living, and in the rise of the early disabled people's movement). Like the preceding stories, the following two examples raise questions about the real life impact of such developments.

Poppy

Poppy was born in the mid-1960s, the youngest of three children. Her father was employed in the Forces and often worked away from home. Poppy also lived away from home, at residential school, only coming home for the school holidays and the odd weekend. Although the family made efforts to include her in home life during her time there, Poppy feels she did not develop close sibling relationships in her childhood, 'I was the youngest, and being disabled, I think I got more attention when I came home. My sister especially resented this, at the time'. Poppy's impairment was not diagnosed until she was over a year old, 'My mother knew that I wasn't developing as I should have'. After the medical diagnosis at the age of two, a senior medical specialist suggested to Poppy's mother that she should be placed in an institution, 'to just forget about me, and to go on and have more children. Apparently, this was common practice at the time. Luckily, my mother refused to consider this option!'

Poppy was sent to a residential special school at the age of four, partly because her parents had to move house regularly. She remained there until she was 16. The school became her social world and she remembers feeling bored and lonely at home during the summer holidays. Her ability to move around independently was limited by an inaccessible environment. At school there was a strict institutional regime with an emphasis on normalisation. This included intensive physiotherapy and speech therapy programmes, 'the more dependent you were, the less privileges you got. I remember how happy I was when I was allowed to bath and shower alone – I hated the rushed bath and bedtime regime'. Poppy still feels that these experiences left her with a fear of using a wheelchair or depending on other people. There was corporal punishment for non-compliance and allegations of sexual abuse from some children, 'I knew it wasn't right, but there was no one to tell'.

However, during the 12 years she was there, Poppy also saw changes towards a more enlightened ethos in the late 1970s. Academic expectations for the pupils were not high but Poppy was able to gain enough basic qualifications to enrol at a residential further education college for young disabled people in the early 1980s, where she spent another four years. The regime was less institutionalised and expectations were higher. She finally left residential special education at the age of 20. After re-sitting some of her exams in a mainstream further education college in her home town she went on to study at a mainstream higher education institution, away from home. However, accessibility in the college was poor, 'The library and Students' Union was up two flights of stairs, I had to ask fellow students to carry my walker and laptop up and down the stairs which was annoying'. Poppy encountered a lack of awareness about disability among other students and the teaching staff but benefited greatly from the friendship of an older disabled student who gave her advice and support. She left college with an Honours degree.

As Poppy spent the majority of her childhood living away, there were friendships with other disabled children at boarding school but not in her home town. She remembers from special school that 'it was assumed that you wouldn't have relationships, you wouldn't have sex, or a family like everyone else. I was caught kissing a boy and punished quite severely for it but this only made me more determined to seek out relationships. The whole experience made me distrust non-disabled people'. She discovered romantic relationships at college, and met her husband before going to university in her mid-twenties. After a bad experience with health care, which resulted in the premature birth and death of her twins, she later went on to have a child and the family life she had wanted since adolescence.

Poppy entered her first job after leaving higher education, organising and delivering recreational activities for other disabled people in a social services day centre, 'When I first started, it was Bingo, Bingo or Bingo and you got a cup of tea with that. I was annoyed that disabled people had such low expectations! ... I like to think I started something'. Through this experience, and meeting other disabled people, she also became involved in disability arts and politics – later helping to set up a local cooperative with other disabled people to raise awareness of disability issues in the 1990s, 'we became Disability Equality Trainers, and we were making good money'.

Poppy's first memory of feeling different was as a young child, 'I was very small, being pushed by my mum in my wheelchair, down the street ... this woman came out of the Church ... she kissed me and she said, "Go to Church, God will heal you and make you better" – I believed her for quite some time after.' Poppy became frustrated with her feelings as a teenager and struggled to find an identity that she felt comfortable with, not knowing if she would ever have an independent adult life and a family of her own. Going to FE college proved a turning point, through which she discovered greater independence and choice but 'it was through disability art culture that I became political and found a strong cultural identity which has allowed me to follow my own dreams and aspirations'.

Poppy says that she has seen a lot of changes since the 1995 Disability Discrimination Act but that public attitudes still need to move forward, 'on the surface it does look like things have changed but there is a whole undercurrent of practices and attitudes that are not changing'. She feels that it is actually harder for disabled children to feel accepted now, being the minority in mainstream school, 'there is more pressure to do more, to compete on a non-disabled level'. She also feels there is not enough information available for people who are now ageing with lifelong impairments like hers.

Ian

Ian was born in the mid-1960s. His mother gave up paid work after he was born and his father moved into a more secure a job with the local education authority. Ian remembers a happy childhood, as an only child, with support and encouragement from his parents, 'it's never been a case of, you can't do this because you're disabled'. His grandfather also lived with them, spending time with Ian at home, 'We would read each other to sleep. And I think that reading has kind of led on and helped me'. Ian's father died some years ago but Ian continues to live with his mother in the same house where he grew up.

Ian's impairment was recognised soon after he was born and he spent the first months of his life in hospital. It was a rare condition but he feels he was lucky that the same hospital had seen two other children with it, 'as they said, you could go through your whole career and not come across somebody with that!'. The family received some financial assistance from the new social security Attendance and Mobility Allowances, introduced in the early 1970s. Later, the local authority social services also provided them with grants for equipment and housing adaptations to increase Ian's independence at home, 'we got a grant to build an extension because dad wanted to extend the bathroom so I could get my wheelchair in more easily, and put a shower in 'cos I couldn't get in and out of the bath'. Their local MP also helped them secure tax relief on additional building work that was needed.

When he was four years old, Ian was sent to a special school for 'delicate children', which he remembers as a large Victorian house in the countryside, where 'kids that were recovering from operations were often sent'. Although the school was in the same county, and his parents had a car, the orthopaedic doctor advised that Ian should live there as a weekly boarder to reduce his risk of injury in travelling. For Ian, this had some advantages and he enjoyed the extracurricular and evening activities.

With encouragement at home, Ian had learned to read at a young age, 'I've been immobilised and the only thing I could do was read'. This was quickly recognised by his nursery teacher who 'pushed me up a year because my reading was so advanced'. In general, Ian had a good experience at the school and feels that the head teacher had a significant influence on his life by focusing on ability, 'might not be fantastic academically but ... it was not what can't you do but what can you do'. In addition to academic subjects, in the early 1970s, there was growing interest in new methods such as Conductive Education'. Staff from the school had travelled to the Pető Institute in Budapest to learn techniques that they were keen to impart. Ian's experience of physical therapy was a negative one as he felt pressured to function normally, 'I accepted very early on that I wasn't going to walk, and physiotherapists have always tried to get me walking.'

At the age of 11, in the mid-1970s, Ian moved on to a new secondary special school, which had been recently built in his home town. Unlike his previous school the intention was to locate the building within a local community, rather than isolating it away from the town. However, the experience was much less happy. Academic expectations were low, offering students only a maximum of five CSE public examinations. The school, situated on a difficult local authority housing estate, also became a target for petty crime, 'like a patch in the Bronx'. Later on, at college, Ian remembers a chance encounter with the former headmaster, 'he caught me up and said "what are you doing here? ... I never thought one of my pupils would be clever enough to do A-levels"'.

There had been some developments towards more integrated education policies by the time Ian reached 16, at the beginning of the 1980s. However, the only option available to him was to continue at one of two residential special colleges of further education, neither of them in his home county. He spent a year at one of them and was 17 before he had his first taste of mainstream education. He found the transition difficult, 'that first couple of days was like dropping me on another planet'. He was a year older than the majority of his peers and it was hard to make friends because, 'they'd all been to school and then come on to college together'.

Ian had no opportunity to talk to a careers advisor at school but started work on a voluntary basis, after being at the residential college, when his father volunteered him to help out at a local Disablement Information and Advice Line service (DIAL). Ian continued to work there during college holidays and has since worked in other voluntary organisations, mainly doing secretarial and administrative work. Having to rely on public transport was a barrier, 'having never driven I was reliant on taxis ... but it kind of restricts you'. He now works part time from home for a local politician, answering letters and queries (his employer has recently moved to a new office because it would be more accessible in terms of the Disability Discrimination Act).

The development of internet sites, like Friends Reunited, has helped Ian to keep in contact with some people. Other changes in technology have made a difference too, like the size and appearance of wheelchairs, 'the ones I used to have to push around were like pushing a tank around'. Technologies for independence at home, like stair lifts, have also improved. Ian is now in his mid-forties, and for the past decade, his life has been limited to his home. Previously this would have meant occupying himself with books and television but broadband internet and laptop computing have enabled him to remain employed and in contact with others, from his bed. The years of being at home have dented his social confidence, however.

Ian has seen advances in medical treatment that he feels improve quality of life for children with his condition, 'I just missed out on that ... I was already too old'. He sees much value in such treatments and in prevention, but admits this is a 'controversial' opinion. Although Ian believes that special education benefits some disabled people, he also perceives changes that would have made a difference in his own life, 'If I was born now I could go to [the local] primary school and it would be very different from day one'. His previous secondary school now offers courses leading to higher qualifications and the students have mainstream further education options too. There are more opportunities for employment and, '... attitudes have changed, it isn't a sin any more, it's nothing to be ashamed of'.

Key points and discussion

Poppy and Ian's life stories raise some similar questions to those highlighted earlier by Florence and Dan but they also reveal traces of significant changes in public policies. A reading of the academic literature might suggest that their generation grew up at a time when public assumptions about the social exclusion of disabled people were rapidly changing. For example, the literature points to emerging critiques of residential institutions of all kinds (Goffman, 1961; Caputo and Yount, 1993). Yet the 1970s saw a rapid growth in the number of special schools for disabled children and most of this cohort were already in secondary school before the Warnock Report (1978) highlighted educational segregation and signalled changes for the next generation (see Clough and Corbett, 2004).

In terms of support for family life, both Ian and Poppy's experiences reinforce the importance to children of acceptance and normality at home. Poppy's childhood was marked by growing estrangement from parents, siblings and neighbourhood friends as a consequence of long-term placement in a residential special school from an early age. Although Ian came home at weekends there were similarities in his experience. In this sense, it was friendships with other disabled children (in an institutional environment) that characterised the everyday world of their childhoods. Within these segregated environments there was also a lack of social expectation, or role models, for a future family life in adulthood. However, both Poppy and Ian suggest some advantages in attending special school, fearing potential isolation and stigmatisation in the mainstream.

Poppy and Ian's early residential school experiences in the 1960s and 1970s reveal highly institutionalised regimes, framed by a therapeutic ethos of compliance with physical normalisation, and a risk of abuse (including abuse arising from fad therapies and treatments). Since this time, the approaches described in the stories have been widely debated and critiqued (see Oliver, 1989, and Read's 1998 response, for example). Both stories do, however, hint at a liberalisation of approaches to special education during the 1970s and the emergence of second-chance academic opportunities in the further education sector (albeit with very patchy provision). For both Poppy and Ian their first exposure to mainstream education, as young adults in college, came as a significant culture shock.

Poppy's experience of access barriers at college highlights the absence of non-discrimination policies and reasonable adjustment responsibilities prior to the 1990s. Like those in the older generation, practical solutions to environmental barriers came often from ad hoc interventions by close family or individual staff members (rather than routinely from public providers). However, Ian's story also reveals traces of new public policies recognising the additional costs of living with impairment (such as Attendance and Mobility Allowances, equipment provision and home adaptation grants). These, in particular, had been highlighted at the time by the Disablement Income Group (founded in

1965) in its objections to the draft Social Security Bill in 1973 (*Hansard*, 6 February 1973, v850, cc212-13) and research by Hyman (1977) on *The extra costs of disabled living* (see also Large, 1991).

Why Poppy chose to pursue employment working with other disabled people is not entirely clear (Ian was volunteered by his father). On the one hand, these disability-related jobs might be seen as continuing segregated life trajectories begun in childhoods spent in residential institutions. On the other hand, Poppy's job led to new encounters with the emerging sub-culture of disability arts, in which radically different disability identities were being explored (see Morrison and Finkelstein, 1993; Sutherland, 1997; Masefield, 2006).

Unlike previous generations, disability awareness and equality policies generated opportunities to discover alternative disability identities through paid or voluntary work. From the mid-1980s, a new micro-industry of self-empowered 'trainers', such as the Disabled Trainers' Forum (established under the auspices of the London Boroughs Disability Resource Team), was beginning to challenge the presumed authority and expertise of medical and social work professions over disability issues (Gillespie-Sells and Campbell, 1991). As Poppy notes, the emergence of consumer-driven information and advice services (like the DIAL project where Ian gained his work experience) has been viewed as significant to disabled people's empowerment.

Reflecting on their adult lives, both Poppy and Ian point to the 1995 Disability Discrimination Act as a key reference point for comparing past and present public policies. Inevitably, this raises questions about whether life has indeed been any 'different' for young disabled people growing up since then. Ian's story also draws attention to the importance of technological developments in access to employment (such as the greater accessibility of public transport or information and communication technologies). For today's generation of young people, it is important to recall that neither portable computing nor the World Wide Web existed until the mid-1990s, well after Poppy and Ian entered their adult working lives.

Children of the 1980s

The youngest cohort, those born in the 1980s, are the first generation to reach adulthood in the era of comprehensive non-discrimination and human rights legislation, following a decade of implementation of the 1995 Disability Discrimination Act and, more recently, ratification of the UN Convention (as highlighted in Chapter One). However, the following two stories raise new questions and concerns about exactly how far we have really come since the 1940s.

Holly

Holly was born, several months prematurely, in the 1980s, 'I had to wear dolls' clothes … back then there wasn't, you know, clothes on the high street for premature babies'. Her parents separated after her impairment was diagnosed, when her biological father was unable to come to terms with the fact that, 'he'd created something that was imperfect'. Holly lived with her mother, who gave up her career, and a step-brother from a previous marriage. Her mother remarried and Holly has always seen her step-father as her father. There were supportive family relationships in early childhood, especially from grandparents. Later on, these relationships became more difficult and Holly is largely estranged from her parents now, 'I've never really worked out whether that was because I was the only girl or whether that was because, obviously, I was the only one in the immediate family with a disability'.

She remembers an active childhood, being largely unconscious of difference until she was in her late teens but, once she went to a residential special school, there were few opportunities to develop close friendships in her home environment – 'when I got home I was at home and there was nothing for me outside of home'. The special school provided the same small circle of friends throughout childhood and Holly found it difficult to make new friends when she left, 'getting used to being the only one with a disability, all at the same time. It was a very big thing to do.' The pre-conceptions and attitudes of non-disabled men also made it difficult to date or develop romantic relationships but Holly is currently in a long-term relationship where, 'to this day my disability has never been brought into anything'. She would like to marry and, if pregnancy is not an option, adopt a baby.

When Holly was born, she was not expected to live for more than a few days and doctors advised her parents not to bond with her. The precise nature of her impairment was not diagnosed until she was 18 months old, however. She was sent to a residential special school when she was two years old, and stayed there until she was 18. Looking back, Holly feels that this restricted her social and academic development, and sheltered her from the realities of mainstream society: 'I personally feel that I was kind of kept within this safety zone'. The school environment was wheelchair accessible and her peers were other young people with physical impairments: 'Instead of seeing the disability you just saw a person … so it kind of just didn't register at all'. There were some social advantages to living with friends as a weekly boarder but Holly feels that low academic expectations at the school left her with limited qualifications and employment opportunities in adult life.

When she left school at the age of 18 Holly also left home, partly because she had become more distant from her parents, and because she had experienced some domestic violence and abuse. She turned to social services who told her that she would need to go into 'a home'. This was not something she was could accept, 'she was like, "well, that's really the only option, if you want to leave home that is the only option we have for you"'. Holly did not know what her rights were in this situation but she was able to access an advocate, who helped her to move temporarily into a women's refuge, 'there's not many hostels or safe houses that would accept somebody with a disability'. Holly was offered a council flat, which she went to look at independently, and decided that she could live in. However, social services also sent an occupational therapist to assess it, who decided it was not suitable, '... maybe it's not the best flat for wheelchair access ... but because I understand my own body I know I can deal with it'. Holly won the argument and lives there with assistance from 'carers', who 'come in and support me with domestic tasks and bathing and meal preparation and laundry'. Her reliance on housing benefits restricts her relationship with her partner because 'Somebody can only actually stay at your property two nights a week otherwise you lose your benefits'. She would like to get married but sees reliance on benefits as a barrier to this.

Although Holly was determined to follow her childhood dream to be a dancer, she had never seen, or heard of, disabled dancers, such as those working in disability arts companies like Candoco or Salamanda Tandam. She remembers talking to the school careers advisor about her ambitions, 'that just completely and utterly threw him'. His advice was to become a secretary instead. Holly enrolled on a performing arts course at a mainstream college in the late 1990s (against advice from her mother and teachers). She was the only person who used a wheelchair and it was the first time she encountered significant barriers. She wanted to be inconspicuous rather than drawing attention to herself by using assistance, 'maybe if I had my time again I would have taken the option ... I wasn't going to be singled out by having a support worker'. She enjoyed the course but completed only one year before a worsening of her impairment condition led her to leave. She enrolled on a different course later, where she felt more confident to ask for student support services. This was after the extension of non-discrimination legislation into educational provision, after 2001, but Holly still found the provision patchy.

Holly does some voluntary work for a local disability organisation. She sees it as a stepping stone to paid employment: 'The reason that I'm here really is to prove myself'. She thinks her limited qualifications have been a big barrier: 'I don't think I'm intellectually at the standard people would want me to be at for the kind of money I need to survive'. She also volunteers with another charity that supports children and young people who have experienced abuse. Given a choice, Holly would prefer not to work for a disability organisation; 'just because I have a disability doesn't mean I have to work for a disability organisation' but the opportunity came up and she needed work experience. She remains concerned about her financial dependency and the benefits trap.

Looking back, Holly feels that she knew nothing about 'the outside world' when she was at school, about her rights to an independent life or about the Disability Discrimination Act. She thinks that 'special needs schools do need to prepare their students a lot, lot more for the kind of attitudes they're going to come across'. Technological developments have helped her – 'you can't even think of getting a kind of wheelchair that I have in the 1940s, 50s, 60s' – and she sees positive changes in public attitudes but, 'I don't think it's changing at the pace that it should be'. She feels that these attitudes still stereotype disabled people as 'eternal children' who are unequipped for sexual relationships. Her feelings about disability identity have changed greatly since she has grown up, 'I'm far more into disability rights and disability equality than I ever was … I'm very much a disability activist'.

Harvey

Harvey was born in the early 1980s and describes a 'working-class' family background, embedded in traditions of male manual labour that were somewhat at odds with growing up as a disabled child. When he was quite young, his mother left his father, following episodes of domestic violence, to stay with the children in a women's refuge but, 'while I lived with the effect of that I, myself, was never the victim of domestic abuse'. They went back to the abusive relationship after leaving the refuge due to a lack of accessible social housing and local service provision to support them: 'my mother was faced with a choice; you either take this inhospitable residence or you go back to your abusive partner'.

Harvey's mother formed a new relationship and, from the age of ten, he developed a more positive relationship with his step-father. Although his mother had made sure the children were never separated, Harvey sees his childhood as very different from that of his brother (who took less interest in education and could be violent sometimes too). He was closer with his sister, who 'always helped me out from an early age'. These days, Harvey lives independently with assistance and support provided from social services and from friends – 'my mother looked after me for 18 years and I don't want me mum looking after me any more'. Although Harvey feels that he needs 24-hour support he receives funding for only 15 hours per week.

Harvey remembers having friends at the local junior school, 'they used to come round to my house and we used to play on the computer games'. At this point disability was not an issue between them but when Harvey reached his teens, in a mainstream secondary school, he became much more aware of it. This had quite a negative impact on his self-esteem. Being excluded from the everyday activities of his immediate peers in the neighbourhood, Harvey focused more on his academic work: 'I was always the geek who only got top grades because he was in a wheelchair'. Socially, things improved at university, where Harvey made lasting friendships with both disabled and non-disabled peers and met his first girlfriend. Sexual and romantic relationships had been a difficult and sensitive issue growing up, and not having a girlfriend at school led on to homophobic taunting from other boys there, so 'once I got a girlfriend that was a big kind of social pressure off my back'.

Harvey says that the doctors told his mother when he was born that he had a 20 per cent chance of living. As an infant, he began intensive physiotherapy, which continued until there were diminishing gains in his mobility and he was too old to use the children's services centre. There was a strong pressure towards normalisation and cure, although Harvey remembers going to hospital for an operation when he was about ten but being refused because the surgeon was not confident it would work: 'I finally realised then that there was no chance of me being able to walk'. There were subsequent attempts at surgery, and experimentation – 'these crackpot American doctors came over and decided that hey presto! They have discovered a cure'. Harvey and a friend were invited to participate in a medical trial, which was tempting, given Harvey's unhappiness at the time, but his mother resisted.

Harvey went to a local mainstream school when he was five, struggling at first but catching up, 'once I got used to it, I took to it like a fish to water'. Despite changes towards more inclusive educational policies in the early 1980s, there was an expectation that Harvey would go to special school but his mother was determined he should go to the local mainstream school and live with the family. There was considerable scepticism from professionals about this but 'I'm really pleased that my mother fought against that ... and to ensure that I had the support to succeed' (he had learning support assistants in class from the beginning).

Harvey remembers that his mother had high expectations of him, knowing he would not go into manual labour like most of the young men in the town. He also remembers disabled friends at school who, he feels, encouraged him socially and academically. Harvey went on to pass his GCSEs and to enrol for A-levels. By this time, in the late 1990s, his teachers also had higher expectations, although Harvey rebelled and spent less time on his studies. Eventually, he went on to university and is currently studying for a postgraduate degree. In the future Harvey would like to have a job connected with disability rights, if his employment support needs can be met.

Looking back, Harvey attributes much to his mother's resilience and intervention when he was a child. There were teachers who helped him too. He feels that he has become more resilient but his bad experiences have also left him with some lasting mental health problems. He has only become 'comfortable' with a disability identity since enjoying a more integrated social life at university. Meeting other disabled people was important in this respect, providing peer role models. Harvey has seen real changes since the late 1990s in the support available for independent living but feels there is a much still to do. He sees big gaps between policies and practices, as disabled people are 'still less likely to go into further education; still less likely to have a job and still more likely to be living in poverty'.

Key points and discussion

Like the examples from the first two generations, Holly and Harvey's stories raise important questions about the times in which they grew up. In historical context, the stories from this generation are of particular interest in addressing the core questions for this book – in particular, has life 'changed' for young disabled people growing up today?

They were born in the 1980s while public policy debate in Britain, under the Thatcher Governments, was increasingly dominated by neo-liberal critiques of public welfare provision (see Pierson, 1994). At the same time, they have grown up during perhaps the most significant period of development in British public policy and debate concerning disability rights issues.

Considering experiences of family and friendship, both Holly and Harvey's stories convey accounts of parental separation and step-parenting. These experiences are by no means unique to this generation (Florence was the child of a single mother in the 1940s; Dan's father remarried after his wife's death). However, their stories draw attention to significant changes in marriage and household patterns in Britain since the 1970s and 1980s. For example, the British divorce rate had tripled between 1960 and 2002, to one of the highest in Europe, although not simply as a consequence of changes in divorce laws (González and Viitanen, 2009). Although the two examples should not be seen as representative of wider populations they do raise questions about the extent to which changes in family relationship patterns have impacted differentially on disabled children and young people (for example, see Mauldon, 1992 for a corresponding analysis of data from the US).

Holly's and Harvey's stories also connect family separation with episodes of domestic abuse (although in different ways). Both Harvey's mother, and later Holly, lived temporarily in women's refuges as an escape from violence in the 1980s and 1990s (both draw attention to a lack of physical accessibility for people with significant mobility impairments). The first such refuges and supported housing schemes had emerged only in the early 1970s, building on the activism of feminist movements, but grew rapidly in number by the mid-1980s (Pahl, 1985; Dobash and Dobash, 1992). Legislative protection for 'battered wives' was not implemented until the late 1970s, following the 1976 Domestic Violence Act. The 1980s and 1990s saw a similarly increasing awareness about the risk of physical, emotional or sexual abuse for disabled children (Helfer, 1973; Martin and Beezley, 1974; Westcott and Cross, 1996; Ammerman, 1997).

The lack of accessible supported housing provision is acutely highlighted in Holly's story, when, at the age of 18, social services offered her a place in a residential 'home' as the 'only option'. It is significant that this occurred after implementation of the 1990s 'community care' reforms, and the initial introduction of direct payments for people with physical impairments aged 18–64. The principles of support for independent living had been well established in user-led pilot projects for at least a decade (for example, Davis, 1981; Priestley, 1998a; Barnes and Mercer, 2006) and Holly's example questions the extent to which the aspirations of community care policy had become a reality. The importance of disability information services (highlighted in the stories of Poppy and Ian) are underlined by Holly's lack of knowledge about her rights. However, her access to an advocate proved a turning point away from the trajectory towards institutionalisation.

Harvey's comments on the amount of support he needs, and Holly's account of finding her flat, highlight the public/private tension between self-assessed and professionally-assessed needs within community care management (see Priestley, 1998b). However, both Harvey and

Holly now live independently of their families, with practical support provided through personal assistants, care agency staff or friends. In this way, their stories do provide recent traces of the policy shift towards more individualised, user-controlled support. Holly felt unfamiliar and uncomfortable with using assistance at first but gained confidence through her experience of student support services (just after implementation of the 2001 Special Educational Needs and Disability Act).

In terms of medicine and treatment, Holly's extremely premature birth hints at the scale of technological developments in neo-natal care that have led to increased survival rates for children born with significant physical impairments, when compared to earlier generations (Tin et al, 1997). Technological developments have also been identified as highly significant in relation to wheelchair design and environmental accessibility (see Woods and Watson, 2004; Watson and Woods, 2005). In contrast, Harvey's recollections of the normalising discourse that framed his intensive physiotherapy are reminiscent of those described in earlier generation stories, albeit within a shift from hospital-based to community-based rehabilitation services. The offer of an experimental surgical 'cure' recalls Ian's story of experimental therapies in the 1970s but Harvey's mother's resistance also draws attention to the increasing ability of parents and children to question medical authority in decisions about treatment (Alderson, 1993; McLaughlin et al, 2008).

Educational provision played an important part in the stories. For Holly, being sent to a residential special school from the age of two to eighteen was a factor in estrangement from her family (as it was for Poppy and, to a lesser extent, Ian). Her accounts of low academic expectations, and confinement with a small cohort of other disabled children, are very similar to the stories conveyed by those born in the 1960s. Unlike Holly, Harvey attended mainstream schools. His opportunity for individualised support from learning support assistants in the classroom arose from a shift of emphasis in integrated school policies in the 1980s, but he would not have had the opportunity without his mother's resistance to the professionally-induced trajectory towards special schooling. For both Holly and Ian, going on to further and higher education provided life changing opportunities. As students, coinciding with implementation of the 2001 Act, they experienced sometimes patchy accessibility but benefited from individualised student support services and the Disabled Students Allowance (introduced in 1993).

Harvey's academic success (he is still studying) suggests a very different life course pathway than might have been expected for Dan, born in the 1940s. Both men were born into traditional working-class communities, in which there were established trajectories of manual labour within localised industries. Harvey's story raises questions about the factors that led him away from this trajectory. On the one hand, his impairment appeared to rule out the obvious range of occupational choices (and these occupations were also diminishing, from the 1980s, with the wholesale restructuring of British manufacturing industry). On the other hand, the opportunities to pursue an academic career, from his class background and with his impairment, might not have materialised without policy initiatives to improve accessibility for disabled students and to widen university participation for children from low income families.

Mainstream college provided a positive social environment for Harvey and, eventually, for Holly. Both draw attention to the significance of gaining belated access to mainstream youth culture but also to the specific benefit of meeting other young disabled people with whom they could identify. Unlike Poppy in the previous generation, Holly's engagement with creative arts was not framed by access to a radical disability culture. Like Poppy and Ian, she did find work experience through a disability organisation but she would prefer not to work there. There are, however, still traces in the stories of the disability identity politics that became more widespread during the 1980s and 1990s. Harvey now describes himself as being 'political' about disability issues and Holly calls herself a 'disability activist' (although she is not directly involved in disability politics), providing examples of identity scripts that were not necessarily available to young disabled adults in the 1950s or 1970s.

Conclusions

This chapter gives a flavour of the life stories contributed for this book via six short examples, two from each generation. The stories are not intended to be 'representative' of the generational cohorts from which they come but they reveal the kinds of questions that arise when individual biographies are read in historical policy contexts. As explained in Chapter One, the approach to this book seeks out these connections between the individual and the social, between biography and history, and between structure and agency.

As the six short stories show, the connections between private lives and public policies are blurred and shifting. Changes in policy frameworks can create new opportunity structures, which open the possibility of new life choices. However, as policy implementation research repeatedly demonstrates, there is often a significant gap between policy rhetoric and reality in individual lives. Changes in policy discourse may take many years to materialise in legislation and many more to gain any systemic hold on practice. Established institutions, environments and social relations may continue to frame old expectations about life trajectories, long after new policies have been introduced.

When we look at individual lives, we find valuable evidence about the reality of the real choices available to people in their personal circumstances. Narrative accounts draw particular attention to the significant turning points that determine the course of subsequent biographical pathways. It is at these moments of opportunity that public institutions and policies often provide, or block, transitions. To understand such turning points it is essential also to consider the kinds of resources, or capital, on which people draw to exercise choice and agency. As the examples in this chapter show, successful transitions and independent lives are often forged in spite of, rather than because of, the opportunities presented by public policies. The importance attributed in the stories to resilience, resistance, role models, familial and social capital underlines this. Understanding the circumstances and human relationships within which life choices are made is essential to formulating better policies. The remaining chapters in this book use examples and moments from a much larger number of life stories to examine, thematically, some of the key policy issues that have been raised so far. They focus, in particular, on family life, medicalisation, education, employment and disability identities and politics.

Questions for discussion

- How useful are the individual stories of disabled people in stimulating critical reflection on the development of public policies?
- What has been the real life impact of policies to improve disability rights and independent living choices by comparison with the kinds of support available previously?

Keeping it in the family

The stories summarised in Chapter Two showed just how important it was for people to be able to draw on the resilience or resources of those closest to them at key turning points in their lives. The same stories showed what can happen to people's lives in the absence of such support. This chapter examines experiences of family life, using examples from the three generations to illustrate how social trends and public policies have affected choices and opportunities for young disabled people to develop and sustain kinship relationships. The discussion identifies a broad distinction between two competing life trajectories – inclusion in the private life of the family and exclusion from family life in public institutions.

This first section deals mainly with family relationships in the private domain. The examples highlight the importance attached to family as a site for acceptance and social inclusion. They also illustrate how people sometimes attribute disruptions in family relationships to disability issues. The discussion draws attention to gendered divisions of emotional and caring labour between birth parents, including the significance attributed to maternal advocacy and paternal abandonment. However, it also points to the positive influence of extended family resources, such as step-parenting and grandparenting. These experiences are set in the context of policy developments and changing family patterns during the 20th century and their implications for disabled children.

The second section focuses on childhood experiences of separation from family life arising from institutional segregation for the purposes of medical treatment or schooling (these contexts are then addressed in more detail in Chapters Four and Five, respectively). The examples illustrate, often graphically, how public policies and institutions can create real barriers to family life with sometimes lifelong implications. They also point to some of the important changes that have taken place since the 1940s.

Life at home – acceptance and rejection

The life stories collected for this book conveyed much about intimate family relationships between mothers, fathers and disabled children but they also revealed traces of wider social changes since the Second World War. These included changes in public policies affecting disabled families and demographic patterns of change in the structure of families more generally.

In terms of family life, the policy framework of the 1940s and 1950s could be seen as offering people with physical impairments a dichotomy of life course trajectories – between an uneasy social inclusion and the total institution. For those in the oldest generation whose families were able, and determined, to cope with life at home there were opportunities for a relatively 'normal' family life but with a lack of targeted help or support from the state (an absence of disability-related cash benefits, community-based health care, social services, or learning support in mainstream schools). Although post-war welfare legislation following the Beveridge Report introduced some limited disability allowances, new policies maintained many pre-war assumptions about the kind of support that would be provided within families, primarily through the unpaid caring labour of mothers and daughters (Williams, 1989; Pedersen, 1993). For children whose families were unable, or unwilling, to cope then the alternative life trajectory tended towards institutionalisation, in a long-stay hospital, residential school or children's home.

In terms of family life, Dan's story (discussed in Chapter Two) conveyed this dichotomy well. There was a clear sense of the ordinariness of growing up in a supportive network of family relationships in which impairment was not a significant marker of difference. Physical impairment and 'crippled' children were by no means unknown to poor urban families who had experienced pre-war depression and wartime bombing, lived in insanitary and over-crowded housing, and who worked in manual occupations (for example, Daunton, 2000). While disability issues quickly emerged for Dan when he went in search of adult employment, disability policy did not reveal itself within the family. Similarly, May felt that her impairment was accepted at home and that it was 'never a big deal':

> ... they had a lot of problems themselves because my mum was always poorly. My dad was a bit of a womaniser ... we just got on with it really. Left to our own devices.

Hillary recalled how her parents brought her up in a 'normal' way so that she was never 'closeted away'. Akeelah described support within the family, particularly from her father, as the 'backbone' in her life.

Maggie described her family as 'brilliant' and 'really close', although she suspects that it was not like that for everyone in her generation:

> *... you do hear stories how, about people, like some people are shoved in rooms if anybody came, you know, they were never allowed to meet the family. No, it was good, yeah, it was.*

So, although there was a remembrance of assumptions that children with physical impairments were sometimes shut away in institutions or the back rooms of family homes (and not everyone from the oldest generation felt accepted at home) this was not generally the experience conveyed in the narratives. Indeed, family support and advocacy was often critical to the negotiation of private lives in relation to public policies and institutions.

Advocate mothers

Past research has consistently shown that, even in two-parent families, mothers are more likely to mediate between a disabled child and service providers, or to attend routine appointments, compared to fathers, whose involvement tends to occur in more isolated incidents (for example, Strong, 1979; Graham, 1985; Beresford, 1995; Read, 2000). The same kind of pattern was evident in the stories collected for this book. Irrespective of the presence of fathers in the family household, mothers usually took responsibility for the health and welfare of their disabled children. The following two examples provide a flavour of this maternal agency, resistance or resilience.

> *I remember hearing mum have a conversation, and I was about eight ... , and me mum said this doctor said 'she's not going to walk properly ... she'll never have children and she won't get married' and she [mum] said 'Pah, I'm going to prove him wrong'. ... in them years to actually go, leave your consultant [here] to go [there], well it wasn't done ... It was me mum who took me, 'cos there was three girls and me gran and we didn't have a lot of money. My dad was a plasterer by trade in the village, so mum had to take me to hospital on the train ...* (Maggie, born in the 1940s)

> *The doctors told her to put me away in an institution. You know what it was like in those days. She was told to forget about me. But my mother was very strong willed and she fought for me tooth and nail not to put me away. My mother had waited seven years*

> *for a baby ... [after I was bullied at school] I had a home tutor*
> *... She wasn't very patient with me and got me very upset. So*
> *my mother kicked her out ... [later, as an adult] I went into [the*
> *general hospital]. They neglected me. They didn't wash me, bath*
> *me, feed me. They didn't change my dressings. There was dirt and*
> *dust on the floor and no doctors came to visit. My mother came in*
> *every day and did everything for me.* (Hillary, born in the 1940s)

The latter decades of the 20th century saw a significant increase in the labour market participation of mothers yet clear evidence remains of gendered divisions in family care and support (Daly and Rake, 2003). The stories from the youngest generation provide traces of this enduring maternal presence in the lives of young disabled adults today. For example,

> *when it come to hospital appointments and stuff like that, mum*
> *would take us for those and, you know, be there after school ...*
> *so I suppose, you know, in terms of relationship I was slightly*
> *closer to me mam 'cos I spent more time with her.* (Steve, born
> in the 1980s)

Across the three generations there was a great deal of continuity in the significance attributed to the presence of mothers at key turning points in childhood and youth. However, this presence was narrated much less in terms of mundane domestic help or intimate care than in terms mediation and advocacy with professionals in the public sphere. Although there were exceptions, the characteristic anecdote was one in which it was the mother who actively resisted an undesired life course trajectory introduced by a professional authority or a public institution. This might involve, typically, refusing to accept a medical prognosis, refusing to abandon a child to a residential institution or challenging a special school placement.

Such examples of maternal challenge to professional authority are clearly evident in the next two chapters but they mirror wider changes in the social roles of both women and professionals. For example, Roberts (1984/1996) drew on the oral histories of working-class women, to illustrate the 'domestic ideology' that framed gendered divisions of family labour at the beginning of the 20th century and (1995) the changes that took place from 1940 to 1970. In addition to an increase in paid employment outside the home, and new domestic and contraceptive technologies, she pointed to a significant shift in women's perceptions of professionals – from authority figures to providers of care services.

Compared with the near universal significance attributed to maternal advocacy in the stories, the recollection of paternal roles varied much more. Fathers were important, often providing essential help and assistance in dealing with practical barriers to inclusion, but they were often absent too (for reasons of national service, employment or because they had simply left the family). Gendered divisions of labour meant that even supportive fathers were more likely to be away from the house and that mothers (sometimes siblings or grandparents) provided the majority of informal support at home.

Absent fathers

In their study of early 20th-century experiences, Humphries and Gordon (1992) suggest that fathers exhibited the felt stigma of parenting a disabled child more acutely than mothers did, perceiving it as a challenge to their 'self respect and masculinity'. This led some of them to avoid contact with their child as far as possible.

> *I never saw my father much when I was little … By the time he came in from work then he wanted me to be in bed kind of thing. He wouldn't even sit at the same table as me. I was a thorn in his flesh so I tried to keep out of his way. He thought I was a one off. He never met another spastic and he thought I was something terrible.* (extract from Humphries and Gordon, 1992, p 26)

In all three generations there were examples where parental separation, or paternal absence, was attributed to this kind of inability to cope with parenting a disabled child. It was the father who withdrew from the family in every case of estrangement except for Florence's abandonment in the hospital by her mother (summarised in Chapter Two):

> *… she decided that she would just leave me there, and part of that was because she was in a different relationship and I was the child of a different relationship and there were all sorts of things and I think she just felt she just couldn't cope with the problems of sort of having a child that wasn't going to be able to do things normally. So I then stayed in the hospital.*

Florence's story highlights a number of social factors and it is easy to imagine the dilemmas that her mother might have faced. There were still strong social taboos surrounding both unmarried mothers and disability in the 1940s and a distinct absence of community-based support services. Catherine (also born in the 1940s) was sent to live with her grandparents, and then to boarding school from the age of five, but she still feels that disability played a part in her parents' subsequent separation. It then surfaced again in adulthood:

> *when I left school I lived with my mother and my step dad until I got married ... I can't say I got on well with my stepfather because it was a difficult situation. He resented the attention my mother gave me.*

A number of studies have suggested that fathers are more likely to experience greater distress at the diagnosis of a child's impairment than mothers (for example, Hornby, 1992; Herbert and Carpenter, 1994) and may find their adjustment more lengthy and unpredictable (Harrison et al, 2007). Meltzer et al (1989) highlighted the increased risk of relationship breakdown among parents with disabled children and it is well documented that a greater proportion of disabled children live with lone mothers compared to the general population (for example, Lawton and Quine, 1990; Beresford, 1995; Read, 2000). Mothers of disabled children were more likely to enter single parenthood, to carry full responsibility for the care and upbringing of the child, and to have a reduced chance of securing future relationships compared to mothers of non-disabled children (Read, 2000).

Looking at the youngest generation (born in the 1980s) there were several examples of parental separation to choose from. For example, Holly's impairment was not diagnosed until she was 18 months old but:

> *coincidentally that's when they split up ... it was down to my natural father not accepting that he'd created something that was imperfect. To him having a disability was imperfection and — and he couldn't process that in his — in his mind that — that a daughter of his was going to have a disability for life.*

Disability was certainly not the only factor at play in parents separating (Rachel and Helen were born to single mothers, while Zoe's parents separated over domestic violence, for example) but it was often invoked as relevant.

Like disability, the institution of the family in Britain has been socially constructed, historically produced and contingent upon economic, cultural and political developments. There have been some significant changes in household composition and family roles since the 1940s, and former conceptions have been much challenged and re-negotiated. The nuclear family (consisting of parents and dependent children) has remained the most popular family form for at least four hundred years (Giddens, 2008) but patterns have changed. For instance, Gittens (1982) points to the dramatic decline in household size since the Second World War. The average household size in England, around 2.4 people, is about half of what it was in the 19th century (HMSO, 2004). An ageing population, rising divorce rates and geographical mobility mean that the total number of households will continue to rise but with a notable increase in the proportion of single person households (DCLG, 2009).

There have been increases in lone parenting, co-parenting and step-parenting. In the 1930s and 1940s, family bonds and relationships were more often disrupted by parental or child death than they are now (Laslett, 1977) but in terms of public policy, marriage was regarded as virtually indissoluble. Divorce was granted only in a minority of cases until legislative reform in 1969. At the same time, the introduction of oral contraception for women and abortion were beginning to reframe parents' expectations about family size and structure, and influencing the choices they might make. Women born in the 1960s have been less likely to marry than, or at least to marry as young as, those born in the 1940s (Frejka and Sardon, 2005). Most adults do still marry but there has been a considerable increase in unmarried parenting, with or without parental cohabitation (Irwin, 2000). These trends have affected disabled children more than non-disabled children.

Although family breakdown is not at all uncommon for disabled children it is not the norm. Re-analysis of samples from the 1991 Census suggested that the vast majority of disabled children in Britain were living at home rather than in institutional settings (Gordon et al, 2000). The same data indicated that more than 90% of disabled children were living with at least one of their birth parents (2.2% in foster homes and 0.7% with a relative).

The vast majority of those living with only one parent were in a household with more than one adult (usually including a step-parent). Indeed, the stories from the youngest generation placed a great deal of positive emphasis on the supportive role of step-fathers (including Holly's and Zoe's stories) and of grandparents (for example, Helen). In these stories, the mother's new partner was often referred to as a 'real father', accompanied by clear examples of high levels of support and practical help. These anecdotes, in particular, tended to challenge the gendered discourse of birth parenting alluded to earlier (that is, step-fathers were often seen as much more involved than birth fathers).

Sisters and brothers

When reading childhood stories within the intimate context of family relationships, comparisons between the lives of siblings can be revealing. Experiences of differential treatment from parents, or of separation when one child lives away from home, resulted in very different life expectations for siblings within the same family. At home, there was certainly a widespread recognition of everyday help and support from sisters and brothers. For example, Akeelah (born in the 1940s) remembers how her father would spoil her, compared to her siblings, but still wonders sometimes if he only did this 'out of pity'. Steve (born in the 1980s) attributed his 'very close relationship' with his brother to the way their roles in the family were negotiated.

> *That's probably because, you know, he's had to grow up pretty quick 'cos I think there's a bit of pressure on him because, or there was when we were younger anyway. 'Cos, despite him being younger, he was expected to look after me, you know ... just more of a supporting role but most younger siblings don't have to do that.*

There were few stories of real difficulty or resentment in such relationships but negotiating fair and equal treatment between siblings could become a significant issue when children had to live away from the family for extended periods of time. For example, although Worton now has a very good adult relationship with her sister, things were not so easy when they were children in the 1950s.

> *I went to boarding school when [my sister] wasn't even a year old, so most of the time I wasn't there and she was the only girl in the house and every now and again I came home, and looking back now I realise that the problem was she saw me as the interloper who took her place in the household ... when she was older we had problems with her wanting to get back at me for me taking her place as she saw it when I kept reappearing every now and again.*

Sibling rivalries are by no means unique to disabled children but Worton's story hints at how public policies (in this case segregated residential schooling for disabled children) can influence private lives and relationships in unintended ways. Most of those born in the 1940s experienced forced separations from their families before the age of seven due to long periods spent in hospital, often from infancy, or because they were sent away to residential schools. It is easy enough to assert, from a contemporary children's rights perspective, that public policies should seek to avoid forced family separation but it is only by exploring qualitative life experiences that the relational and psycho-emotional consequences of such policies are revealed (see Reeve, 2002). As Worton continued her anecdote, the more private consequences became clearer.

> *[Mum] used to try and get her to take me out and play with her and her mates, but ... the one thing she didn't want to be doing was to be seen pushing her 'crippled' sister in a pushchair, wheelchair. She didn't want to so she had this little thing, which I've hardly told anybody about, she would take me out because she was told to do so and, when she got far enough away from home so it was unlikely that she would get caught, she'd hide me in the bushes and go off and play and retrieve me about the time we were due to go home. And she'd say 'don't you ever go and tell anyone because I'll do nasty things to you'.*

Worton's experience conveys a strong social stigma attached to her physical impairment in public space (see Goffman, 1968) but also highlights how the negative association with disability was felt by her sister too. Later, Birenbaum (1970, p 196) would refer to this as a kind of 'courtesy stigma' transferred to those close to the disabled person: 'their normality is obvious in their performance of conventional social roles; their differentness is occasionally manifested by their association with the stigmatised during encounter with normals [sic]'.

The stories collected for this book, showed how non-disabled family members sometimes sought to evade this kind of stigma by developing a social life that kept them as distant as possible from a disabled sibling or child. Some parents cut off all links with their disabled children (retaining contact with their non-disabled siblings). In other cases, families were forced to accept separation because the opportunity structure presented by the policies and institutions of the time presented them with no alternative. Bridging the deficits of support required for children, parents and siblings to live an ordinary family life together needs to be key objective for a disability policy focused on full participation and social inclusion in the community.

Public policy and family life

Looking at the life stories it is clear that professional authority, particularly medical authority, played a big part in decisions about separating disabled children from their parents and siblings (either for hospital treatment or for special schooling). This was particularly evident in the childhood accounts of those born in the 1940s and 1960s although there was very little evidence that the same professionals had much involvement or influence in family lives at home. Many of the strong critiques of the professional colonisation of everyday life, offered by disability activists and scholars in more recent years (for example, French, 1994; Swain and French, 2001), would not necessarily have been recognised by the oldest of the three generations.

Through the 1950s and 1960s there was little coordination of the limited support available to families (with a focus on hospital-based rehabilitation services in the case of children with physical impairment). Local authorities maintained responsibility for health visitors, home helps and child welfare clinics after the 1948 National Assistance Act, which also gave recognition to the Home Help Service. This led to a rapid increase to the latter's role and client numbers, which rose by 42% between 1949 and 1953 in England and Wales (the majority of clients being older people). Dexter and Harbert (1983, p 20) suggest that continuing expansion of the Service through the 1960s and 1970s was due, in large part, to changing demographics and family structure (including the dislocation of intergenerational support, the increased survival of children with significant impairments, and increasing life choices for women).

The establishment of local authority social services departments in 1970 was accompanied by a much more concerted public interest in the family and professional interest in private family relations was burgeoning by the mid-1970s. This included a marked increase in professional interest with family dysfunction and breakdown (for example, in the work of the Tavistock Institute, combining psychoanalytical traditions with new social sciences). A good deal was being written also about disability and the family, mainly from a similar social work or therapeutic perspective. Such studies were often concerned with individualised psycho-emotional issues, such as self-esteem (see Harvey and Greenway, 1984) or, for local authority practitioners, how to manage the expanding networks of intervention by the different 'caring professions' (for example, Black, 1978).

Disability was still mainly characterised as a negative and traumatic disruption to normal family relations, as a 'family crisis'. Such writings remained heavily grounded in personal tragedy models of disability and turned, increasingly, to the experiences of parents and siblings rather than the experiences of disabled children themselves. There was, however, also an emerging recognition of the 'disabled family'. As Topliss (1979, p 129) put it:

> Although the precise impact on family life depends upon the position within the family of the disabled person, a growing body of literature suggests whether it is the disabled husband, wife, child or elderly person who is affected disablement has an important effect on the relationship and opportunities of the family as a whole.

This kind of approach had both positive and negative implications for young disabled people within the family. On the one hand, it highlighted the lack of public support for inclusion at home and the need for public services and household income (for example, as acknowledged with the introduction of new care Attendance Allowances in 1971). On the other hand, public policy debates became increasingly preoccupied with arguments about the 'burden of care' rather than with disabled people's rights. The National Children's Bureau had drawn attention to the needs of siblings of disabled children in the early 1970s (Parfit, 1975) and Kew's (1975) book *Handicap and family crisis* portrayed a narrative of 'tragedy' and the 'problem of care' (see also Beresford, 1994; Nixon and Cummings, 1999). It is ironic that, while the professional narratives of the period convey the presence of a disabled child in the family as the problem for family relationships, the stories from disabled people convey their enforced removal from the family as the much bigger issue.

The absence of flexible and affordable community support services made it difficult for other family members to work (Baldwin, 1985). Disabled people were more likely to live in a family where no one worked, where family income was below the average and where there was a greater reliance on public transport (Barnes, 1991). Inadequate levels of income from employment and welfare benefits created a situation in which many disabled families experienced a higher cost (and lower standard) of living than non-disabled families (Martin and White, 1988; Berthoud et al, 1993). Impairment-specific dietary requirements, clothing needs, extra heating bills and transport costs all add up to make daily living an expensive business for some families (Disability Alliance, 1987; Thompson et al, 1990). In national survey research three quarters of parents said they did not have enough money to look after their disabled children (Beresford, 1995).

The language of the social model of disability was not widely available when Topliss (1975) wrote about the 'disabled family' (although the Disablement Income Group and UPIAS had begun to advance such ideas). More recently, and drawing more directly on social model concepts, Dowling and Dolan (2001) showed how families with disabled children continue to experience inequalities and reaffirm that, 'social organisation disables not just the family member who has an impairment but the whole family unit' (p 21, see also Connors and Stalker, 2003). However, the most dramatic manifestations of public policies affecting the family unit are evident in examples of institutional segregation and it is these that we turn to now.

Life away from home – the total institution

Much has been written about the removal of disabled people from community life to segregated residential institutions, epitomised by Goffman's (1961) account of the 'total institution' in which 'a large number of like-situated individuals, cut off from the wider society for an appreciable period of time together lead an enclosed formally administered round of life' (p 11). The experiences of those who lived in hospitals and special schools as children are examined in more detail in the next two chapters. The focus here is on the implications of that removal for family life and friendships at home.

The number of children with physical impairments sent to special schools was rising in the post-war period. The Board of Education (1958, p 133) were pleased to report more 'physically handicapped' children attending school because of the increased provision of 'special school accommodation for the severely crippled' but this was achieved at the expense of community integration. By 1964 there were 6,615 children attending special schools designated for 'the physically handicapped' while others spent long periods in hospital (at the end of the 1960s there were still around 3,500 children registered in hospital schools).

On the other hand, the Department of Education and Science (1972) identified more than 10,000 'physically handicapped' children attending mainstream schools in 1970, of whom 20% required some assistance in school, 15% using wheelchairs or walking aids (see also Topliss, 1975). These children would certainly have been known to their non-disabled peers at school but with few, if any, physically accessible buses, public spaces or street crossings to enable them to socialise freely outside school hours (see Watson et al, 1999). Indeed, there was no legal provision for such access to public buildings until the 1970 Chronically Sick and Disabled Persons Act (and no widespread enforcement until after the 1995 Disability Discrimination Act).

Several of the older participants drew attention to the lack of visibility or presence of disabled people in the communities in which they lived as children. Judy (who was born just before the Second World War and went to mainstream schools) attributed this to their isolation at home and to institutionalisation:

> *I don't know where I'd been but I had never known any other disabled people or families with a disabled child. But of course in those days disabled children often did not have any education at all, they were in institutions. On the other hand, I just wasn't in the world of disability.*

Judy's perception points to a dichotomy in the life stories between those who lived at home as children, largely unaware of disability issues, and those living in institutions, whose lives were dominated by them. Institutionalisation affected children and their families in all three generations and a reading of individual experiences cast some doubts on grand policy narratives that portray enlightened progress towards support for community living.

Family separation in hospital

The stories of those in the oldest generation underlined the predominance of medicine, and medical authority, in segregation from family life. Although the new National Health Service brought many changes, post-war medical and rehabilitation services for children with physical impairments were still predominantly hospital based. Among the stories collected for this book there were numerous accounts of long periods of childhood spent in hospital for treatment or rehabilitation, with minimal family contact.

The impact of medical treatment on children's lives is examined in the next chapter but suffice to say that a number of factors contributed to the net effect on children's experience of family life and friendships. The prolonged time then required for major invasive treatments and recovery was compounded by the absence of community-based services to support early discharge from hospital. The relative scarcity of local specialist hospital facilities required many families to travel long distances (further compounded where there was also a lack of access to private household transport). In addition, as Lomax (1996, p 12) notes, the institutional regimes of the former Victorian hospitals did little to encourage the maintenance of intimate connections with family:

the tendency continued for hospitals to isolate themselves from the community, as also evidenced by repeated medical demands to cut back on visiting hours in an effort to reduce the risk of infection from outside. One suspects, however, that it was also proving easier to run an efficient ward without too many parents on the scene.

The stories reinforced a sense of widespread acceptance and compliance with medical or nursing authority that, once admitted, parents could expect to leave their child in the care of the hospital until their discharge or death (Johnson, 1990). Despite the fact that daily visiting had been strongly recommended from the 1950s, it was not uncommon for visits to be limited to parents only, and then only once or twice a week, at the discretion of hospital staff (who sometimes thought it best for parents not to visit at all if a child appeared particularly upset). Public health concern with infectious disease reinforced such regimes in post-war isolation hospitals (see Chapter Four). The stories of those born in the 1940s provide clear insights into the family separation experienced. For example, Bella described how as an infant:

> *I was taken into an isolation hospital … my parents were only allowed to see me through a glass window in the door of the room that I was in … I was there for several months and then transferred directly from the isolation hospital to an orthopaedic hospital without going home … I came home again when I was four.*

During the four years that Bella was in hospital she had no contact with her brother because hospital policy dictated 'no visitors under the age of 15'. Her separation from family then became extended with her transfer to the orthopaedic hospital, from where she made only short visits home.

Grace also spent the first five years of her life in hospital under treatment for polio, during which time her mother died of the same disease. She never saw her again:

> *… my mother and I were both in iron lungs in an isolation hospital, and I can just about remember being there and I can then remember going home and being looked after by a nanny and by my grandmother. I hadn't realised how ill my mother was, obviously at five you don't.*

When Daisy went into hospital she was not aware why she was being sent away from her family or for how long she would be away:

> *It was just I was four years old I think and I didn't understand anything that was happening ... I wasn't told a thing. I mean my parents, all they said was, I think, was something like 'well, you know, the doctor is going to make you better'... And so they just kind of left me there and it was just absolutely devastating to be left in this huge hospital with these strangers who just seem, you know, as a child your sense of security is based in adults you can trust, isn't it?*

Worton's father had been brought up in an orphanage and was determined that his daughter would not have the same experience. However, she was sent to boarding school from the age of six until she was almost 18 (coming home only in the holidays). Parents were allowed to visit only one Sunday a term.

> *They went to great lengths to keep telling me that it was for my own good and they'd come back and fetch me soon ... I still remember [my mum] walking away and I was convinced I'd never see her again ... I missed just not having a home life really.*

The 1948 Children Act, based on recommendations from the Curtis Committee, sought to establish a more coordinated and enlightened approach towards children in public care. Although the Act increased protection from abuse and deprivations in children's homes, it was not taken to include institutions catering specifically for children with physical impairments or learning difficulties. In this sense, disabled children remained somewhat overlooked in the emergence of the early child protection policy agenda (Hardiker, 1999). However, concerns with familial separation were already well known at the time and much discussed (partly because of the recollection of mass evacuations of city children away from their families during the war).

In a letter to *The Lancet*, Rickman (1939) had argued that early detachment from familiar faces and relationships would 'show itself in unsatisfactory or unhappy social relationships later in life'. A more specific concern about deprivation from 'maternal care' during long stays in hospital was highlighted by the psychologist John Bowlby, who recounted 'vivid and distressing' examples and advocated change towards more 'regular visiting by the parents' (Bowlby, 1951; Moncrieff and Walton, 1952). Stacey et al (1970) and Rutter (1972) added further evidence on the lasting adult effects of prolonged periods of hospitalisation in childhood. Daily visiting for children in hospital was encouraged by the NHS from 1954 but this policy guidance did not seem to have filtered down to the experience of those we spoke to.

Bella, Grace and Daisy all found themselves in hospital on a regular basis throughout early childhood. For Daisy, it was a traumatic experience that she feels had a lasting impact on relationships with her parents and sister but she thought that things had improved for children growing up today:

> *The children are respected as human beings and not just people to have things done to. And the parents are able to go into hospital, or at least one of the parents is able to go into hospital with them, and stay with them. So there's a constant continuity of parental support. And nowadays people would be very supportive of the child, but in those days they weren't at all.*

The kind of isolation and family estrangement described in some of the stories was exacerbated in the 1940s and 1950s by the fact that paediatric surgery was only beginning to gain real recognition as a specialism (see Chapter Four). The opportunities for complex paediatric treatment were limited to relatively few hospitals – often in the cities, often a long way from the family home. As Daisy continues:

> *I remember going up to London, because I was in hospital in London, we lived in [another city] at the time, quite a long way from the major London hospitals ... I think my parents came every other weekend 'cos they didn't have a car or anything like that to start off with, so they came up on the steam train ... they still couldn't get there that often because obviously Dad had to work and after work didn't really want to make the journey.*

The availability of transport to visit children in hospital was reported as an issue for parents by Baldwin (1976) and Rutter (1972). Both studies suggested that the expense and inconvenience of arranging transport posed a significant barrier. This had a further negative impact on family relationships as it also reduced the opportunity for parents to discuss the child's fears and worries. Looking back now, Daisy still believes that early detachment from family when she was in hospital had a lasting effect on her capacity to develop relationships in adulthood:

> *And here I am at the age of 58, living on my own, no family, no children, you know, it's almost as if it pre-determined the rest of your life when that happens.*

However, family estrangement was by no means an inevitable consequence of prolonged stays in hospital for those born in the 1940s. For example, Maggie spent regular periods in long-stay children's hospitals from a young age, with stringent visiting hours, but never felt this came in the way of maintaining a close sense of family. Emma kept a close relationship with her brother, parents and grandparents even though she spent a substantial part of her childhood in long-stay hospital, from the age of four and a half. However, in this case, her mother had maintained contact only by subverting the institutional regime.

> *You weren't allowed visits from your parents 'til you'd been in a month but mum, with her being a nurse, would walk in, in her uniform ... mum always told us everything.*

As Emma's story illustrates, families were not always passive in the face of institutional authority, even if they were not always sure what was best for their children. In general terms, though, the stories from the oldest generation provided little evidence of active resistance to separation arising from stays in hospital (examined in Chapter Four) but rather more resistance to educational segregation (examined in Chapter Five).

From hospitals to schools

The stories from the middle generation, those born in the 1960s, were also marked by significant episodes of childhood separation from family life. What is perhaps significant is a change in the context for that segregation, primarily a shift from the long-term hospital to the residential school. There was, however, still much evidence of medical authority in decisions to place them away from home.

Flora was the eldest of ten children and recalls that she was very much part of family life with her siblings at home during her early years.

> *I grew up like a tomboy because I wanted to keep up with them ... I had a walking frame, it was like a baby walker on wheels but bigger ... I used to turn it into a go-cart and stand on the rails and my brothers and sisters used to push it as far as possible ...*

However, like many others from this generation, she was sent away to residential special school at the age of ten (to a charitable foundation school, established in the early 1950s by the National Spastics Society). She recalled the significance of this turning point in her family life.

> *I loved school 'til I got sent away and after that everything went down hill ... I used to go for three months at a time and I never understood why I couldn't go home at weekends ... That was traumatic being away so long when you are young ...*

Flora went home only in the school holidays and grew further and further apart from her parents and siblings:

> *It was very bad because when I came home, they weren't used to having me around and it went pear-shaped. I didn't get on with my mum and I got very depressed ... I was so depressed and I thought of killing myself.*

Similarly, Sonia had attended a primary level special school, near her family home, until she was 11 but was then sent to a residential special school some distance away (another non-maintained school, originally part of a philanthropic hospital for 'cripples' in the early 20th century). Sonia remembers questioning why she had been removed from her family home:

> *I used to feel that, you know, just so isolated, and strange thoughts do go through your head like, well, 'why am I here?'. You know, 'am I not wanted?' kind of thing.*

Amy had also felt very secure and loved by her parents in early childhood and was surprised and hurt when they sent her away, although she now understands that they did this on the advice of doctors. She spoke about the lasting psycho-emotional impact of three years spent in hospital in the 1960s:

> *I mean the idea of keeping you in hospital for three years with little excursions home now and again, that's probably had the largest, if you like, influence on my life ... I actually had mental health issues from the age of 14, and it probably was triggered by many factors. And even now, that's travelled with me throughout my life.*

While echoing some of the segregated childhood experiences of the oldest generation, there had been some liberalisation of visiting rules by the 1970s and children at residential schools were often allowed to make telephone calls to their families. It is worth noting that none of the oldest generation recalled using telephones from hospital. Home telephones were still considered something of an expensive luxury before the 1960s and personal letter writing (without computers or voice recorders) was a difficult challenge for many of those with physical impairments. Worton, from the oldest generation, would have loved to receive letters from home but relied on Braille, which her mother could not read or write. Where they were available, telephones would be fixed landlines in adult-supervised locations or public payphones. It was not until the 21st century that children really began to have any independent access to the privacy of communication by mobile phone, SMS, email and internet social networking. For Sonia, in the 1970s, the opportunity for telephone contact was some consolation but:

> But when you're in that kind of situation it is difficult to maintain a kind of close bond with your parents ... I was only going home, what, once every six, seven weeks ... I used to go home to sit in my bedroom and not really communicate with them.

When we compare the experiences of the youngest generation (born in the 1980s) it is notable that sustained separation from family relationships, as a consequence of public policies and institutions, was still very much a part of growing up for some. Holly's story (summarised in the previous chapter) is an obvious example but so too are the experiences of Zoe, Terry and Schumacher. For example, although Terry had lived at home while he attended a county special school the completion of compulsory schooling led to his placement in a residential college of special education (although unlike earlier generations he notes how provision for visits and phone calls made a difference here). This transition, away from inclusion, occurred simply because of a lack of provision for personal support.

> Where I live you see, I haven't got the support there that I would need. I need quite a bit of support in living, you know, and I haven't got it where I live.

Schumacher expressed the 'homesickness' she felt on transferring to the same residential college. Indeed, concerns about young disabled people living away from home were raised increasingly during the

1990s. For example, Russell (1995) reiterated the importance of family contact while Morris (1998) drew on the personal accounts of disabled children to highlight significant concerns about segregation and isolation. These latter studies were framed within the policy context of social care, child protection and children's rights, pointing to the increasing significance of such policies towards the end of the 20th century (notably, after adoption of the UN Convention on the Rights of the Child).

It is important to put these experiences into perspective. While the situation of disabled children living away from home raises very significant concerns about human rights and about the psycho-emotional consequences, the vast majority of disabled children do live at home with their families (Gordon et al, 2000) and as many as 10% may live in a household in which there is also another disabled child (Lawton and Quine, 1990; Shah, 1995; Cowen, 1996).

There has been increased attention to disabled children's voices in policy evaluation and the Audit Commission's (2003) review of services for disabled children and their families drew extensively on children's own experiences. This highlighted the limited service options available to support transitions to adulthood (including the inappropriateness of placements in adult residential homes) but it did not consider the situation of children who were living away from home. The Government's much-vaunted *Life chances* report (Prime Minister's Strategy Unit, 2005) noted that nine out of ten families with disabled children reported problems with their housing. It called for services to be 'centred on disabled children and their families' and for 'giving disabled young people access to a more transparent and more appropriate menu of opportunities and choices' (p 7). Yet, surprisingly, it too failed to identify connections between family separations and residential placements.

Conclusions

There have been some substantial social and demographic changes in family life since the 1940s and family breakdown has impacted disproportionately on disabled children. There is, however, also a certain optimism about the ability of re-constituted and step-families to generate new informal networks of mutual support. Disability cash benefits, community-based services, the availability of direct payments and non-discrimination legislation may not have solved all of the problems of family life but they have made a difference to families. In the absence of such public policies, previous generations remained rather more reliant on the resilience and goodwill of close family and friends.

It is important not to judge the past by the standards of the present but it is useful to make comparisons (for example, Johnson and Sherman, 1990). Article 23 of the UN Convention on the Rights of Persons with Disabilities, ratified by the UK in 2009, is based on the principle of 'respect for home and the family'. This includes adult rights of freedom to marry and to have children but also emphasises the requirement on the state to ensure that children and parents are never separated solely on the grounds of disability. The brief examples used for illustration in this chapter indicate quite graphically how public policies have often failed to ensure such rights in the past. Moreover, today's policy framework still permits, sometimes requires, a minority of disabled children and young people to live away from home (especially as looked after children in full-time 'educational' placements).

Fewer children with physical impairments today spend extended periods in hospitals or children's homes, compared to the 1940s, but there has not been an even or continuous pattern of decline in institutionalised living arrangements since then. Indeed, the stories of those born in the 1960s highlight the rapid expansion of special school provision, including residential school provision, during the 1970s and its impact on family relationships. Rather than suggesting a progressive decline in institutional constraints on family life the evidence in this period points rather to a shift in the institutional context for family separation – from the medical institution to the educational institution.

At the same time, the rapid expansion of local social services in the 1970s and 1980s brought some unintended consequences, turning a post-war policy framework somewhat sympathetic to the concept of equality and rights into one more characterised by professional colonisation of the family. Despite the subsequent introduction of more user-directed forms of support and anti-discrimination legislation, many young people with physical impairments are still unable to access public buildings, leisure facilities and educational establishments on an equal level with others. This affects not only them but other members of their families. Disabling environments as much as residual institutionalised services continue to make it hard for disabled families and their friends to share in normal patterns of everyday life together.

Questions for discussion

- Was practical support from family and friends any more important in achieving adult independence prior to the development of extensive community social services in the 1970s than it is now?
- What impact did the expansion of public social work and social services have on disabled people and their families in the 1970s and 1980s?
- How have social changes in divorce, separation and family structure since the 1960s impacted on the lives of disabled children and young people?

FOUR

Living with medicine

The examples in Chapters Two and Three drew attention to claims about the influence of public medicine in the private lives of young people with physical impairments. The stories suggested at least three kinds of influence. Medical diagnosis and opinion appeared to frame future life expectations or trajectories, even from birth. Medical treatment regimes appeared to shape early life experiences, particularly in relation to hospital stays. Medical authority appeared to be significant at key turning points, particularly in choosing schools. The stories also raised interesting questions about medicine and social change. To what extent have life expectations been shaped by medical knowledge? Have challenges to medical authority altered power-knowledge relationships between health professions and disabled people? How have developments in medical technologies and health care institutions affected young people's life chances and choices? The chapter examines these kinds of questions by examining the influence of health professionals, policies and institutions on the life expectations and life pathways of the three generations.

The role of medicine in society was increasingly scrutinised and debated during the second half of the 20th century. Its role in disabling social relations has been much asserted in the critical disability studies literature (for example, Barnes and Mercer, 1996; Thomas, 2007) and there are frequent references to the 'medical model' of disability. Although such references are often juxtaposed with discussions of the 'social model' this misses an important point. For the original exponents of social model analysis, medicine played its role within a larger scheme. As Oliver (1996, p 31) put it:

> The individual model for me encompassed a whole range of issues and was underpinned by what I called the personal tragedy theory of disability. But it also included psychological and medical aspects of disability. ... In short, for me, there is no such thing as the medical model of disability, there is instead, an individual model of disability of which medicalisation is one significant component.

Numerous writings have credited medicine with policing normalcy and constraining life expectations for disabled people. For example, American functionalist sociology in the 1950s appeared to characterise impairment, along with illness, as a form of 'deviance' from social norms that required correction. Thus, Parsons (1951) described a system founded on individual responsibility to comply with 'technically competent' professionals. Within an expanding rehabilitation 'industry' (Albrecht, 1992) both professionals and public institutions contributed to the governance of disability but their legitimacy began to be more openly challenged during the 1960s and 1970s.

While Goffman's (1961) *Asylums* revealed extremes of medical authority in the 'total institution', critics, like Illich (1976) also drew attention to a pervasive 'medicalisation' of everyday life beyond their walls. Borsay (2005) argues that professional power and influence made it particularly difficult for disabled people to resist institutional medicine before 1970. However, by this time, public trust in medicine began to waver and new challenges to medical authority were emerging in consumerist and rights-based social movements (Zola, 1977).

Medical knowledge and authority have been viewed as giving powerful expression to individualising and tragedy-laden discourses of disability that preclude engagement with social barriers and discrimination (Barnes and Mercer, 1996; Thomas, 2007). It has not been the intention in these debates to characterise all medicine as inherently negative but rather to highlight where medical power has been inappropriately applied to social problems. Thus, Oliver (1996, pp 35–6) also makes it clear that: 'doctors can have a role to play in the lives of disabled people ... The problem arises when doctors try to use their knowledge and skills to treat disability rather than illness.'

Disabled writers have drawn particular attention to the colonisation of their lives by health and welfare professionals. For French (1994, p 103) this relationship has 'never been an easy one' and imbalances of power in the design and delivery of services have been accentuated by micro-politics of socio-economic class between, often poor, disabled people and, often affluent, health professionals. Similarly, Morris (1989), Lonsdale (1990) and Thomas (2001) highlight gender power imbalances for disabled women in male-dominated medical environments. Yet, there has been reticence among some disability activists and researchers to address medical issues directly. For example, drawing on disabled women's accounts of general practitioners in the 1990s, Begum (1996, p 157) argued that: 'the fear of disability being construed as a catalogue of medical problems, has made disabled people wary of putting health issues on the public and/or academic agenda'.

The stories collected for this book clearly highlight the significance of medical professions and institutions in people's lives and so the topic demands attention. However, this is not a history of medicine and our main interest is the ways in which medical institutions and relationships have influenced private lives. Our analysis is, therefore, mainly concerned with the medicalisation of private lives and the normative influence of 'professions allied to medicine' (Finkelstein, 1999). At the same time, the discussion seeks to acknowledge evidence of the positive consequences of changes in medical practice where appropriate.

Medical prognosis and life trajectories

The influence of medicine was evident at different points in the stories beginning with the accounts people gave of their own birth stories. These episodes draw, necessarily, on the family stories that people were told about their own lives rather than their own memories. Anecdotes become shared family stories in the telling, and it is well known that parents often construct selected remembrances into moral narratives that convey life lessons to younger children (Fiese et al, 1995). Childhood stories also provide scripts for the life stories we then construct about ourselves in adolescence (Habermas and Bluck, 2000) while the re-telling of our identity stories reinforces who we think we are at significant turning points later in life (McLean and Pratt, 2006; McLean et al, 2007).

In this way, the negotiation of very early life narratives, between parents and professionals, plays a part in establishing early life expectations and trajectories. Medical opinion and prognosis featured prominently in the birth stories of most of the people who contributed to this book, and across the three generations. These narratives pointed to the influence of medical opinion well beyond the medical sphere, informing family expectations about the more social implications of disability in future adult life.

Birth stories

Accounts of the medicalisation of childbirth in the 20th century are well known from the feminist literature, compounded by a male-dominated medical authority that constrains mothers' decision-making in both subtle and overt ways (Cahill, 2008). When medical diagnosis and prognosis are communicated by health professionals, and when families interpret them, social messages are also conveyed about expectations for life choices and chances in the future – and these messages have consequences. For example, the stories summarised in Chapter Two remind us that Florence's mother abandoned her when doctors diagnosed that she would never walk (in the 1940s). Poppy's mother was told to place her in an institution and forget about her (in the 1960s). Holly's parents separated after her impairment was diagnosed (in the 1980s). In this way, medical opinion can be important in framing early life course trajectories for children with impairments – although medical knowledge may also be embellished or resisted in the stories parents then tell (Landsman, 1998). The following examples provide a flavour of the family stories people told about their own birth, and how the medicalisation of disability featured within them.

Worton's story (from the mid-1940s) conveys themes common to other stories. Her survival of a premature birth, and diagnosis of significant physical impairments, had been narrated in terms of her limited chances of living a 'normal' life:

> ... the day after I was born they took me into the centre of the city to X-ray me at the main hospital as the maternity block had been moved out because of all the bombing. They discovered that my joints were malformed and wherever two bones meet they didn't do it properly and that became more obvious as I grew. In fact within a few days my parents were told that I would probably never walk, probably wouldn't talk and that I would probably be an 'idiot' or words to that effect.

The stories handed down by parents about early diagnosis and prognosis were often conveyed in terms of limited life expectancy, functional limitation, progressive decline, poverty of future relationships or of lives lacking in social value. Indeed, medical prognosis often seemed to introduce assumptions of a future life trajectory that could be characterised, in Hobbes' (1651) terms, as 'solitary, poor, nasty, brutish, and short'.

There was a clear sense of the underlying personal tragedy model of disability that Oliver describes, weighted by the authority of medical knowledge and opinion. The characteristics of specific body parts or symptoms were often extrapolated as predictions about future social lives and relationships. For instance, Maggie (who, in her 60s, is now a mother of three and a grandmother of four) described the birth story she had been told in this way:

> *My feet were turned completely the other way so he [the doctor]*
> *said 'she won't live, you'll have her for a few days and she definitely*
> *won't live' ... I think it was [the doctor] said 'she's not going to*
> *walk properly', and 'she can't, she'll never have children and she*
> *won't get married'.*

Negative and medicalised expectations at birth were, thus, often juxtaposed against real life accounts of positive and socially embedded roles in adulthood (for example, in terms of fulfilment in work, friendships or family life). Thus, people pointed to life course pathways that contradicted or deviated from the rather negative and limited life trajectories introduced by medical opinion and prognosis. Birth stories were often told alongside a powerful counter-narrative of resistance and resilience, in which the family or the individual had denied or defied medical prediction (that is, by surviving and by achieving a fulfilling life in adulthood). For example, for Matt (born in the 1960s) the defiance of a life-limited prognosis was an important and recurrent factor in his early life.

> *They were told that I wouldn't live beyond six weeks or whatever*
> *... then I think they were told at some point I wouldn't live beyond*
> *being two. And even when I was seven they said 'well, he won't*
> *live past 14' and at 14 they said the same thing. Then you get to*
> *21 and I thought 'he ain't going anywhere'.*

Harvey and Terry (born in the 1980s) were not alone in telling similar stories two decades later:

> *When I was born, me mum said to me, the doctors gave me a 20*
> *per cent chance of living ... you know, lucky to be here, let's make*
> *the best of it type of attitude.* (Harvey)

> *I was born early, and I was fighting for my life. When I was born,*
> *there was a boxer, who was also fighting, at the very same time.*
> *Because I was fighting for my life, my middle name's [the same*
> *as his].* (Terry)

These representations of personal resilience in infancy were more common in the stories of young men that we spoke to. However, there was a strong sense across the generations of lives lived in defiance of medical authority or against biomedical odds.

Medical opinion was also seen as important when it introduced a narrative trajectory towards abandonment and institutionalisation. For example, Hillary and Worton (born in the 1940s) suggested that doctors advised their parents to 'forget' about them and to place them in an institution. This was a narrative repeated in stories from those born in the 1960s. For example, Poppy and Flora's parents had told them of a medicalised construction of disabled lives that held no rightful place in the family home.

> ... *my mum was actually told by one specialist to put me in an institution and to just forget about me, and to go on and have more children, but luckily she didn't do that.* (Poppy)

> *It was very traumatic for my mum because she was young and it was her first child. She said that the worst thing was not that I had cerebral palsy but they asked her did she want to give me up. She said that was worse. She didn't know what they were on about. It never occurred to her but that's what they did in those days, they encouraged parents to give up disabled children.* (Flora)

While most, across all three generations, asserted that their parents had no intention of giving them up, it did happen, especially for parents with limited familial or financial capital to draw upon (as Florence's story in Chapter Two illustrated). Health care workers' understandings of disability can influence how parents see the future for their disabled child. In a highly medicalised birth and neonatal care environment there may also be few alternative sources of knowledge for parents to draw upon.

As Goodley and Tregaskis (2006) show, medical prognosis continues to frame parents' initial understandings of the prospects for their disabled baby's future life. Vehkakoski (2007, p 288) concludes that it is 'important for health care professionals to provide many-sided elements for parents to consider in the construction of the image of their baby other than traditional tragically and negatively biased cultural interpretations'. However, Tregaskis (2006) also suggests that there is a greater sense of parental resistance to medical advice among families today. Comparing her own experience of disabled childhood with evidence generated through research, she argues that parents are more likely to resist the objectified depersonalised image of disabled babies presented by professionals in the 1960s and 1970s.

From medical authority to the expert patient

The examples of medical opinion in family stories of infancy highlight a wider concern with the role of medical authority in shaping people's subsequent lives. The life stories collected for this book revealed the significant influence that medical professionals had in decision-making at key turning points (particularly in relation to choice of school, as discussed in the next chapter). However, they also revealed traces of important changes in relationships between doctors and disabled people, as patients, since the 1940s. The stories of the two older cohorts often conveyed a sense of medical authority that appeared beyond challenge for ordinary people. Several of these stories described hospital consultants with the status of 'gods'. For instance, Amy, who spent the first 20 years of her life under the surveillance of medical professionals, said:

> *My Mum and Dad were in awe of medicine, and whatever the doctors would say, they would do ... At that time, you know, the doctors were God.*

Maggie drew on the story her mother told her, that she would cry when the doctor approached the waiting room:

> *He was frightening, he thought he was ... in them days consultants were gods. And he was THE god.*

These narrative constructions of medical authority in the hospital context are not without some foundation. The new NHS involved a public coordination of health services but it required the compliance of a powerful, often resistant, medical profession. Placating professional concerns required substantial concessions to medical autonomy from policy makers, and the Minister for Health strongly underlined this in his inaugural message to them: 'My job is to give you all the facilities, resources and help I can, and then to leave you alone as professional men and women to use your skill and judgement without hindrance' (Bevan, 1948).

Repeated public commitments to the overriding autonomy of the medical profession continued from the initial NHS White Paper proposals of 1944 throughout the post-war development of the NHS and well into the 1970s. Consultants, in particular, retained a unique level of professional authority within hospitals. However, a steady decline in medical control has been well documented during the latter part of the 20th century – declining autonomy in prescribing treatment, declining authority over other professions and declining influence in institutional decision-making processes (Freidson, 1988; Allsop and Mulcahy, 1996). Both the social status and the autonomy of medical practitioners gave way somewhat with the increasing public management of health services. To quote the Chairman of Council of the British Medical Association in 1961:

> The more unintelligent members of society ... frequently regard the doctor almost as their servant ... They are only aware that they pay large weekly contributions towards social security, and the symbol of that security is the general practitioner, who, the politicians assure them, is at their service ... The status of the doctor in their eyes has gone down ... (Grant, 1961, p 1279)

The causes of declining medical authority have been attributed, variously, to financial crisis and managerialism within the welfare state, the professionalisation of other health occupations (including nurses and therapists) and challenges from increasingly knowledgeable patient-consumers in an information society (Harrison and Ahmad, 2000).

To take one theme from these debates, there were clear traces in the life stories of change in the extent to which children and families from the three generations were consulted in discussions about treatment. The earlier stories were marked by a distinct absence of such consultation. For example, Daisy presented a colourful memory of surgery as a young child in one of the first NHS hospitals:

> *I remember one morning the lady passing me by with breakfast, she went to that bed then to that bed and as she went round the ward I sort of went 'me, me' and she kept passing me by ... the next thing I know I'm being wheeled along the corridor and I said 'where are you taking me?' and they said 'to the theatre' and the only context I knew the word theatre was of course pantomime. So I didn't know what the theatre was ... they wheeled me into this room and again it was very strange with all these people dressed in green ... and a green rag coming towards me ... There was chloroform on this green rag and they just said 'I want you to try and blow this away'. And as he came towards me I just said 'no, I don't like it' and I tried to push it away.*

Reflecting on changes since the 1950s, Daisy and Dan (from the same generation) compared their own early hospital experiences with those of children today in terms of information and personal respect, as well as technological developments:

> *And nowadays people would be very supportive of the child, but in those days they weren't at all.* (Daisy)

> *I think it's totally different now, I mean you get a lot more explained to you, you spend less time in hospital because of, you know, the advances in medical technology and everything else.* (Dan)

Encounters with medical authority, especially within the hospital, gave rise to stories of objectification under a powerful, normalising, gaze. Tan's story (born in the 1960s) epitomised this. She felt that her 'imperfect' and 'rare' body was continually judged against normative measures as an object of curiosity and experimentation for doctors to inspect and correct.

> As a child all I remember is being poked and, you know, stripped off and made to walk across the room in your knickers and stuff like that ... I feel the medical profession has experimented with me and my body trying to make it into something which is acceptable in the way that I eat, the way that I walk, the way that I sit, the way that I do stuff. You know, that's what the medical profession wants. It wants for you to look and act and be like the majority, and if you don't fit in then it has to try and bend your limbs, and twist your head, so it's all in the right direction.

The exercise of uncontested professional authority within institutionalised environments can create substantial vulnerability to abuse for both children and adults with physical impairments (see also Hollomotz, 2009). For example, Westcott (1994) drew on interviews with adults to illustrate graphic examples of abuse by staff in hospitals (including hospital porters, nurses and therapists), many of which echo other accounts related by disabled people who grew up in the first half of the century (Humphries and Gordon, 1992). In their extensive review of the abuse of disabled children, Westcott and Cross (1996) drew particular attention to degrading medical routines and practices like those described by Tan previously (including public stripping, parading, medical photography, and so on). The list is extensive – physical segregation, social isolation, poor access to services, discrimination, physical restraint, medical photography, forced feeding, denial of basic choices, and so on. Greater frequency and duration of institutionalised encounters, and their normalisation from an early age, compound this vulnerability to emotional, physical and sexual abuse. As Sanghera (2007, p 29) argues, such abuses are often 'shrouded under normal clinical routines and continue unchallenged'.

It is important to underline that degrading experiences in medical encounters were by no means limited to childhood. For example, Worton (born in the 1940s) described an encounter with a hospital consultant when she was a young adult in the early 1970s.

> *All these students trooped in and he then starts explaining about my deformities. He literally started with my toes and worked his way up manipulating my joints as if they were his, not mine. And I just sat there and let him get on with it until he got to my hands … and [he] waved my hands around, like that, and started flexing my fingers and said 'you see, she doesn't hold things properly she claws at them' … I said 'excuse me, they might not be standard hands but they'll do most things I need. I can wash and dress myself, I can feed myself and what's more I can play the piano'. And he turned around and said 'don't be silly, of course you can't play the piano with hands like that'.*

Wendell (1996) describes the kinds of 'epistemic invalidation' that disabled people experience when health professionals doubt their knowledge of their own bodily experiences. The invalidation of patient knowledge in medical encounters was compounded by narrow medical specialisms, in which the person's primary impairment diagnosis acquired a kind of master status that was then attributed to other, unrelated, health complaints. For example, William (born in the 1960s) recalled a recent experience of unbearable pain, which he knew had 'nothing to do with' his impairment but he felt that doctors at his local hospital 'were not listening' to him (the real cause was only discovered when he went, privately, to a physiotherapist). Similarly, Bob (also born in the 1960s) illustrated the potential for expert patient knowledge to contribute to medical knowledge.

> *About two years ago I had some tests and my red blood cycle count was higher than normal … went to three doctors who didn't understand it. So I said, 'right I've got cerebral palsy yeah, I don't breathe deeply. Could it be that over these years my body's adapted,*

because I'm a shallow breather, so the amount of oxygen I actually take in and circulate is less? Could it be that affecting the blood cycle?' They said, 'we never thought of that'.

It is fair to say that there has been very considerable progress in policy and practice for involving disabled children in discussions and decision about their medical treatment. Although the 1948 Universal Declaration of Human Rights had implicitly included children as well as adults, a further Declaration of the Rights of the Child was adopted by the United Nations in 1959. Agreement on the United Nations Convention on the Rights of the Child, and the 1989 Children Act proved a catalyst for subsequent developments. In particular, much debate was aroused by Article 12 of the Convention, which states that: 'States Parties shall assure to the child who is capable of forming his or her own views the right to express those views freely in all matters affecting the child, the views of the child being given due weight in accordance with the age and maturity of the child'.

During the 1990s attention turned to understanding how this could be achieved and implemented through information and consent in health service contexts (for example, Alderson, 1993; Bradbury et al, 1994; Alderson and Montgomery, 1996; Lightfoot and Sloper, 2003; Cavet and Sloper, 2006). The British Medical Association (2001) produced practical guidance on children's consent and choice (see also Tates and Meeuwesen, 2001). Patient Advice and Liaison Services (PALS) are now available in most hospitals and the National Children's Bureau has recently worked with them on new guidance for their staff to work more effectively with children (see also Heaton et al, 2008).

The youngest generation (born in the 1980s) still had quite mixed experiences of medical encounters and consultations in the 1990s but they did convey a much greater sense of active engagement with medical knowledge and medical authority.

> *I remember going to see another doctor when I was about 16 ... And he sat there with me at 16 and started asking mum 'what type of school does she go to? How old is she?' etc., etc. ... So he kept asking the questions and I kept answering 'cos my mum didn't know the answer. And he did this throughout, even though I was giving the answers. At the end I turned round to him and I came up with some convoluted scientific explanation of what I thought was going on in my body and his face dropped.* (Helen)

Kay had relatively little involvement with hospitals as a younger child but became a regular consumer of health services as a teenager. She recalls her discussions with doctors as patronising and unhelpful:

> *He [the doctor] talked to me like I was a baby. He talked to me like I was completely thick and he would continuously tell me, yes, you've got scarring on the brain. That's causing your epilepsy, yeah. I was born with cerebral palsy. Of course I've got scarring on the brain. You telling me that every few months is not going to change my brain.*

After two years of consultations with the same paediatrician, Kay felt the medical advice she was receiving was not making any difference to her life and, the day after she received her GCSE results:

> *I turned around and said 'well, actually you're not really helping me, I'd like to be taken off your books' ... I remember walking out the door and going 'by the way I got one A, five Bs, four Cs. Yes, you've really made a difference to me'.*

As Alderson (2006) argues, although children and parents today have considerable rights in treatment decisions under English Law, their choices are limited in practice by the options offered by the medical team, by what considered to be in the 'best interest' of the child, and by financial resources. Noyes (2000) argues that children with communication impairments are still particularly marginalised from involvement or that they are not taken seriously (see also Sudbery and Noyes, 1999). For example, Rachel, who uses assisted communication, remembered both positive and negative experiences when she was due to have surgery at a specialist children's hospital (vocalised by her mother in the interview):

> *The actual consultant that did your surgery was wonderful. He ignored me [mother] completely and spoke to you [Rachel], which is how it should be. But then when you came to meet the anaesthetist you wanted to know what gas they were going to use, you asked him and he said, 'oh, it's special sleeping gas'. So patronising!*

However, such examples aside, there is little doubt that disabled children and young people today are, on the whole, much more consulted about their hospital admissions and treatments despite continuing difficulties in developing trust and communication (for example, Avis and Reardon, 2008). There were certainly no experiences from the two older generations to compare with Holly's account of admission to hospital at the turn of the 21st century.

> *I had to have extreme tests that took about a year, and I was spoken to an awful lot about the dangers and the pros and the cons and the this and the that, and it made me dizzy in the end because there was so much going on ... They didn't try and deter me from doing it but they made certain that I actually understood that my life was going to be at risk.*

At the end of the 20th century the concept of the 'expert patient' was formally acknowledged in public policy (DoH, 2001) as the basis for greater self-management and involvement by people with 'chronic disease'. Initial implementation met with some scepticism within the profession and:

> The suspicion is that for many doctors, the expert patient of the imagination is the one clutching a sheaf of printouts from the internet, demanding a particular treatment that is unproved, manifestly unsuitable, astronomically expensive, or all three. Or, possibly worst of all, a treatment the doctor has never heard of, let alone personally prescribed. (Shaw, 2004, p 723)

Looking at the evidence from the life stories it is easy to find traces of the changing relationships and expectations of patients and their doctors. The stories suggest an increasing knowledge and assertiveness among young disabled people, fuelled by peer information networks and the internet but also facilitated by a greater recognition of patient voice and rights in health care policy and decision-making. Such developments are both positive and significant, although health care provision still seems to have been less impacted by the activism and claims to self-determination of the independent living movement (when compared to parallel developments in the social care field over the same period). Despite some positive changes, it is also clear that medical opinion and authority retained a substantial influence on the life course trajectories and pathways of individuals in all three generations (although more so in the older generations). Historical processes of medicalisation and de-medicalisation were particularly evident in the context of education (that is, in decisions about schooling and in regimes within special schools). This is examined in more detail in the next chapter. The remainder of this chapter turns from relationships with medical professionals to the institutions of health care delivery.

Changing policies and institutions

The life stories revealed much about the types of medical institutions, treatment regimes and technologies that people encountered, particularly as children. Biographical experiences showed how changes in the infrastructure of medicine and rehabilitation altered the everyday life choices and chances of people with physical impairments during the second half of the 20th century. In particular, the stories illustrate a shift from hospital-based to community-based service provision, a reduction of confinement in hospital, a humanisation of everyday hospital regimes, and a de-medicalisation of non-medical services.

The institutionalisation of medicine

As outlined in Chapter One, the foundations for national health provision had been laid in the early 20th century but were transformed in the immediate post-war period with the establishment of the NHS. The approach to disability, in employment as much as health policy, focused on the rehabilitation model. This policy model focused on a medically-embedded response, based largely on the infrastructure of the hospital with a focus on prevention, cure and rehabilitation. The rapid expansion of rehabilitation services affected both children and adults, although the infrastructure was initially less geared to the specific needs of children.

With the exception of Coram's London Foundlings Hospital, special hospitals for children in England had only really emerged in the mid-19th century (for example, the Great Ormond Street Hospital for Sick Children was founded in 1852). In addition, it was not uncommon for children with physical impairments (resulting from rickets, joint disease or spinal 'scrofula') to be officially excluded from specialist children's hospitals, although it is clear that they were increasingly admitted in practice (see Holmes, 1869). Although such hospitals had proliferated by the beginning of the 20th century few of them were originally intended to carry out major surgery, which remained the province of the general hospitals. At the same time, children's wards in these general hospitals were by no means as common as they are today.

Aneurin Bevan's strategy of nationalising hospitals, towards a universal health service, provided new options for many families of children with physical impairments, particularly poorer families, but the financial cost associated with the birth of a child who needed hospital medicine remained a real concern. As Humphries and Gordon (1992) show, although middle-class parents could usually afford to pay for private treatment in voluntary hospitals, those from working-class backgrounds often relied on charity and folk practitioners within their communities (including midwives, herbalists or barber surgeons/dentists). Under the National Insurance Scheme fathers had often been the only family member entitled to free health care, meaning that treatment for a child with physical impairment could impose significant family expense. As Worton noted:

> ...*before the NHS came in, in '48, that was a real problem. My parents took me to see lots of people to see if they could help. They always wanted an X-ray, which would be half my dad's weekly wages. In the end they gave up because nobody seemed to know what to do or what was 'wrong' with me.*

The transition of voluntary hospitals into public control took time and it was often necessary for families to travel considerable distance to find a hospital that could provide surgery or rehabilitative treatments. Daisy recalled her early separation from family when she was admitted to a hospital away from home in the early 1950s (see Chapter Three). Her narrative explanation for this sought to balance both private and public factors – her parents' search for the 'best' and the availability of free treatment.

> *I don't know why my parents wanted me to go to a London Hospital but I can only think that maybe the regional ones weren't yet NHS ... my mum used to say it was because she wanted me under the best surgeons ... when they got up there he [the doctor] apparently said to my parents that, you know, there was a bed for me there and then if they wanted to leave me, and if they didn't want to leave me he didn't know when they might be able to get me in, they might not be able to get a bed later on. And so they just kind of left me there ... the status of the surgeon in those days was like god.*

Leaving aside the 'god' status, discussed earlier, consultants were pivotal to the new institutional framework in relation to the development of specialist services, like paediatrics and orthopaedics. Early NHS guidance encouraged the creation of new salaried positions for specialist doctors to balance their 'haphazard' geographic distribution.

> In the main specialist practice has been a matter of unpaid hospital responsibilities, coupled with private consultant work which has provided the whole or greater part of the specialist's income. The inevitable consequence has been an uneven distribution of specialists who are too few to meet the needs of the whole population. (Ministry of Health, 1948, para. I.1)

Independent paediatric departments, treating children up to the age of 14, were to be established in each large hospital centre and NHS Region, often linked to a University Institute of Child Health. However, it was accepted that it might be 'necessary to provide in-patient accommodation at some distance from the main hospital group', including 'long-stay orthopaedic cases'. Importantly, the guidance also reflected an important link between the institutional infrastructure for paediatric care and other medical challenges of the time. Thus:

> It is of the utmost importance that hospitals or wards for infectious diseases should be closely associated with paediatric departments, since so many of the patients are children and the problems are similar. Equally, the work of orthopaedic surgeons, cardiologists and tuberculosis specialists must be co-ordinated with paediatrics. (Ministry of Health, 1948, para VI.50)

Infectious diseases, such as tuberculosis and polio, became endemic after the war and were major causes of childhood impairment or mortality (there were 50,000 new cases of TB in 1948, with half of the infections in children under 14). The epidemiology, the associated treatments and the institutional provisions all left traces in the stories of those from the oldest generation (especially those who contracted polio in infancy, like May, Tom, Bella and Grace).

Although polio had been clinically described as a paralysing condition in the 18th century, and the virus identified in 1908 (Sass et al, 1996) children were not vaccinated in Britain until 1956. So, during the major polio epidemics of the 1940s and 1950s, suspected patients were placed in immediate isolation (often with children and adults on the same ward). Social isolation was compounded somewhat by the rural setting of many hospitals or sanatoria used in the treatment of tuberculosis and other childhood illnesses up to the end of the 1950s (with urban smoke pollution, 'fresh air' remained very much a part of treatment up until the 1956 Clean Air Act). This complex mix of factors affecting hospital provision for children with physical impairment was very evident in Bella's account, for example:

> *I was on a children's ward but there was adults there as well because they had patients who had TB as well as just a mixture of people really needing orthopaedic surgery, it was an orthopaedic hospital. And so the wards were enormous with really high ceilings and the top of the ward was open. I don't know why, I don't know if it was because of the TB patients, but it was absolutely freezing in the winter ... It was a really bleak place.*

These kinds of hospital ward, often in distant or remote locations, provided the environmental context for many of the childhood experiences recounted in the life stories. Some of the earlier accounts portrayed an environment reminiscent of the 'total institution' (Goffman, 1961) characterised by de-personalisation and a (literal) stripping of identity. For example, as Florence (born in the 1940s) recalled:

> *When you were admitted to hospital in those days you were automatically stripped of your clothing, given a bath and put into hospital pyjamas ... no taking in your toys, none of your own clothes, nothing.*

Bella described how practitioners would identify patients according to medical diagnoses rather than as people, and how the depersonalisation of the hospital environments and regimes still haunt her:

> *When my parents came to visit me they walked the whole length of the ward and back again and couldn't see me. And they'd shaved my hair off and so they just didn't recognise me ... You didn't wear your own clothes either... I went in and out of that hospital over the years and one thing I hated was that I couldn't wear my own clothes. So you were supplied with these sort of hospital nightdresses ... I don't know, it just felt like you had nothing that was personal really.*

By the end of the 1950s, the number of NHS beds occupied by children had risen and an awareness of the social and emotional consequences (discussed in Chapter Two) was beginning to emerge, prompted in part by the Association for Welfare of Children in Hospital and studies published by the Nuffield Foundation. The policy implications were finally highlighted in the high profile Platt Report (Central Health Services Council, 1959), which drew attention to the 'emotional and mental needs of the child in hospital' and 'the importance of mitigating the effects of the break with home'.

The report called for an end to the admission of children on adult wards and for (a rather gendered) involvement of parents in care and decision making. For very young children, sleeping accommodation was proposed for their 'mothers', while fathers were to be fully consulted about admission so that 'nothing should be allowed to detract from their authority'. The Committee found that daily visiting was permitted in most children's hospitals and concluded that anything less should 'be condemned' (some of the biographical evidence reported in Chapter Two appears to contest the extent of this reality). It also highlighted how surgical inpatients were at particular risk of being overlooked and that paediatric medicine now needed to focus more on addressing long-term impairment than mortality. It argued for the avoidance of hospital admission where possible and reductions in length of stay, via an increased role for family doctors and home nursing services.

Many of these issues were addressed in hospital management and nursing practice, certainly by the late 1970s. However, it is clear that the kind of concerns raised in the Platt Report continued to mark the life experiences of many young disabled people in years to come. For example, they framed the first half of Amy's life (born in the 1960s), which revolved around her long stays in hospital:

> I was in and out of hospital on and off from the age of about eight, until I was ... about 22 ... I hope they don't do that any more ... I mean the idea of keeping you in hospital for three years with little excursions home now and again, that's probably had the largest influence on my life.

Signs of change

Compared to those with similar impairments from previous generations, children like Kay (born in the 1980s) were not so often detained in hospital as newborns and reported much less sustained contact with health professionals during childhood. Initial proposals in the Court Report (Committee on the Child Health Services, 1976) to devolve paediatrics to local medical practices had been heavily resisted (they had included proposals to establish new community-based 'handicap' teams). The 1970s, however, heralded a period of great institutional change, not least in separating health provision and social service provision (following the Seebohm Report, the 1970 Local Authority Social Services Act and the 1973 NHS Reorganisation Act). This introduced new professional boundary conflicts in public responsibility for children and young people with physical impairments but it meant that the management of day centres and home help passed from health services to social services. In this formal sense, at least, there were signs of a de-medicalisation in public policy towards disability (but a re-medicalisation of specific focus within the health service).

By the mid-1970s, the epidemiology that framed demand for, and supply of, hospital treatments had also continued to change, with many fewer children receiving long-term orthopaedic treatment (for example, as a consequence of the eradication of polio and TB, the replacement of certain complex surgical interventions with growth hormone treatments, and the onset of selective abortions based on neonatal screening using ultrasound). There was also a diversification of medical specialisms within acute hospital-based paediatrics and, by the 1980s, a shift towards the involvement of community-based paediatricians for children who might previously have received the bulk of their medical contact in hospital. There was an increase in the number of children living at home with the aid of assistive medical technologies (such as home dialysis or assisted ventilation).

Notably, the focus of disability policy development within the Department of Health had also begun to shift towards a less medically dominated approach, in which social barriers and support service needs were also being recognised. By the early years of the present century, the development of a National Service Framework for disabled children and young people set new standards for the promotion of social inclusion and successful transitions to adulthood. In general terms: 'Children and young people who are disabled or who have complex health needs receive co-ordinated, high-quality child and family-centred services which are based on assessed needs, which promote social inclusion and, where possible, which enable them and their families to live ordinary lives' (DoH/DfES, 2004b, p 5).

In delivering health services there have been attempts to minimise hospital and clinic visits (by coordinating multiple appointments) and to schedule them around everyday life (for example, outside school hours or in the holidays). There has been greater recognition of the regional inconsistency of physical therapy and equipment services, with increased funding to reduce waiting times and to offer services at home or at school. However, the Healthcare Commission (2007; 2009) still found significant deficiencies in hospital care for children in the majority of local areas, and United Nations Committee on the Rights of the Child (2008) concluded that access to health services for disabled children remained a problem.

From survival to prevention

The examples used to illustrate the first part of this chapter drew attention to narratives of resilience and survival in defiance of pessimistic medical prognoses. That discussion was framed by interpersonal relationships between doctors and families but it is equally important to revisit those stories in the context of historical developments in medical treatments and technologies. As noted earlier, technological developments since the 1940s led to an increase in the survival rates of infants with significant physical impairments and, particularly, to the survival of babies born prematurely. At the same time, developments in medical technologies also led to the increased detection of foetal impairment characteristics. When combined with parallel socio-legal changes concerning parenting and abortion this led to the increasingly selective prevention of lives that would otherwise have been lived. In this sense, there has emerged a particular discursive tension between medicine as saviour and medicine as executioner of disabled lives, a tension evident in the narrative accounts.

To return to those from the oldest generation, Catherine and Worton were born prematurely in the immediate post-war era. As Catherine's story illustrates, the delivery and care of premature babies was still in its early stages and neonatal mortality rates were high.

> *I was three months premature ... I was born at two and a half pounds and I went down to one pound eleven ounces ... I mean they didn't have all the neonatal care then that they do now. So I mean they were very proud that they kept me going.*

Both premature birth and 'congenital malformations' were among the top five causes of child death in the 1940s. In addition to epidemic polio and tuberculosis, there were higher rates of less-common congenital conditions like hydrocephalus and spina bifida (Carter, 2008). Thus, while infant mortality rates in general had been dropping steadily since the beginning of the 20th century, those arising from 'congenital malformations' appeared to have increased (Record and McKeown,

1949). Medical effort turned simultaneously to the survival of born children and to the prevention of congenital impairment.

Although medicine has been rightly criticised for reproducing disabling relations it is important not to overlook some of the positive impacts its development has had on young disabled lives. The first special care units for premature babies had been created during the war and many infant deaths had become preventable through the use of antibiotics (Anderson and Lerner, 1960) as Daisy's story highlights:

> *I think prior to the last century, people used to die. They just used to die – they didn't survive if they had disabilities. I mean I wouldn't have survived. Just because I've grown up in the generation I have, they have antibiotics to clear up infections, 'cos that would have killed me, the infections, the infections getting into my bloodstream.*

The development of hospital-based paediatrics, intensive care facilities and 'special care baby units' led to new techniques for sustaining babies who would previously have died (House of Commons, 1980). Through the 1980s and 1990s survival rates continued to improve but there were corresponding increases in the incidence of certain neuro-developmental impairment diagnoses, like cerebral palsy (for example, Pharoah et al, 1996; Wilson-Costello et al, 2005). Indeed, prematurity and low birth weights featured in several of the birth stories from the youngest generation (born in the 1980s) like those of Helen, Steve or Schumacher, for example.

Looking back to the previous generations there is also recognition that some of the valued lives that were lived and told might not have been lived in this youngest generation, simply because they would now be terminated before birth through pre-natal screening technologies and selective abortion. Sonia (born in the 1960s) notes that, 'In those days they didn't do any examinations' and for Yvette the timing of her birth occurred in a narrow historical envelope between the chance of survival and the likelihood of prevention:

> *... nowadays parents would have amniocentesis tests but at the time my mum and dad didn't know about my disability until I was born ... I [also] have a feeling if I'd have been born ten years earlier the technology might not have been around and I might not have even been alive.*

Developments in screening technology occurred very much in parallel with social developments in family planning and birth control. For example, ultrasound was introduced in obstetric care in 1955 while large-scale medical trials of birth control pills began the following year. The availability of 'the Pill' in family planning clinics from 1961 highlighted, most dramatically, concerns with detecting physical impairment in the associated Thalidomide scandal. By 1965 there was some evidence of declining birth rates as (married) women made more choices about family planning and, in 1967, the Abortion Act was passed amid considerable controversy.

From a disability perspective this Act was significant in legislating detectable impairment characteristics as greater reason to request termination of pregnancy, and consolidating medical opinion and authority as the primary arbiter in decision-making. In principle, the 1967 Act permitted very different parameters for considering termination of unborn babies who would be 'seriously handicapped' (in the opinion of the doctors). In 1990, with the increasing survival of very premature babies, the general time limit for legal abortion was reduced to 24 weeks. However, exception was retained for the 'handicap' clause: there is no legal time limit to abortion where there is 'a substantial risk that if the child were born it would suffer from such physical or mental abnormalities as to be seriously handicapped'.

The most significant medical developments of recent years have been in the area of genetic knowledge, arising from the Human Genome Project, raising concerns about the eugenic potential of new scientific knowledge in formulating and implementing health policies (see for example, Armer, 2007). These debates mirror some of the concerns raised early in this chapter about conflicts between professional and lay knowledges (Kerr and Cunningham-Burley, 1998a; 1998b). Thus, Shakespeare (1998) draws particular attention to the 'lack of a disabled voice in genetic policy', especially in the information and choices provided to prospective parents of children with impairment characteristics.

With the growth of critical disability studies and activism, a great deal has been written about disability, impairment, birth selection and eugenics since the youngest of the three generations were born in the 1980s (for example, Shakespeare, 1998; 2006; Parens and Asche, 2000; Kerr and Shakespeare, 2002; Raz, 2005). As they reach adulthood in the 21st century they are confronted both by new technologies, new social debates and difficult choices. Based on her own experience of growing up with prejudice and discrimination, Maggie (born in the 1940s) acknowledges that her view now would be controversial:

> *I'll be honest and people aren't going to like it, but if I found*
> *out I was having a [baby with my impairment] I would have it*
> *terminated because of, not what my mum went through, but because*
> *of what I went through. And it wasn't the schooling, the kids were*
> *brilliant, but afterwards, there's a lot of ignorant people out there …*

What is significant here is the message that negative social factors, rather than impairment, could make a life not worth living. Perhaps more than any other message in the stories, this underlines the need for policies and social changes to support greater inclusion.

Conclusions

The methodological framework for this book (outlined in Chapter One) focuses on the ways in which change in environments, institutions and relationships have impacted on the life course trajectories and pathways of young disabled people since the 1940s. The examples used for illustration in this chapter provide a flavour of the accounts that people gave about life choices and chances that were influenced by medicine. They point to the significance of medical opinion in relationships with powerful professionals and, in combination with the examples in Chapter One, to medical institutions as contexts for physical segregation and surveillance. They also suggest some important elements of social change in Britain since the 1940s affecting both of these dimensions.

Medical opinion, in the form of early stage prognosis, continues to be an important factor in shaping early life expectations and parental understandings of what it means to have a child labelled as disabled. Such prognoses have often contained social opinions that extend well beyond biomedical or functional assessments, to include other predictions about adult social roles and the social value of disabled lives. When coupled with uncontested medical authority, such messages have had life-changing consequences (including abandonment to public institutional care or separation from family and community life). Dependency on hospital-based care and denial of voice within that context have resulted in increased vulnerability to inhuman and degrading practices under the guise of medical treatment.

Although there is great diversity of experience among individuals there is also evidence of collective biographical experience in the interactions with hospitals and doctors. Reading the stories in the context of policy analysis it is reasonable to conclude that changes in medical practices, treatment and technology created different opportunity structures for the different generations. Changes in medical technologies and treatment regimes have resulted in dramatic reductions to time spent in hospital and an increase in the participation of children and families in treatment decisions. Medicine has less influence over non-medical services and life decisions than it once did, while increasing lay knowledge and patient choice has provided opportunities to resist or contest medical authority. However, the accounts also suggest that doctors' perceptions of childhood disability have sometimes been slow to change and that medical authority, coupled with advancements in technology, can still have a substantial influence on private lives beyond the narrow sphere of medical treatment.

Questions for discussion

- Have challenges to medical authority and a shift away from hospital–based rehabilitation resulted in more socially integrated lives for disabled children since the 1940s?
- How have regimes of institutionally based physical therapy affected disabled children's experiences of school and family life, and has this experience changed since the 1970s?
- To what extent are disabled children and their families now more able to participate in, and resist, medical or professional decisions about treatments, therapies and the provision of assistive equipment?

FIVE

Learning about life

This chapter examines experiences of education, particularly schooling. The main focus, as in other chapters, is to examine the impact of public policies on private lives in the context of change over time. The stories in Chapter Two, the accounts of family life in Chapter Three and the discussion of medicalisation in Chapter Four all drew attention to the significance of educational policies and practices in young people's private lives. Across the three generations, the separation of children from their families and friends was perhaps the most obvious example. The complex policy relationship between health and educational provision highlighted the extent of medical authority in educational settings (for example, in determining choice of school and in daily school routines). There were also strong suggestions in the stories that low academic expectations for disabled children had impacted on life course trajectories and later opportunities in adulthood.

School and college experiences frame peer cultures, role models and identity construction (discussed in Chapter Seven). Successful participation in education is also an important enabler of social and economic inclusion for adult life (this is very relevant to the discussion of employment in Chapter Six). The examples in this chapter focus on some key issues at the interface between private lives and public education policies – on the personal and policy factors that influenced choice of school and college, the ways in which institutional provision shaped those choices, on the social experience of educational settings and on academic expectations and achievements.

Selecting pupils, choosing schools

Within the stories, choices and decisions about sending a child to special school featured prominently as key biographical turning points. These decision points illustrated much about the interaction between public policies and private lives. They were often points at which individual agency and familial resources collided with professional authority or with institutional barriers to inclusion. They established life course trajectories that would persist into adulthood, or marked turning points towards alternative biographies and life chances. There were both similarities and differences in the experience of those from the three generations.

Professional authority in selection

Those of the oldest generation were born into a rapidly changing policy context. Among the 'five giants' identified in Beveridge's wartime analysis of social need, 'ignorance' was of great concern and the 1944 Education Act (pioneered by Rab Butler as President of the Board of Education) ushered in sweeping changes to the organisation of schooling in England. It marked a greater involvement of public authority in the strategic and operational management of schools – free secondary education for all but with greater control over the admission and selection of pupils (notably, via the infamous 'Eleven plus' examination gateway to grammar schools).

Butler's education reforms also embodied 'an entirely new approach' to special education (Griffith, 1955) as local authorities acquired duties to consider special educational needs and powers to establish publicly funded special schools, under a new Ministry of Education. Although special schools had existed previously, the post–war period saw an increase in their number and a greater targeting of children labelled with particular types of impairment. Each local authority had long been required to maintain a school for the education of blind and deaf children (under the 1893 Blind and Deaf Children Act) and provision for 'mentally defective', epileptic and 'physically handicapped' children was also evident by the end of the First World War. By the early 1920s special schooling was well established in England for almost all disabled children.

The 1921 Education Act had defined five separate categories of impairment. It also enabled local authorities to require parents of 'certified' children to send them to special schools (or residential institutions). Particular emphasis had been placed on the measurement of IQ in distinguishing 'mentally defective' children, as established by the Mental Deficiency Committee (1929). Following the 1944 Act, the 1945 Handicapped Pupils and School Health Service Regulations provided for 11 categories of special educational need (reduced to 10 categories in 1953). Like Tomlinson (1982), Barnes (1991, p 29) sees clear connections between greater academic selection in general secondary education and the proliferation of special schools during this period. Indeed, he concludes that 'selection by ability sanctioned selection by disability'.

Intelligence testing was still viewed as the main arbiter of special school placement but, by 1956, more than a third of special school pupils were attributed an IQ score above the 70 point 'ESN' threshold, and nearly half of all pupils in rural special schools (Chief Medical Officer, 1962). Straightforward IQ 'certification' had been replaced with a more generic 'ascertainment' of a child's educational attainment. In this sense, the new category of 'educationally subnormal' (ESN) was intended to describe low achievement in school rather than some intrinsic low ability. In effect, it also brought children with physical and intellectual impairments into the common administrative system (see Ministry of Education, 1946).

Williams (1965, p 137) saw this as particularly significant for 'children who were making no progress with their school work, but who were not of low intelligence'. The ascertainment process applied to any child who was falling behind their age peers, for whatever reason (including, for example, the kind of long absences in hospital described in Chapter Four). Neither did the regulations assume that 'backward' children would be placed in special schools but, rather, that they would receive 'some specialised form of education wholly or partly in substitution for the education normally given in ordinary schools'. It is also worth noting that there were also few special school places available.

However, Tomlinson (1982, p 51) suggests that the guidance did promote a view that ordinary schools could not meet the needs of children in 'subnormal' categories and that medical authority remained the most appropriate mechanism for sanctioning decisions to remove them from the mainstream. As noted in Chapter Four, medical authority in special school placement decisions was asserted by several of those in the oldest generation. For example, Bob, who was sent to a residential special school at the age of five, believed his educational experience in the 1950s was shaped in this way:

> *The education of disabled children ... was actually controlled by the health service and not by education, so they had quite a large say in where disabled children went ... they felt it was best to send me away to a special school, for my mum and for me.*

For May, who also went to a special school at an early age:

> *I think it was the consultant who we saw, yeah. And it was them that said I should go to this school, yeah, it was down to the consultant really, that I should go there.*

These early recollections (no doubt informed by parental accounts and subsequent reflection) lend some support to the medicalisation thesis described in Chapter Four but it is useful to place them in context. In terms of educational provision, there had been a significant de-medicalisation in the transfer of responsibilities to the new local educational authorities (LEAs). There was no unitary system for deciding who went to special school and, in addition to IQ results, the Handicapped Pupil assessment forms included comments on physical and emotional condition, academic progress, behaviour, social history and home conditions (see Williams, 1965). They included both educational opinion (from the head teacher) and medical opinion, often supplemented with psychological and social evidence. In this sense it was not a 'medical' process although, in practice, the overwhelming majority of decisions were taken by Principal School Medical Officers within the local education authorities (Segal, 1961).

It is likely, then, that the biographical recollections of medical authority in school placement often relate to these officers, within the LEA, rather than to consultants within the NHS. On the one hand, this could be seen as a creeping colonisation of education by powerful medical professionals (a 'medicalisation' of everyday life). On the other hand, it should be seen as a policy shift from the medical to the educational domain (that is, the legislation had invested authority in LEAs, not in medical professionals per se). Indeed, the Chief Medical Officer (1958) had sought to ensure 'arrangements for consultation ... instead of leaving the medical officers with responsibility for an educational matter which is really outside their sphere'. It was also the Ministry of Education (1961) that urged the early selection of pupils for special education 'treatment', to stimulate their development. The expansion of special schools during the post-war period appears then to have been driven more by educational than medical concerns.

Resistance, negotiation and choice

As suggested in the previous chapters, the stories provided many examples of resistance to the kinds of professional authority alluded to earlier. This was as evident in relation to education as it was in the context of medical treatment. For example, Dan was unsure exactly why he was withdrawn from special school to return to his local school but linked this to his own and his parents' agency.

> *I used to complain, at home you know, saying 'I want to go to school with all the others'... I don't know what happened, whether*

my parents had put pressure on, but I remember leaving the school and then going to an ordinary secondary school.

When Daisy's mainstream class teacher was unable to cope, Daisy was excluded but, here too, a narrative of maternal resistance and resilience was invoked to explain the outcome:

The headmaster said to my mother 'we need to get her into a special school', and my mum didn't want that at all ... she fought to get me back to this mainstream school and managed to get me back there.

On a similar note, Maggie recalled opinion from medical and educational professionals (presumably within the LEA procedure discussed) that she would be better supported at a special school. However, she attributed the outcome to her mother's determination and the availability of networks of informal support amongst siblings and friends in a close-knit community:

I think why I had the life I had was because me mum wouldn't let me go to a special school ... The council, or whatever they call them, and the school wanted me to go to a special school. And my mum put her foot down and said 'no way, she will go to that school' ... And I remember her sort of saying [to me] 'you're bright enough to cope and so I know you can do it'. And I think I must have said I don't want to go to a special school. Because my friends were here, it was a village, we knew everybody, and people would say 'oh, we'll look after her'. I suppose when you think about it my life could have been totally different, totally different.

Grace also had parents who resisted recommendation for special school placement. Here too their informal negotiation of environmental barriers was invoked as enabling the positive outcome.

I learned later that I was to go to a special school but dad refused, bearing in mind this is [mid-1950s]. Dad absolutely refused point blank. I wasn't to go to special school. I was to go to mainstream school ... I went to the same school as my brother ... There was no way I could have managed to walk to school, and mum also arranged for me to go to school on a bike. Nobody else was allowed to go to school on a bike but I was allowed to go on my three-wheeler so that's quite, quite good ... bearing in mind it was the

> *fifties, the school was quite receptive to disability. The classrooms were upstairs and I was allowed extra time to get upstairs.*

In the absence of statutory frameworks on disability discrimination, several stories from this period revealed creative, practical solutions that were informally negotiated between families and schools. Thus, they conveyed a sense of disability being addressed more as an everyday 'personal trouble' than as a public 'social issue' (Mills, 1959).

This kind of agency at critical turning points was attributed to individual teachers, as well as to parents, shaping subsequent life course pathways (also reported by Shah, 2005b; 2008). For example, Bob (from the oldest generation) attributed much to a particular primary teacher at a residential special school in the 1950s, who recognised his academic potential and persuaded the LEA to place him in a more academically-oriented secondary school:

> *The teacher felt you know I would actually start to go backwards if I stayed there so she persuaded the local authority to try and get me into a different school ... I was 11 and it was [early 1960s].*

Helen's story, some 40 years later, revealed a very similar turning point, which she believes changed her life substantially.

> *I was very, very lucky because the only reason I left my special school was that the teacher who had been assigned to my class ... saw that I had the potential and the ability to survive in a mainstream environment. So she took her free periods off when she wasn't teaching. She took me to the local primary school and made sure that I did maths and science along with kids at the local primary school. But she fought against the rest of the school and to some extent the apathy of my parents to get me out of the school.*

In these examples, the narratives suggests that individual agency or resilience were determining factors in achieving positive life course outcomes, achieved more in spite of than because of the opportunity structure provided by public policies and institutions. However, it was also recognised that choice and resistance were substantially constrained by institutionalised barriers. The extent of physical and social barriers and the general absence of individualised learning support in mainstream schools were still very evident in the accounts of the middle generation (born in the 1960s). For example, Eileen perceived real differences in policy and provision, then and now.

I was in the mainstream school. I think now I would have had a fantastic DDA case for being excluded from school for a period of time ... I fell down the stairs; the school said it was too dangerous for me to be there and they just told me to go home that afternoon, and come back when I was better ... after I fell down a hill, I wasn't allowed to go on field trips with geography because they deemed it to be too dangerous, which was actually probably true, although it could have maybe been dealt with in a different way. There was no method at school to kind of sit down and say okay, this is the itinerary for this field trip, you can't do this bit but you can do this bit.

It is worth noting that, although the Disability Discrimination Act was enacted in 1995 it was not applied to educational provision until amended by the 2001 Special Educational Needs and Disability Act. So, the kind of 'DDA' rights to equal treatment and non-discrimination Eileen refers to were not in force even for the compulsory schooling period of most of the youngest generation (that is, those born in the 1980s).

Proposals for the 1976 Education Act had sought to implement Labour's comprehensive education pledges but allowed continuing loopholes in the placement of disabled children. While those in categories of special need were to be educated in mainstream schools this remained subject to the important proviso that special schooling was appropriate where a mainstream placement would place them or other pupils at an academic disadvantage, or where it would result in unreasonable expense. As Barnes (1991) and others have argued, this reinforced LEAs' very considerable discretion in excluding a disabled child from a mainstream school.

Goacher et al (1988) argue that, despite the rhetoric of greater integration in the much vaunted Warnock Report and the 1981 Education Act, there had been little change in the professional power relationships associated with school placement decisions. However, they draw attention to the replacement of medical authority by educational psychologists in this process (see also Bennett, 1998). Alderson and Goodey (1998) also expressed concern about the persistent influence of health professionals' advice in cooperation with LEAs. Thus, while there was some degree of de-medicalisation, professional authority was little challenged.

At the same time, new rights and opportunities to contest professional authority were emerging. Within a strident policy agenda for parental 'choice' in education, promoted by the Conservative Government, the

1993 Education Act (consolidated in the 1996 Act) introduced a new Code of Practice and a Special Educational Needs Tribunal system with the intention of allowing greater rights of parental appeal. Riddell et al (2000, p 631) argue that, particularly in England, these developments highlighted 'a shift away from a policy framework based on professional control' towards more bureaucratic and managerial approaches (see also Vincent et al, 1996; Harris et al, 2000). In practice, there has been much critique of the Tribunal system's effectiveness in facilitating mainstream access against professional opinion (for example, Kenworthy and Whittaker, 2000; Bagley et al, 2001; Runswick-Cole, 2007).

Rachel spent the final year of her primary education in a mainstream school (in the mid-1990s) but was refused admission to local secondary school. As her mother articulated:

> *The LEA said there was no accessible secondary school so she will have to go back to special school ... So off we went to the High Court and Special Needs Tribunal and they agreed that [Rachel] should go to the local comprehensive.*

Ultimately, the 'comprehensive' school in question was not prepared to accept Rachel. Harvey, now aware of the policy changes that occurred during the 1980s, also narrated his mother as actively contesting administrative and professional authority to secure his inclusion in a mainstream school.

> *When I first started at school the Tory Government had introduced mainstreaming disabled people in education. However, my mother still had to fight the entrenched values of the education system to enable me to go into mainstream education. There was a lot of pressure on me to go into a special needs school ... round about the time when I was starting school there was this kind of accepted thing that disabled children went to special school ... I'm really pleased that my mother fought against that to put me into mainstream school and to ensure that I had the support to succeed, because there was a lot of doubt amongst the professionals as to whether I would be able to succeed.*

Such stories are characteristic of many reported in the parent, activist and academic literature. They often seek to convey parents as the passionate and committed agents of educational inclusion for their children but the bigger picture is not so clear cut. Indeed, Croll and Moses (1998, p 22) showed that the Tribunal was actually hearing 'more cases from parents appealing *against* an LEA's refusal to grant a special school place' (our emphasis). The Tribunal's more recent records indicate that the number of appeals began to decline, following steady increase, after implementation of the 2001 Special Educational Needs and Disability Act. In 2008 the Tribunal structure was reformed into a 'two-tier' system and there have been policy moves to encourage mediation rather than formal judicial processes (echoing parallel policy developments in family law proceedings). However, as Riddell et al (2010) point out, there is little evidence that mediation has been widely used in practice. In 2010 the responsibility of the Local Government Ombudsman was also extended to consider complaints about LEA provision for special educational needs.

The motivation and capacity of parents to contest decisions, and to advocate for mainstream placements, was also framed by new forms of social capital arising from the growing movement for inclusive education. Both disability advocacy groups, within the disabled people's movement, and parental advocacy groups, in a climate of educational consumerism, played a part here (Clough and Barton, 1999; Clough and Corbett, 2004; Halpin, 1999). For example, Steve cited the importance of informal parental networks as a resource enabling his mother to contest professional opinion that he should go to a special school.

> I think me mum looked to specialist, because she didn't realise mainstream was an option ... [then] she spoke to a few other parents of children around my age who were looking at the possibility of sending their kids to mainstream school.

Halpin (1999, p 225) places great emphasis on the significance of social capital and civil involvement in achieving inclusion, asserting that:

> getting people involved in this way is not just a necessary condition for the development of more inclusive schools. It is a crucial element also in the process of reconstituting and revitalising civil society as a whole both to countermand the excessive powers of the interventionist central state and to foster people's confidence in their ability to direct their own lives.

It is clear that children and their families had access to different kinds of resources (or capital) when choosing schools. Some of the stories showed how the social capital provided by extended family and community strengthened their agency at critical turning points. Others revealed weakened family structures, parental resignation to professional judgements, and parental advocacy for segregated education. Such examples revealed that, where public policy or provision introduces a trajectory towards segregation, lack of access to advocacy for inclusion affects the outcome. The discussion in Chapters Two and Three highlighted concerns about weakened family structures in recent decades (including parental separation, single parenting, migration, and so on) but the stories also revealed new kinds of familial and social capital, including the emergence of parental self-help networks and the inclusion advocacy groups.

Although the stories conveyed a strong sense that agency and social capital were critical, it was clear that their influence was constrained by the kinds of schools available (as well as by professional authority in the decision-making process). In practice, professional authority and a lack of accessible schools often meant being sent away from home to a residential special category school.

Categorising children and schools

The proportion of children attending special schools was fairly small in the post-war years and such schools were intended primarily for those whose 'backwardness' had been attributed to low IQ. Between 1955 and 1965 the number of day and boarding special schools increased from 621 to 789. However, expanding provision continued to target those designated as 'educationally sub-normal' and there was actually some decline in the number of children with physical impairments attending special schools (see Cole, 1986; Hurt, 1988).

Policy envisaged that children assessed as needing special educational input should receive it in ordinary schools if possible. However, many 'physically handicapped' and 'delicate' children were sent to special schools for social, practical or therapeutic reasons rather than academic ones. For example, Hillary recalls being at mainstream school for a term, before her parents were persuaded to remove her:

> *When I was five, the LEA suggested that I should go to the local primary school for three mornings a week. My parents were happy with the choice. But my mother soon recognised that it wasn't working. For example, at play time the other children bullied me and segregated me from their games. When they did include me, the children would delight in playing 'push and shove' with me as I sat in my buffer chair, which was on wheels ... After a few weeks, the headmistress admitted that having me in the school*

> *wasn't working and I need personal one-to-one teaching. So I left
> after a term and I had a home tutor. She was hopeless ... Now
> the local school and home tutor had failed me, the LEA had to
> provide financial support for me to be educated out of the county.*

In Hillary's case, this meant a National Spastics Society boarding school providing specifically for children with cerebral palsy. Impairment-specific schools were seen as progressive in offering concentrations of specialist support (Hurt, 1988) but, although policy categories of 'handicap' shaped new institutional provision, children did not always 'fit' neatly into them (Plowden Report, 1967). Worton's experience provides an obvious example as she acquired a mix of impairment labels during her school career in the 1950s.

> *Basically when I went blind I spent a couple of months being towed
> round all the boarding schools and being turned down by them
> because the blind ones didn't want me because I didn't walk very
> well and the physically impaired schools didn't want me because I
> was blind, and some schools didn't want me because, once I went
> blind, it became obvious that I was actually quite deaf.*

For the purposes of education policy, 'physically handicapped' children had been defined as those:

> not suffering solely from a defect of sight or hearing who by
> reason of disease or other crippling defect cannot, without
> detriment to their health or education be satisfactorily
> educated under the normal regime of ordinary schools.
> (Ministry of Education, 1959)

Schools catering for this category admitted children with a very wide range of impairments. For Daisy, it was difficult to identify any commonality of impairment amongst her peer group at school.

> *There were lots of people there that didn't look disabled at all and
> there were some people there that were very disabled ... It was
> like a human rubbish dump in a sense, and that is awful but that's
> what it was, in a sense. And anyone that they didn't know how to
> handle, or that was causing any problems, be it a cough or a severe
> disability, put in this school and shut the door on it.*

Haskell and Anderson (1969) reviewed the situation in the mid-1960s and noted that, of the 20 thousand or so 'physically handicapped' and 'delicate' children receiving or waiting for special education in England and Wales, only a minority went to ordinary schools. Special schools were expensive to run but the support required to ensure full inclusion in mainstream schools was generally viewed as more costly (Cole, 1989). By 1975, the Schools Census form listed 21 different 'categories of Handicapped pupils' and, between 1970 and 1980, the number of children enrolled in special schools increased by 44%. However, there was also evidence of increasing integration for those with less significant mobility impairments.

Publication of the Warnock Report (1978) and the subsequent 1981 Education Act are widely acknowledged as significant turning points towards integration. From the early 1980s there was a reduction in the proportion of children attending special schools, from 1.87% to 1.30% by 2001 (see Norwich, 1997; 2002). The 1981 Act replaced categories of 'handicap' with categories of 'special educational need' (SEN), gave a legal entitlement to individual assessment and promoted greater parental involvement in the process.

The expectation that children with 'special educational needs' should attend mainstream schools was re-emphasised in the 1996 Education Act, and bolstered by the 2001 Special Educational Needs and Disability Act (extending the Disability Discrimination Act into educational provision). The stated objective of government policy increasingly focused on inclusion, whilst admitting that special schools would continue to provide for a 'small minority' whose needs were not met by mainstream schools. Yet, since the implementation of non-discrimination legislation, and in the 21st century, the total proportion of children attending special schools has remained relatively static.

The designation of special schools in England requires approval of the Secretary of State, in accordance with the 1994 Education (Special Schools) Regulations. This continues to specify the nature of 'special needs' catered for. Most are still targeted to pupils with particular impairment labels, including schools for children labelled with visual impairments, hearing impairments, speech or language impairments, learning difficulties, or 'emotional and behavioural difficulties'. However, Helen's experience, some two decades after the 1981 Education Act, recalled rather similar anomalies to those of Worton or Daisy in the 1950s:

> *a boy who was deaf, blind and in a wheelchair with severe learning difficulties and behavioural problems; someone with cerebral palsy*

who was ambulant but had severe behavioural difficulties and had a tendency to bite people, someone with cerebral palsy who also had moderate learning difficulties, was partially sighted and partially hearing, someone with spina bifida who had moderate learning difficulties, the fourth one was a deaf student with severe learning difficulties. And me. So it was an interesting combination for anyone to try and teach.

In England, special schools are generally smaller than mainstream schools and more likely to include a wider age range of pupils (for example, from nursery to age 19). This means that there are often smaller classes and progression from one class to the next is more often dependent on teacher judgements. Eleven school categories were identified in the 2007 School Census, including 329 special schools in England approved for the primary need of 'physical disability', with around 4,500 pupils (DfES, 2007).

There are still more than a thousand publicly maintained special schools in England, employing some 17,500 teachers. According to data from the Pupil Level Annual Schools Census (PLASC) for 2006/07 there were 89,400 children enrolled in special schools in England, the overwhelming majority in publicly funded schools. This data suggests that, despite considerable policy change since the 1940s, approximately 40% of children with 'special needs' in England continue to attend special schools (DfES, 2007). Although the number of children with physical impairments in the mainstream has increased, at the beginning of the 21st century the overall number of pupils enrolled in special schools was higher than it was in 1970 (Office for National Statistics, 2000).

Public policies for the categorisation, selection and school placement of disabled children have dramatic consequences for the kinds of private lives those children live. There has been a shift from medically administered institutions to educationally administered ones, and a transfer of professional decision making away from medical authority. There have been increased opportunities for parents to contest that authority and non-discrimination legislation, including a Disability Equality Duty that promotes accessibility in schools (see Beckett, 2009). However, as some of the examples in the next part of the chapter show, the stories still reveal some remarkably similar experiences of segregation between the youngest and oldest of the generations.

The personal impact of schooling decisions

The stories from all three generational cohorts conveyed much about the institutional regimes experienced in different types of schools, and the impact these had on young people's private lives and social worlds. Academic achievements at school are clearly important in shaping adult life choices and chances but schooling has important social dimensions too, which also impact on adult lives. The following sections focus on the life course implications of segregated social environments and limited academic or social expectations.

The school environment

The expansion of special schools in England produced a patchwork of institutions offering educational 'treatment' for designated categories of need. Specialisation, and uneven development, meant that pupils often travelled long distances. Provision included a number of rural establishments converted, by charities and public authorities, from country houses or sanatoria and the stories of those who attended residential schools in the 1960s and 1970s conveyed many images of such places. For example:

> *It was terribly cut off. It started off as a Victorian businessman's hunting lodge and gradually worked its way to being a school for what were called 'delicate children' ... kids that were recovering from operations were often sent there because being in the countryside ... the air quality was better and was thought to be conducive to your recovery.* (Ian)

> *... like a massive big house in these huge great big grounds, and in the middle of nowhere. Twenty-five miles away from [my home town], and I got took to school when I was four years old ... And I was crying my eyes out 'cos my mum and dad had left me, and I was all frightened.* (Tan)

> *I mean I do think there is a place for specialist education but when it's, when it's residential as well and it's living in [some rural county] amongst loads of trees, it's not what you want.* (Sonia)

Within these relatively isolated environments, school became the primary social world of childhood. Moreover, the isolation from family and community was often accompanied by institutionalised environments and social regimes:

> *There was no carpets in the school, it was stone floors, wooden floors. There were hospital beds with rails on them 'cos when we were little we had cots. And you were in a dormitory with probably about 20 other people in a room … We didn't have no tellies, no carpets, no … you know, it was really horrible, hard blankets, there was hardly any heating 'cos the building was like, I don't know, it must have been pre-Victorian this building …* (Tan)

> *Looking back it was horrendous behaviour, but at the time we just accepted it. The school was very institutionalised, and you got up at seven every day, including weekends, which I wasn't too happy about. And they had set meals, you had set bath times, set bed times, the day completely structured … every break time we had to sit on the toilet, whether we wanted the loo or not. I couldn't understand this at all, and one day I said 'I don't want the toilet' and I got told off for that, and I did it again and I got a good spanking.* (Poppy)

As illustrated elsewhere (Shah, 2007; Shah and Priestley, 2009) there was some ambivalence in the stories about the social implications of attending mainstream or special school. For example, Daisy (born in the 1940s) saw benefits in her exposure to the realities of mainstream peer culture but this was not without personal cost.

> *I have mixed views on schools because I did experience a lot of bullying, rejection and things like that. But on the other hand it toughened me up and helped me to deal with the world … If you go to a mainstream school I think you need a very, very supportive family to give you skills for life if you like.*

Conversely, some of those who experienced mainstream school prior to the provision of learning support, physical accessibility or protection from abuse saw benefits in a segregated setting where their specific needs might have been more readily recognised. There were issues of peer acceptance to consider too. Florence (born in the 1940s) would have preferred to go to a special school simply because she knew other children there (from hospital), although her mother was strongly opposed to this.

> *... none of the people that had grown up with me went to the school that I ended up going to. I think there wasn't an acknowledgement of being different and trying to cope with adolescence and being different, whereas a lot of the children I knew at the special school, because I met them in hospital quite regularly and I knew them, but they didn't consider me their pal because I went to ordinary school.*

The clustering of children by administrative categories of handicap', and the particular isolation of certain schools for those with 'physical difficulties', meant that many grew up almost exclusively in the company of other disabled children. This had implications for the construction of peer friendship networks, personal identities and role models (discussed in Chapter Seven, with extended examples in Shah and Priestley, 2009).

Like several of those from the preceding generation, Holly (born in the 1980s) attended the same special school from infanthood to adulthood. It became her primary social world:

> *I went to a special needs nursery and then started a special needs school at the age of five. So a lot of the people I went to nursery school with I actually went to my main school with. I've actually been with the same bunch of people from the age of two to the age of 18 ... A lot of students spent two weeks at home, then a week boarding at the school which is what I did. It was nice staying at school because I got to spend time with friends ... when I got home I was at home and there was nothing for me outside of home so it was quite nice to actually spend that week at school boarding.*

Brandy and Zoe (also born in the mid-1980s) were both still in full-time education at the time of telling their stories (in 2007). Both women had been living in residential school placements continuously since they were three years old. Zoe recalled how remaining in the same school differed from normal patterns of life course transition experienced by young people in mainstream schools:

> *Fifteen years is a long time. I think if you stop there 'til you're 11, like you do any normal [school], I think that's long enough.*

While most special schools are now day schools, there are still around ten thousand children attending residential special schools (about four per cent of children with SEN statements). However, the population of those institutions has changed considerably since the 1940s, with the large majority now being teenage boys, often labelled with 'emotional and behavioural difficulties' (EBD). Some schools and colleges still accommodate disabled children throughout the year in 52-week 'educational' placements and an official report in 2003 showed just under half of the 1,320 residential placements for 'looked after' disabled children were in schools (DfES, 2003a; Priestley et al, 2002).

Pinney (2005) shows a declining number of residential school placements and provides more detail. Although information about impairment has only been collected since 2004 (and only in publicly funded schools) it is clear that children with EBD as their main category of need are over-represented in residential schools (at around 35%), with hearing impairment at 13%, visual impairment at 9% and physical impairment 10%. The reasons for placing disabled children in residential education continue to vary, according to local policy and provision, but research evidence cited by Reed and Harrison (2002) suggests many placements result simply from local schools being unable to accommodate children's access needs.

Following consultations in 2001, national standards for residential special schools assert that, 'In accordance with their wishes', children should be 'able and encouraged to maintain contact with their parents and families while living away from home at school' (DoH, 2002, p 37). The provision of 'space for children to meet privately with parents and others' is required (p 7) and the 'prevention of contact by telephone or letter with parents' is prohibited (p 18) except where there is clear risk to the child. Yet, research indicates that many disabled children placed in residential schools remain cut off from their families for significant parts of the year (for example, Reed and Harrison, 2002). Despite guidance in the 1989 Children Act to ensure disabled children and their families maintain appropriate and regular contact, a substantial proportion of residential school pupils, at the end of the 20th century, were neither going home nor being visited by their family on a regular basis (Gordon et al, 2000).

Expectations and achievements

There were numerous examples in the stories suggesting lack of access to a challenging academic curriculum for children with physical impairments. This arose not only from sustained absences from school, such as long stays in hospital, but also from low expectations at school. This was particularly evident in accounts of special schooling. For example, Dan (whose story was summarised in Chapter Two) was able to make comparison between the mainstream and special primary schools he attended in the early 1950s:

> *It was more about doing things like making raffia baskets and playing with, you know, clay, and they had gardens at the back and used to let us potter about, digging things up or planting things, but it didn't seem to be, you know, really academic type of thing … I remember leaving the school and then going to an ordinary secondary school, where you know, it was more maths and English and what have you, rather than making raffia baskets.*

For those, like Worton and May, who spent many years in such schools, there was a cumulative impact on their opportunities to progress in adult life:

> *I do think that it was a wasted opportunity from an education point of view. I think one of the problems was they underestimated my academic abilities.* (Worton)

> *… the standard of education was very poor. They never had any expectations of you at all. Never was entered for the Eleven Plus, didn't do any O-levels, it was very basic education.* (May)

For May, the choice of school was influenced by its provision of physical therapy rather than its academic resources (highlighting, again, the post-war transfer of provision from the NHS to LEAs).

> *[I went there] Because you had physiotherapy, which you could have had anywhere really, could have gone to the hospital for it, but that was one of the reasons … I mean, you did reading, maths, things, you know, things like that. But it was very sort of basic things. I used to try and stay off school as much as possible … Just hated it. So I didn't have any expectations of myself, I just wanted to, couldn't really wait for the day until I left school … I left at 16.*

Daisy was sent to an 'open air' school at the age of seven. These schools had developed for the treatment of 'delicate children' before the war (first as day schools and later as residential schools). In the 1930s many of their pupils had come from the urban slums, suffering diseases of poverty and overcrowding like tuberculosis and rickets before returning to mainstream school (Cole, 1989; Oswin, 1998). However, they offered only basic education so that disabled children, like Daisy, lagged behind their peers academically when they returned:

> *It didn't seem like a school, we had to go to bed in the middle of the day and things like that! [laughs] It was horrible really, I didn't learn a thing in those two years. Through Friends Reunited, I recently met up with a friend that I made there. And she came down here with her dad and he said to me as well, the couple of years that she spent at that school, left a big gap in her learning. So I think it really is better if children can go to mainstream schools.*

Not all the accounts in this period were negative in this respect. For example, Hillary and Catherine both attended residential special schools run by the Spastics Society where they recalled a greater emphasis on academic potential. Catherine, unlike many in her generation, emphasised the positive expectations of teachers:

> *It was the only grammar school in the country for people with cerebral palsy … the original headmaster was the most exceptional man and he used to say 'you're all the cream of the cream'. And he fought for us to have exactly the same lifestyle as any other 11- to 18-year-old, and have the same chances. So the [school] is what made me what I am today.*

As discussed in Chapter Four, academic progress was constrained by stays in hospital or adherence to intensive therapeutic treatment schedules. For example, Bella (also born in the 1940s) described the punctuated nature of her academic experience.

> *I missed quite key things in my education and very early on I must have been in hospital when they did the alphabet. And so I went back to school and it was almost like everybody had a secret code that I wasn't aware of, and I just couldn't understand how you worked this out, you know, what letters followed each other … I spent about seven and a half years in hospital. So I was coming and going all the time.*

The implication, as Daisy explained, was a tendency to fall further and further behind:

> *What they always used to do whenever I came out of hospital, or when I started school late they always said to me, 'We'll put you*

in the lowest stream and see how things pan out and then we'll move you'. But what I found was I never moved up, I was always kept low ... I failed miserably at most subjects.

Such experiences drew attention to the schooling provided to children in hospital. Among the concerns raised about child welfare in hospital in the 1950s (see Chapter Four), James Robertson, a psychiatric social worker, was prominent in arguing that hospitalised children should have the same opportunities as other school-age children. The provision of educational services within hospitals was increasingly seen as relevant to mitigating academic deprivation and the psycho-emotional effects of falling behind in school (for example, Barker, 1974; Murphy and Ashman, 1995).

While hospital teaching provided some access to education it was not always tailored to academic need. Maggie spent much of her childhood in hospital and recalled that, although there was schooling, it did not offer the same opportunities as her local village school.

In the summer all the beds were pushed out onto the balcony and you were sat in your bed in the sun. Yea, and the teacher came and we had schooling ... it's not the same as being at school, you know, and I wish I could say by missing school that's why I wasn't so intelligent but I don't know ...

Similarly, Bella recalled her hospital education in the 1950s:

They would come in the mornings, and I know it's very different now for children who are in long-term hospital, but they would just come, they would arrive, and hand out a card with sums on or something like that ... And then there was nothing else you see, even though I can remember asking if there was things that I could have or more work that I could have. So if the work hadn't been sent in from my school, which only came periodically, it would have been very minimal really ... I mean in that sort of era occupational therapy seemed to be about making things, so I'd make 20 rabbits or something. I did a lot of basket work.

There were similar accounts from those born in the 1960s. For example, Eileen recalled a very basic education during her extended stays in hospital:

*I was off school for between four and six months each time. And
there was no support whatsoever. So actually it was only that a
friend brought all of my — all of the notes, she took notes in class,
she photocopied them and gave them to me — that I actually did
my O-levels. And when I think about it now, it's bloody ridiculous
… they provide you with teachers when you're in hospital for any
period of time. But they couldn't do an O-level syllabus. They could
let you draw pictures and they could give you books to read, but
I mean I could read a book! I could bring my own books to read
but there was no syllabus.*

Not all of these experiences were negative, however, and Amy felt
the hospital schooling she received for much of her childhood was
important in her subsequent academic progression:

*The doctor who was in charge of this unit, she was very, very up
on your education … she absolutely wanted you to be as educated
as you could be, and if I hadn't been in that hospital unit, and
back at the daily boring special school, I never would've taken any
exams … our days were literally split into three hours probably of
physiotherapy, and three hours of schooling, every day … because
she didn't like any disruption, the head honcho, she didn't like
any disruption to your schooling, as much as to your physio … I
went from my whole school life there, apart from the odd little bit
of time where I did go back to the other day school.*

It is notable in these examples that individuals often narrate the forces
that shape their lives in terms of personal relationships and agency,
rather than institutions and social structures. Thus, low expectations
and lack of challenge from teachers featured prominently in the stories
of the middle generation but were often contested by narratives of
resilience and achievement 'against the odds'. For example, Ian recalled
his experience in special school from the late 1960s, where he felt the
teaching and expectations were particularly sub-standard, as illustrated
by an encounter some years later:

*The head teacher should never have been in the job, apart from one
teacher all the others were basically just marking time … well the
perfect example when I was at [FE college] and I can remember
coming out of a lecture at break time, seeing my old head teacher,
diving down a corridor to avoid him but failing miserably. And he
caught me up and said 'what are you doing here?' And I said 'I'm*

> *a student' ... and his exact words were 'Oh, I never thought one of my pupils would be clever enough to do A-levels'. And that summed up the entire ethos of that school. There was no motivation.*

Low academic expectation in special schools during the late 20th century has been highlighted often in disability research (for example, Humphries and Gordon, 1992; Alderson and Goodey, 1998; Morris et al, 2002; Shah, 2007). Cole (1989) argues that the training of special education teachers had been a low priority on government agendas. Moreover, there remained an institutional legacy of ambiguity in the transfer from places of 'care' and 'treatment' to places of education. Indeed, it was not until the 1988 Education Reform Act that children attending special schools received entitlement to the same National Curriculum as those in mainstream schools. Even then, Halpin and Lewis (1996) argue that it was not designed with special school pupils in mind and note the active resistance of many special schools to the original proposals.

The consideration of expectations and aspirations is important in the context of a biographical life course approach because it helps to reveal how turning points, resulting from life decisions and institutional factors, establish trajectories towards particular kinds of future lives in adulthood (see also Furlong and Biggart, 1999; Shah, 2008). There were fewer accounts of low expectations from the youngest generation (born in the 1980s) although they were certainly evident from some of those attending residential special schools in particular (like Holly). Harvey's experience in mainstream school conveyed a much more positive picture of teacher expectations:

> *They had very high hopes for me 'cos I did quite OK in the GCSEs, you know, I did above average for the school, you know, and they were like you – you know, Harvey, you go to the top for university ... I think if I didn't have those teachers inspiring m, because that's what they did, I wouldn't have done what I've done today.*

In 2010, the Department for Children, Schools and Families issued new guidance on *Breaking the link between special educational needs and low attainment* emphasising that 'interventions put in place should minimise any impact on attainment' (DCSF, 2010, p 9). The Office for Disability Issues now includes school achievement within its disability equality indicator set (combining School Census and Attainment Data). This data does not disaggregate by category of 'disability' but it suggests that the overall achievement of pupils with special educational needs in Standard Assessment Tests (SATS) has risen year on year. It also confirms the low numbers achieving good GCSE grades. Data from the Youth Cohort Study indicate that only 39% of disabled 16-year-olds were studying for Level 3 qualifications in 2003/04, compared to 50% of their non-disabled peers. The same data suggest that 28% of disabled 19-year-olds had experience of higher education (compared to 41%). However, the Higher Education Statistics Agency suggest that, of those who do manage to enter university, 56% achieve first or upper second class degrees, much closer to the 59% of non-disabled students (DCSF, 2010; ODI, 2010). The academic attainment gap thus narrows at higher levels, while concerns remain about the barriers to progression at school.

Social expectations

The kinds of limited social environments and low academic expectations outlined so far were accompanied by concerns that segregated institutional provision also fostered a lack of social preparedness for inclusion in adult life. For example, Mickey (born in the 1980s) hinted at the implications of growing up in limited social space.

> ... it was quite a sheltered environment, so going to university was quite a shock ... I think, in a way, the sheltered environment of the secondary school made me a little weaker as everything was done for us. It may have been easier for me at university if the school was not so sheltered.

Both Brandy and Zoe attended the same residential special school in the 1990s, followed by admission to a neighbouring specialist residential college. Brandy invoked the same narrative of 'sheltering' from the real world, although she acknowledged a degree of improvement at the college.

> [at the school] it's not a real life because you get so sheltered ... It feels like your real life till you get somewhere like here [college]. Here you are sheltered to a certain degree but you're not quite so sheltered. You are sheltered but your decisions aren't made for you here.

Improvements in academic expectations have not always been accompanied by raised social expectations for community inclusion in adulthood. Such concerns were raised by the British Council of Disabled People in the 1980s (BCODP, 1986) – that the special education system was constraining young people from learning the kinds of skills and social knowledge they needed to live as independent adults. As Holly continued:

> *I left school when I was 18 and we were very cocooned ... We weren't told about the outside world and things as a disabled person, the kind of attitudes we were going to come across ... At that point I still didn't know things like the DDA and stuff like that.*

Narratively, such examples contrast with those of the older generations, who more often emphasised a school focus on maximising their 'independence'. However, those references usually referred to a therapeutic focus on the normalisation of physical functioning and mobility (as described in Chapter Four). For example, Poppy recalled her experience in the early 1970s.

> *The aim [at school was] to get us as independent as possible, but not independent to use a wheelchair to get about, but you must walk, you must talk, I had speech therapy ... I had physiotherapy, and we had to dress ourselves, we had to feed ourselves, and the more dependent you were, the less privileges you got.*

By contrast, those in the youngest generation had a more social concept of what 'independence' meant and did not talk about being 'made' to walk at school.

Zoe and Brandy's stories draw attention to the way independence skills have been targeted in the further education sector. Despite a policy rhetoric of inclusion the sector's rapid expansion involved a substantial growth in specialist colleges, units and programmes for disabled students (Barton and Corbett, 1993). Even after extension of the DDA to educational provision, Pitt and Curtin (2004) highlight the experiences of those who are still moving from school into special education colleges simply 'because of the inadequate physical accessibility of their mainstream colleges, the quality of disability services available to them and their previous experiences whilst in mainstream school' (p 387).

In this context, the formalisation and surveillance of 'independence' skills for adulthood has raised some concerns. Zoe's story gives an insight here. Despite previously living independently as an adult, with her boyfriend, in their own flat, Zoe's college would not allow her to leave the campus alone without completing their 'independence training'.

> I was going shopping on my own. I was doing everything you can think of on my own outside of the house … Since I've been back I'm asking for more independence now. [I have to do] more independence training, like how to do my own cooking and do my own washing, because I've had the experience of that and they're thinking you need to be trained to do that. And I've done it. I know how to do it. I was doing it every day for four months and over a year and I feel like I've gone back a bit, kind of thing.

Middleton (2003) has argued that the formalisation and accreditation of independence skills can be viewed often more as a mechanism of social control than a marker of educational achievement. While the overriding emphasis in mainstream further education policy has been to prepare young people with skills for employment (or entry into higher education) specialist colleges have often prioritised curricula for social and independence skills.

Conclusions

There was a great deal of rich description in the life stories about education and schools and it is only possible to give a flavour of this in one chapter. It is also important to read these experiences in the context of the material discussed in Chapter Three (family life) and Chapter Four (medicalisation). Understanding the interaction between these different domains is important at the level of both public policy and private lives. The establishment of a combined government Department for Children, Schools and Families (abolished on the first day of the new Government in 2010) and the promotion of 'joined up' practice between education, health and social care authorities had gone some way to acknowledge these connections.

School placement decisions, especially residential placements, resulted as much from the type of schools available as from professional authority, and it is notable that there has been no steady trend towards inclusion over the historical period in question. Indeed, the expansion of special school places (particularly during the 1970s) intensified, rather than challenged, life trajectories towards segregation. The patchy nature of institutional provision in different localities has been significant and, ironically, the declining number of special schools has intensified the dilemma of separation for some families (when the 'only alternative' offered to them may now be some distance away). In addition, a new generation of residential 'colleges' has introduced new forms of segregation and surveillance under the guise of 'further education'.

Considering change over time, there is less evidence that children's educational opportunities are constrained as they once were by the institutional framework for health care and therapy provision. There are also greater opportunities for families to contest professional opinion or to complain about local educational provision. In this sense, the generational stories suggest changing opportunity structures. However, it remains a matter of great concern to read individual stories from the turn of the 21st century that bear such similarity to stories of institutionalised disadvantage from half a century ago.

Questions for discussion

- How does the support available to disabled children in mainstream schools today affect their academic and social lives compared with those who went to school in the 1950s or 1970s?
- How did the expansion of special schooling in the 1970s, including residential schooling, affect the family lives and friendships of disabled children, and have more recent changes in inclusive schooling policies made a difference for children today?
- To what extent have policies for integrated or inclusive education, developed since the early 1980s, created new academic and social opportunities for disabled children and young people, and why are disabled childen still being sent to special schools today?

SIX

Working for a living

The preceding chapters have emphasised life choices and chances in childhood. They also illustrated how childhood transitions can establish trajectories that affect adult careers. This chapter turns to work and employment as a key factor in transitions to adulthood, and as a key preoccupation of disability policies since the 1940s. It is perhaps worth noting at the outset that few in the youngest generation (born in the 1980s) had yet entered the adult labour market, either because they were still in full-time education or because they had not found paid employment. Conversely, the long work experience of some in the older generations provided useful insights into the changes they had witnessed up to the present day.

Work and employment have been viewed as central to inclusion in adult life, by disability activists and policy makers alike (Priestley, 2000). For example, those who pioneered the development of social model thinking in the 1970s and 1980s asserted a strong structural relationship between employment and social inclusion, arguing that:

> the struggle to achieve integration into ordinary employment is the most vital part of the struggle to change the organisation of society so that physically impaired people are no longer impoverished through exclusion from full participation.... All the other situations from which physically impaired people are excluded are linked, in the final analysis, with the basic exclusion from employment. (UPIAS/Disability Alliance, 1976, pp 15–16)

Like education, employment is an expansive theme and it would be impossible to cover the full range of issues arising from the stories here. As with the previous chapters, the main emphasis is on relationships between public policies and people's private lives. The examples focus on three themes arising from the stories. The first section looks at the kinds of help people drew upon to look for work in changing labour markets. The second section considers barriers to employment and the impact of changing policies. The final section addresses the substitution of meaningful employment with alternative occupation.

Help in looking for work

The experiences of looking for work in the life stories revealed much about the strategies that people used to navigate their way into the labour market, and the kinds of public and private help they received. The older generation's encounters with help from public employment services were not remembered very positively and there was much more evidence that people relied on informal help to find and sustain employment. Neither were careers teachers and advisors remembered as being very helpful, often blocking career aspirations with disabling responses.

There were numerous stories of the ways in which young disabled people had been assisted by family and friends. For example, Maggie left school with no formal qualifications in the early 1960s. As in other areas of her life, she drew on family support to secure her first job in the open labour market.

> *I was sat at home and me uncle who worked at the factory rang up and said 'Are you doing anything?' and I said 'No'. I think I'd been left a week or two. I'd left school a week or two. 'Right get your coat on.' 'Where are we going?' 'Get your coat on.' So I put my coat on, he picked me up and he took me into the middle of the factory to where he worked, sat me in an office and said, 'The boss will come and he might offer you a job'. I'd no make-up on, no hair done. I sat there, this Mr M came in and he just asked a few questions. 'Right start Monday', and that's how I started ...*

Having rejected the limited options offered by the Employment Exchange, Dan also drew on informal sources of help.

> *I had a local Canon from the Church who used to whizz me round in his car, to try and get employment, and he was the one who got me a job in a butcher's ...*

Catherine, who was initially sent to a sheltered workshop, recalled how:

> *I refused to go to any of the places that they suggested I should go and, with my parents' help, we just hawked round all the local places to see if I could get any sort of job and eventually I got a job with the County Council and it worked out to be an absolute boon because it was in the education department.*

Looking at change since this time, Warren (2005) argues that implementation of non-discrimination legislation in the mid-1990s, including the abolition of the employment quota, marked a shift of policy responsibility onto the individual to market themselves to employers. Yet, most of the stories suggested that those who found work in the open labour market prior to the DDA had relied on personal resources despite the availability of structured 'help' from public agencies.

Help from public employment services

Those in the oldest generation (born in the 1940s) did not enter the adult labour market until at least the mid-1950s but there had been considerable change in the policy landscape immediately prior to this. Cohen (2001) and Borsay (2005) point to the significance of the King's National Roll Scheme, established during the First World War, which offered public recognition for the 'noble obligation' of employers to fulfil a voluntary quota of disabled workers (Kowalsky, 2007). This was eventually extended to include disabled civilians, before being replaced by statutory provisions in 1944 Disabled Persons (Employment) Act. Increased optimism about the untapped potential of disabled workers had also been fuelled by the re-assessment of civilians who were found employable in key industries where there were war-time labour shortages (see later, and Stone 1984).

The Tomlinson Report (1943) had argued for a more integrated process of 'recovery' from disability towards active participation in employment. Its focus, as the Committee's name suggested, was on 'Rehabilitation and Resettlement' – targeting those who had acquired impairment after commencing their working lives. Introducing the Bill for new legislation in 1943, the spokesman for the Ministry of Labour emphasised the need for a model based on 'inspiring hope in the mind of the patient' towards economic independence:

> The Bill is based upon the principle that disability is a handicap, not a barrier, to employment, and that the great majority of people ordinarily regarded as disabled are capable of useful and productive work ... There is need, therefore, to consider what the disabled persons can do rather than what they cannot do, and so, on that basis to create the greatest possible opportunity for the disabled to take their places in the ordinary economic life of the country. (*Hansard*, 10 December 1943, v395, c1268)

The 1944 Act established a national register of 'substantially handicapped' persons and a statutory three per cent quota for their employment. It designated certain occupations as 'reserved' for disabled people and formalised sheltered work facilities for those deemed unable to gain employment in the open labour market. The new role of Disablement Resettlement Officer (DRO) was established, monitoring local working conditions for disabled people on behalf of the Ministry of Labour and guiding individual pathways. The processes of work assessment and preparation combined an emphasis on medical authority (see Chapter Four) with a recognition of social rights to participation. Barnes (1991, p 85) suggests that the arrangements might be viewed as 'a compromise between policies of enforcement and those of persuasion'.

Reviewing the provision of employment services in the mid-1950s, the Piercy Report (1956) re-emphasised the medical profession's authority over rehabilitation, and the restoration of work capacity in a work-like environment. It recommended the establishment of medically-based employment rehabilitation centres, linking hospitals and industry, and the expansion of sheltered employment provision. During the same period there was also an expansion of occupational therapy provision in NHS hospitals (see Cromwell, 1985).

The experiences narrated in the life stories highlighted the existence of two rather different life trajectories shaped by this policy framework. Borsay (2005), like Thornton and Lunt (1995), argues that the policy provisions of the 1940s polarised a division between 'effective' and 'ineffective' workers. Thus, while the former were provided with some opportunity to participate in the open labour market, albeit with many barriers and little practical support, the latter were increasingly segregated into various forms of what Barnes (1991) terms 'institutionally secured employment'.

The availability of DROs within local employment offices affected the kinds of work offered to people entering the labour market. For example, among the provisions of the 1944 Act, the Minister for Labour was empowered to 'designate' certain occupations for disabled workers. Although the scheme was heralded as progressive, it was narrow in scope and only two occupations were reserved – 'car park attendants' and 'electric passenger lift operators'. Registered disabled workers were not restricted to these occupations but designation meant that DROs might steer people towards them.

For example (as summarised in Chapter Two) Dan went to the Employment Exchange after being refused entry into the Navy. He was presented with the offer of a designated vacancy.

Like most kids in the 1960s, I wanted to get out of school and start earning some money, you know ... well I went to the Job Centre as a 16-year-old, I had a Green Card. I had my disability, my Green Card, and he actually said, 'well, there is a lift job at this big store in [another suburb]'. He said, and 'you'll be able to sit most of the time' ... it was like the old jobs, that was kept for people with disabilities, you know, you could be a lift attendant, car park attendant, these really brilliant jobs, you don't want to be [laughs] ... I never got offered a car park job. I did get offered a lift job.

Within the policy framework, the DRO's options were not limited by occupation but Dan was offered only the designated vacancy. After refusing that he went out to search for a job informally, without support from the public employment services. By the mid-1960s the large majority of those in designated occupations were registered disabled men (although there were no other references to designated jobs in the stories). It is worth noting that these provisions continued, at least in theory, until they were abolished with the implementation of the Disability Discrimination Act in 1996.

Those in the two older generations seemed to have received scant assistance from DROs, or they were directed to workshops and 'training' outside the open labour market (discussed later). The sense was of a narrow range of options and a lack of focus on personal career goals. Indeed, during a 1957 parliamentary debate on improving the employment services (prompted by the Piercy Report) one MP noted, with reference to the work of DROs, that:

These people are the key to so much of this work. I was thinking, as I listened to hon. Members on both sides, that it could be perhaps that by the very nature of their work they are the ones who need rehabilitation. Events are moving at such a terrific pace in industry that a preconceived idea of what a man's functions may be, derived from the fact that he may have gone through a course of training some years ago, may be completely out of focus. (*Hansard*, 13 December 1957, v579, c1696)

Leaving full-time education two decades later, in the early 1980s, Matt found that DROs still lacked the capacity to consider his individual circumstances and that their advice remained constrained within very limited policy options.

> I was going to the Job Centre on a regular basis saying 'I want to get a job'. They said we think you should go to the rehabilitation centre in [a nearby city] to see what you can do ... every time I went in they kept bugging me to go ... In the end I stopped going to Job Centre.

What Matt wanted was help to find a job in the open labour market, rather than to be assessed. The DROs often seemed unable to offer much more than a placement in an assessment and training centre (or a recommendation for sheltered employment). There was relatively little they could provide in the way of practical adjustment and support for mainstream employment, other than to seek enforcement of the employment quota and the goodwill of employers.

By 1965 there were more than 655,000 people registered as disabled for employment purposes (one in 40 of the working population). Of these, only 43,000 were 'unemployed' and 13,000 were placed in sheltered workshops. As Mattingley (1965) points out then, the vast majority were employed in mainstream jobs (and not necessarily because of the quota or designated vacancies). It is worth noting, however, that registration remained voluntary and that those who 'registered' needed to have, in the opinion of assessors, a reasonable prospect of finding work. The employment figures suggested in the official statistics are therefore rather unreliable.

From the early 1980s, and with rising unemployment, increasing numbers of disabled people were being advised by general public employment services (and fewer relying on specialist guidance services). There were also attempts to include more disabled young people in mainstream employment training schemes, like the much-vaunted Youth Training Scheme (Bradley, 1995). In a study at this time Kuh et al (1988) blamed 'the handicapping features of employment services' for the 'static or unstable occupational paths' of the young disabled people they spoke to. By the end of the 1980s policy direction favoured a greater de-centralisation of assessment and training services towards local teams combining the functions of the DRO, the Disablement Advisory Service and the Employment Rehabilitation Service (see DfE, 1990).

Careers advice at school

Another major source of professional advice to young people during this period was at school or college. It was not until the 1960s that the school curriculum included any real focus on 'careers' advice, although this function then expanded rapidly during the 1970s (Law and Watts, 1977). By the 1980s it was envisaged that all schools should timetable careers education, although not within any prescribed model. Within the life stories there were many recollections of encounters with careers advisors and gatekeepers to vocational training. They were, in general, remembered as rather dispiriting encounters. While this echoes the negative experiences that many non-disabled students report too (Watts, 2001), it is important to emphasise that disability figured quite explicitly as a factor in the stories. For example, Tom (from the oldest generation) recalls how the careers advisor discouraged him from his aspiration to become a doctor.

> *They said 'Oh, you can't be a doctor, you're crippled' … I think the doctor actually was solicited at some point. I can remember a conversation saying, you know, showing me how difficult it would be for me as a disabled man to perform as a doctor.*

Similarly, Catherine remembered the reaction when she applied to train as a speech therapist in the early 1970s (leading her to modify her career plans accordingly).

> *I went for an interview at a college in [the city] and they said, 'It's not an occupation for somebody in a wheelchair, definitely not. We suggest you do something else, teach or something'.*

Ian remembers no opportunity to talk to a careers advisor about his choices on leaving special school in the late 1970s, while Yvette, who also went to a special school, remembers:

> *A guy came in to do careers but I can't remember him actually doing anything useful, and, you know, there was no sort of encouragement into a career. In fact, I don't know if I've dreamt this, but I kind of seem to remember that our Education for Life, which I think you'd now call PHSE, we got asked if we wanted to go and visit the local Cheshire Home because that's where we'd be living.*

Amy felt that her aspirations were ridiculed and that this had a diminishing effect on her confidence and motivation at the time.

> *… and they would say things to me like, 'Well, there's no way you'll be able to go to university and do say a journalism degree,*

you know, you're not going to go to university at all are you?'.
And it was all very negative, negative, crushing.

A national study of disabled school leavers in the 1970s pointed to the poor quality of careers information for special school pupils and the under-development of targeted guidance services (Walker, 1980). Similar findings were noted in evidence reviewed by the Warnock Report (1978, pp 165–6) concluding that the state of careers guidance for young disabled people at the time fell 'far short of what is required'. They recommended that there should be nominated careers teachers in special schools, and additional disability training for advisors in mainstream schools.

Since then, and relevant to the youngest generation, a new Connexions service was introduced in 2001, following concerns raised by the Social Exclusion Unit (1999) about the growing number of 16- to 18-year-olds 'not in education, employment or training' (commonly referred to as 'NEETs'). It was also recognised that young disabled people might be particularly at risk. The plan was for a unified transition support service, available to all young people from the age of 13, with access to a 'personal advisor'. In reality, the advisors appeared often to lack the skills and time to work effectively with young disabled people (Rowland-Crosby et al, 2004).

Among the youngest generation, there was no clear sense of who exactly provided careers advice and little sense that professional guidance was playing any great part in the decisions they were taking. Indeed, Holly's story (as summarised in Chapter Two) underlined the extent to which the personal aspirations of young people with physical impairments still challenge the expectations of those charged with advising them.

> *I can remember going to see the careers advisor at school when I was 15, 16 years old and he would turn to me and said well, what do you want to do then? I was like, 'I want to be a dancer'. That just completely and utterly threw him and he said but you have a disability. And I said, 'Yes, I know. I want to be a dancer.'*

It is fair to say that there has been substantial policy development and investment in providing career transition advice to young disabled people (through both employment and educational services). However, and across the three generations, there was little evidence that this had helped much in the search for employment in the open labour market. As shown later, public institutions played a rather larger role in initiating life course trajectories away from that labour market. In terms of finding work, there was thus much more evidence that young people had drawn on private than public networks of support.

Changing labour markets

Finding work was also influenced by the availability of jobs. Early social analyses of disability argued that changes in the structure of adult labour markets had been instrumental in the production of disability as a social category in capitalist economies. Indeed, Stone (1984) showed how policy definitions of who is 'disabled' had arisen directly from state efforts to control labour supply in changing economic conditions (see also Priestley, 1997). From a policy perspective this is important because it highlights the 'elastic' way in which public policies define employment expectations at different times in the economic cycle (Gruber, 2000). Thus, people classed as disabled because they were 'unable to work' at times of labour shortage (for example, during economic recession) may be brought into the labour market at times of high demand for labour (for example, during wars or periods of economic growth).

The Second World War had forced a massive restructuring of the British labour market as thousands of (non-disabled) male workers left their jobs to join the armed services. Labour shortages were significant, leading government to acknowledge an army of untapped labour, particularly among women but also among those previously marginalised from employment on grounds of disability. As Calvocoressi and Wint (1972, p 407) put it, 'by creating an emergency which required the mobilisation of the whole nation, war forced the government to take note of the whole nation'. In this context, increasing numbers of people with physical impairments were brought in to work in essential services and industries. For example, Humphries and Gordon (1992, p 131) cite the example of a disabled woman who spent her childhood in a 'home for crippled girls' where unexpected opportunity for meaningful work emerged:

> *Before the war no nurse was allowed to go in if you were disabled. But as the war was on, nurses were short, they'd gone to war. They just had to put up with whatever they had. I asked Matron if I could do children's nursing and she said as the war was on she would give me a chance.*

In the climate of post-war reconstruction the focus on labour supply turned rapidly to the exploitation of colonial labour and the 1948 Nationality Act quickly recognised the rights of workers from Commonwealth countries to live and work in Britain (Levitas, 1996; More, 2007). As Daisy recalled from her visit to hospital in London in the 1950s:

> *I remember going up there and there were these massive bomb sites everywhere, you know, just total demolition basically. And it was also a time when, because so many people had been lost in the war, people came over from Africa [sic] on the Windrush, and so London was just beginning to become, what's the word? Cosmopolitan or multicultural.*

Both Flora and Anton (born in the 1960s) were children of Commonwealth migrant families and their biographies were intimately tied up with these labour market changes. For Flora and her parents this meant negotiating both disability and racism in England.

> *... when they came here it was a Commonwealth country. They came here as part of an invitation to be Commonwealth citizens to help rebuild the economy ... in the sixties black people were not treated very well. They were given a very frosted reception. There were signs all over the flat saying No Blacks, No Irish and No Dogs.*

By the late 1950s both production and consumerism were growing rapidly and the Prime Minister, Harold Macmillan, was much quoted for his assertion in 1957 that 'we have never had it so good' . The booming urban labour market offered much flexibility to young workers and various writers have argued that the availability of plentiful and low-skilled jobs offered transitions from school to work that were relatively straightforward (Carter, 1962; Ashton and Field, 1976; Vickerstaff, 2003). As Dan recalls:

> *In those days I think, in the sixties and seventies, particularly in the work I was doing then, sort of manual factory or whatever, you could go from one job to another really. And I've left a job because someone else up the road was paying an extra ten shillings, which was a lot of money, and so you'd give your notice in on the Friday and start another job on the Monday.*

This popular narrative was evident in several accounts, although as Akeelah pointed out it took her a lot longer to find employment as a 16-year-old in this market than her peers (either for reasons of disability or racism).

> *They left school on the Friday and they were able to get jobs on the Monday ... it took me six months to find an office job but eventually I did find one ... trying to find a job, trying to convince, going for interviews, etc. I had to work twice as hard to convince that I was capable of doing the job.*

After this initial delay, however, she was able to continue in clerical work for different companies in the city where she lived, and to earn enough to keep herself and to support her younger disabled sisters to make choices in their own lives.

By the beginning of the 1970s official research estimated that there were some 176,000 'substantially handicapped' people in the British labour force (Buckle, 1971, p 35) although, as Topliss (1975) points out, there were nearly 600,000 people on the Disabled Persons' Employment Register in 1973. The dramatic oil crisis of October that year, followed by rapid economic downturn, created a very different labour market, in which excess rather than shortage of labour became the key policy issue. Rapidly rising unemployment was accompanied by widespread industrial and social unrest (often leading to gendered and nationalist claims to protect white, male jobs).

In this climate the labour rights of women, migrant workers and disabled people all came under some pressure in the early 1980s. Alongside curbs on (mainly non-white) immigration, the social agenda of the New Right sought to emphasise women's work within the home. As Barnes (1991) points out, the proportion of employers meeting their obligations under the legislated disability quota also declined dramatically in this period (halving from 53.2% to 26.8% between 1965 and 1986). Campaigners attributed the failure variously to deficiencies in the existing law (for example, the Disability Alliance, via Jordan, 1979) or to employers (for example, Field 1977). However, as Sheikh et al (1980) demonstrate, it is more accurate to say that unemployment for disabled workers mirrored the same ups and downs as general trends, whilst very slowly improving in relative terms. The real concern, however, was economic inactivity.

In a social context of mass unemployment and the expansion of local social services departments after 1970, increasing numbers of young people with physical impairments were subsisting on out-of-work benefits and the provision of social care (Barnes, 1990; Danieli and Wheeler, 2006). Exemption from employment on grounds of disability was being fuelled by rising of claims for Invalidity Benefit and Severe Disablement Allowance (SDA) (Disney and Webb, 1991). Many of those now 'going on the sick' were older male workers from industrial occupations that were now in rapid decline. Many of them would never work again. However, there were parallel experiences for young disabled people entering the labour market too.

Matt (born in the 1960s) claimed his right to disability benefits in the early 1980s, when he finished college. At the time, he saw even his basic welfare entitlements only as a temporary measure to help him while he looked for work (perhaps confusing his continuing rights to Attendance Allowance with a claim for out-of-work benefits). His perspective was not shared by the assessing doctor, who maintained that he was not fit to work and should look towards long-term dependency on public welfare:

> *This doctor came to see me and they did a review, He said 'You can keep this', keep your DLA or Attendance Allowance as it was. He said 'What are you going to do now?'. I said 'Well, I'm going to get a job'. And he looked at me, shook his head and said 'You'll never work. You're not up to working. Don't try and do that.'*

National disability surveys carried out in the late 1980s revealed low employment and unemployment rates for disabled adults but very high rates of economic activity. Martin et al (1989) estimated an inactivity rate of 64% for disabled women and 53% for disabled men, compared to 25% and 8% for non-disabled women and men respectively. By the time New Labour came into power in 1997 approximately 40% of all disabled people aged 18–59 were economically active, compared to 83% of non-disabled people (Barnes and Mercer, 2005). Since that time, during a period of steady economic growth up to the recent economic crisis, there was some improvement in the official statistics. For example, data from the Labour Force Survey indicate that the employment rate of disabled people increased from 38.1% to 47.2% between 1998 and 2007, and that the gap with non-disabled people continued to narrow (ODI, 2009).

As the discussion suggests, the individual experiences narrated in the stories suggested that public policies and services had provided very little practical help in personal searches for employment in the open labour market. Moreover, they also revealed hidden traces of connections between individual biographies and socio-economic changes at the macro level.

Negotiating barriers at work

For those who did find work there were numerous accounts in the stories of both social and physical barriers, including experiences of direct and indirect discrimination. In an imperfect and disabling society this is to be expected and it is hardly necessary to itemise the range of everyday barriers disabled people may encounter at work. The selection of examples here focuses mainly on evidence of policy changes over time, and on revealing private negotiations with public policies at work.

The attitudes of employers

Earlier sections point to a reliance on informal help in gaining work for previous generations, in the absence of enabling public policies. However, the same informality of support meant there were also few opportunities to contest arbitrary employer decisions to hire or fire on grounds of disability prior to the introduction of anti-discrimination legislation. Thus, Dan recalled his first job, in a butcher's shop, in the early 1950s:

> ... one of the jobs there was the big bones ... You used to put them through a band saw, no safety shields or anything ... and I kind of tripped, like I did occasionally, and I fell ... the bloke who owned it went, 'Ooooo, you can't stay here, you know. You can't stay because I've got this mental picture of you falling through the band saw and losing an arm or something like that', and I actually lost my job because of the disability.

Daisy remembered a similar experience, in a baker's shop, as a teenager in the mid-1960s.

> I was slipping over, the floor's slippery. It was quite hazardous but I was coping, but they just decided they weren't covered insurance-wise for me, or maybe they were scared I'd fall over and break my hip or something ... the managers came in and decided, they took me to one side and said, 'We can't have you here, we're not insured and if anything happened to you ...'

Bella (also born in the 1940s) noted how direct discrimination on grounds of gender in the 1960s was just as important, particularly in a male-dominated manufacturing environment like her first paid job in a chemical factory.

> *I went for the interview and the person who was actually the chemist was off, he wasn't there at the interview, and he said afterwards … we got on very well eventually, but when he came back he said, 'Well, I wouldn't have set you on'. Because he said, 'I don't think it's a suitable environment for a female'.*

Catherine recalled both indirect and direct discrimination in her first year as a teacher in the 1970s.

> *The head was a spinster and now an oldish spinster … she always said I was a good teacher but she had no conception of what it was like to be disabled, none at all. She put me in the classroom that was furthest away from the cloakrooms and the layout of the building was hilly, and you had to go down these twisty, windy paths …*

She remembered how the same head teacher barred her from going to the toilet more than once a day, which she was unable to manage. Catherine continued to face discrimination and eventually left for another school. She found out later, from the inspector:

> *'[The head] says you're a good teacher and that the children love you and you're doing a great job but she finds your disability irksome' … I only wish I'd belonged to the union at the time that it happened, because she'd never have got away with that.*

William (born in the 1960s) thought he was consistently unfairly treated by an employer in the 1990s.

> *I had to fill out all the forms, work on finance and all that crap … the final straw was I had accidentally hit a secretary on the leg. And the team manager said that it could be construed as sexual harassment.*

Although it might have been feasible for some to claim unfair dismissal through an employment tribunal there was, in effect, no legal protection against direct disability discrimination in employment until the 1995 Disability Discrimination Act. Even then, protection did not apply to employers with fewer than 15 employees and early claims of discrimination were met with frequent challenges from employers (Gooding, 2000).

There were, however, many positive examples in the stories of more flexible working arrangements and relationships. For example, Ian (who works remotely from home) talked about the positive working relations with his line manager and colleagues as a consequence of a flexible approach to negotiating and managing his workload. By comparison, Emma described the inflexibility she experienced starting out in the 1950s, at the age of 15, in craft piecework (where performance against standardised expectations of productivity was a necessity).

> *I worked at [the factory] to start with and that was paid by ... how much you did, not the quality of your work, by how quick you got your work done. And so that didn't work out too, and my work was fantastic but I wasn't quick enough.*

There is some evidence of change over time and research conducted for the Department for Work and Pensions (Kelly et al, 2005) showed that awareness of rights under the DDA had increased among small employers, although a third were still not aware of their obligations. The more recent Equality Duty has impacted substantially on public sector employers but in the private sector implementation of the DDA still relies heavily on individual disabled people asserting their rights in law. The unprecedented scale of public sector job losses, and historic shift of emphasis towards private sector employment, arising from the 2010 emergency budget and comprehensive spending review, has raised new concerns about the protection available to disabled employees in Britain.

Physical barriers

There were numerous examples in the stories of obvious physical barriers in the workplace, as might be expected. Those who had longer working careers, from the older generations, were also able to reflect on the changes they had seen over time. For example, Akeelah (born in the 1940s) remembers few physical adjustments 'like special seating or anything' when she started office work as a teenager in the 1960s. Comparing her past to her present, Emma reflected on how workplaces have changed in terms of physical accessibility:

> *I mean there's more access for people ... whereas when you were younger there wasn't anything. If you couldn't get up the stairs you stayed out the way.*

Section 8(1) of the 1970 Chronically Sick and Disabled Persons Act was the first legislation to address physical access to buildings and specified that buildings newly open to the public should make provision for disabled visitors (similar provisions applied to school and university buildings). The Silver Jubilee Committee on Improving Access for Disabled People (1979) had raised awareness through its enquiry *Can disabled people go where you go?* (a slogan that also featured as a Royal Mail postmark). Its report recommended that local authorities appoint coordinating 'access officers', and recognised the role of local access groups of disabled people in monitoring environmental accessibility. Its findings led to the establishment of the Committee on Restrictions against Disabled People (CORAD), which first reported on the case for rights-based legislation in 1982.

For Daisy (born in the 1940s), even in the early 1980s, these kinds of basic physical barriers at work still appeared as inevitable impediments to her sustained employment rather than as something that could be challenged or corrected.

> *I did get jobs but they'd be up three flights of rickety stairs in buildings. It was so hard from that point of view. So, often, those sorts of jobs didn't last very long.*

In the late 1990s, despite implementation of the DDA and working in a public sector post, Bella recalls that few adjustments were made for her access needs as an existing employee at the time.

> *[Our team] is three flights of stairs up and the women's toilets are two flights of stairs beyond that. And now they have a disabled toilet on the ground floor, but that's only because of someone who came to work late, much later than I did. But before that the only toilet was right up at the top of the building.*

In addition to workplace barriers, transport to work figured prominently in several of the stories. These stories also illustrated the kinds of private negotiations that public policies required from people. For example, from the beginning of the NHS, in 1948, the Government had provided many 'invalids' with powered tricycles free of charge (see Invalid Tricycle Association, 1960; Woods and Watson,

2005). The Ministry also paid for the insurance, tax, repairs and a small annual petrol allowance. By the early 1960s there were an estimated 15,000 tricycles and it became possible to fund assistance in converting private vehicles too (Joint Committee on Mobility for the Disabled (1963; 1968). By the late 1960s some 27,000 people were receiving state support for vehicles, at a cost of around £2.75 million (*Hansard*, 16 July 1969, v787, c634).

Matt learnt to drive when he was 16 and had one of the 'invalid' cars (which he used mainly to drive to a day centre, where he spent his time applying for jobs).

> *I had one of them blue three-wheelers. So what it did do for me strangely was I was always up in the morning and I would never want to lie in bed ...*

When Catherine went to train as a teacher she had to drive much further in her 'invalid' car (because the college accommodation was not accessible for her to stay there). However, the limitations of the battery on long journeys caused her to give it up in the end.

> *I drove a little blue electric car ... they fixed up on the wall outside in the college, a unit ... a unit where I could plug in my car ... One day I was driving to college and I looked in the mirror and there was a policeman, and he followed me all the way ... And I thought what am I doing wrong? He eventually flagged me down to stop and I thought oh, what is it? And he said 'Oh, I've been so worried about you because traffic cuts you up because you're slow. You must have a sign put on the back of the car saying maximum speed, ten miles an hour.'*

By the time the last vehicles were registered, in 1977, the overwhelming demand was for adaptations to ordinary cars. The Motability Allowance Scheme was established and the Invalid Vehicle Service (IVS) was phased out, closing in 2003. A national 'Orange Badge' parking scheme had also been introduced in section 21 of the 1970 Chronically Sick and Disabled Persons Act. Parking badges were issued by local authorities but were recognised for parking benefits in other localities too (the 'Blue Badge' parking card is now recognised in most European countries).

Catherine's story (outlined earlier) is interesting to follow further, as it reveals the importance attributed to informally negotiated arrangements in the absence of accessible public transport during the 1970s and 1980s.

> *There's an old people's centre near here and they have transport with a tail gate, dropping the old people off every day. And our local councillor arranged for them to come to the school and collect me. So [my husband] could drop me off in the morning and they would come and get me about half past four, quarter to five, and bring me home.*

She also recalled how informally negotiated solutions were thwarted by her employer.

> *At the time there weren't converted taxis ... the local priest arranged for two parents at the school ... they would collect me and bring me home ... the headmistress decided that at the end of my first term she didn't want her teachers fraternising with the parents. And she forbade them to take me home...*

Later ...

> *I discovered that there was this company in [nearby town] that had converted wheelchair taxis. So if I wanted to stay at school for extra time or do something, or go into school late and [my husband] had to be at work, then there was this wheelchair taxi. The guy was really nice, but astronomically expensive.*

The Piercy Report (1956) had recognised the practical barriers that people with physical impairments faced in accessing employment (including a proposal that transport to work should be provided). Several targeted initiatives to assist disabled workers were developed, including support for aids to employment, adaptations to premises and equipment, fares to work, and help from personal readers. There were, in the stories, several examples where people had benefited from grants for adaptations to work premises or from the Special Aids to Employment scheme. For example, Anton described how his employers made adaptations to the toilets.

> *They have a fund there, but it's for conversions, anything that disabled people need for working. I've only scratched the surface in terms of using that.*

The various diverse initiatives were later consolidated in a unitary 'Access to Work' scheme in 1994. The policy aim was to create a more flexible and user-centred provision, in which the type of assistance to be provided was not pre-determined by the scheme (see Thornton and Corden, 2002). Among the stories, for example, Jayne had the controls on her car adapted using Access to Work funds and Matt acquired an electric wheelchair hoist for his car. Importantly, the scheme also sought to include those who were unemployed and applying for jobs. However, it was notable that Holly (who is looking for employment) travels to her voluntary work experience using a taxi funded by the organisation because she is not eligible for Access to Work in this context.

Lack of accessibility at work is often viewed as a form of indirect discrimination, not necessarily resulting from conscious or direct discrimination by an employer. The DDA sought to address this by obliging employers to make 'reasonable adjustments' where existing workplace arrangements put disabled employees at a 'substantial disadvantage'. In reality, there remains much concern about policies that rely on legal interpretations of vague concepts like 'reasonable' and 'substantial' (Lawson, 2008) but within larger companies and public sector employers, in particular, there is evidence of changed practice. For example, Maggie (born in the 1940s) recalled the changed atmosphere at the large company she worked for at the time of the DDA.

> *There was a new thing that came out and it was something that was started through [the company] for disabled and we had a meeting and said, 'Right, if you can't get in that door, [the company] has to do this for you' and they said what you were entitled to ... so we had a committee that was set up and I was on that committee ... after that they knew me so I went all over, I could get into offices and they were real good after that.*

In addition to calls for anti-discrimination laws, early social analyses of disability had placed much hope on the enabling potential of future technologies and flexible working practices in post-Fordist modes of production (see Roulstone, 1998). Perhaps the most evident changes in the stories were new opportunities provided by information and communication technologies (particularly evident for the generation born in the 1960s and now in mid-career). As Gilbert commented,

> *Computers have immensely improved my ability to communicate, work, etc.*

The most striking example was in Ian's story (summarised in Chapter Two). The availability of mobile personal computing and internet connectivity meant that he was able to sustain paid employment (from his bed) in a way that would have been unimaginable when Emma started out in office work in the 1960s. Anton, whose employer had relocated to another town, had also been 'set up for me to work at home', so that he was able to continue working when unable to travel the distance. Anton's employer thought it would be better for him but Anton felt it might be harder to concentrate, and he misses the social aspects of working in the office, so he has decided he wants to travel in at least a couple of days a week. As Michailakis (2001) points out, solutions based on 'technological optimism' often overlook the embeddedness of technologies within economic, social and cultural contexts.

Alternatives to employment

Bearing in mind an apparent lack of public help in finding open employment, and the concerns expressed earlier about high levels of economic inactivity, it is important to consider the experience of those out of employment (as well as the barriers for those in employment, discussed previously). The following sections illustrate the concern, arising from the stories, that public policies often steer young people's lives away from inclusion in work and employment.

Training centres and workshops

As mentioned earlier, the post-war policy framework included a strong focus on vocational rehabilitation, especially in areas of labour market need. With this in mind, Industrial Rehabilitation Units were established in significant manufacturing regions (mostly in the Midlands and North of England). They provided factory-like work experience, job assessment and craft training, typically lasting a few weeks. Although they were within the remit of the employment service, the referral and management of trainees remained the province of medically-oriented rehabilitation services.

Such training was primarily targeted at people who acquired impairment during their working careers and who hoped to return to work. While those with acquired impairments formed the large majority of registered disabled persons, those who contributed their stories for this book had grown up with impairment from birth or infancy. As a consequence, the placements they received tended to be rather different in character. In particular, they provided more examples of direction from the employment services towards placements in sheltered workshops and day centres, beyond the mainstream of the labour market, intended for those with little hope of finding work (see Hyde, 1998).

The Disabled Persons Employment Corporation (later Remploy) had been established at the end of the war to provide sheltered employment for those deemed unable to gain employment in the open market. The 1958 Disabled Persons Employment Act also encouraged local authorities, voluntary bodies and non-profit ventures to develop sheltered provision (Barnes, 1991; Borsay, 2005). As Barnes (1991) points out, such establishments were originally envisaged as a 'bridging experience' to mainstream employment yet they were to become much criticised as places 'where society relegates its unwanted cast-off goods and people' (Mallas, 1976). Moreover, Hyde (1998) argues that such provision consistently privileged the needs of employers over those who worked there.

A review by Greenleigh Associates (1975) indicated that the failure of sheltered workshops to meet policy objectives resulted from a range of factors, including a lack of variety and choice among routine and unchallenging assembly work. In addition, the work was extremely low paid. Such concerns were very evident in the stories of those who experienced them. For example, Hillary (born in the 1940s) remembered working in a sheltered workshop, run by the Spastics Society, for 13 years in the 1960s and 1970s:

> *I had always wanted to work, but this kind of work was not what I envisaged. Each new job was as monotonous as the next. The wages were four pounds a week. I did not complain – until I was given the filthy job of screwing up newspaper for packing around porch lamps. It was the most degrading job I had ever done. Soon I had had enough and demanded the manager to complain. His response was 'Unfortunately, the job befits your handicap. There is no other job for either of you. Get back to work or I will stop your wages.'*

Catherine, who attended the same schools as Hillary, was also directed to a workshop but was able to draw on her family resources to resist the limiting life course trajectory in which she was being drawn.

> *Initially the people from the Spastics Society told me that I should be content with having a job putting soap powders in packets and all that sort of thing. And I said 'Well, you've spent an awful lot of money on educating me, it seems awful to just encourage me that I should be going to a centre' ...*

The fact that Catherine subsequently became a teacher (noted earlier) sheds a rather tainted light on the capacity of the workshops to assess and respond to the employment aptitudes of those who worked within them. Flora's story (born in the 1960s) conveyed a very similar narrative of wasted education in light of her workshop placement, but she lacked the cohesive family resources to mobilise much resistance to the initial decision.

> *When I came home [from residential school], they weren't used to having me around and it went pear shaped. I didn't get on with my mum and I got very depressed. The careers officer dumped me in a work centre. I was packing nuts and bolts for 11 pounds a month ... After spending all that money on me, educating me, that was the best they could do, that's the best career move.*

With little job satisfaction and feeling exploited, Flora left. Many of her colleagues, however, continued there for the rest of their working lives.

Ian (born in the 1960s) had certainly gained the impression that there would have been few opportunities for the generation preceding him, 'apart from sheltered employment I guess, like Remploy', whereas now he sees more job opportunities in the mainstream. He also believed that:

> *In the eighties, when Remploy had to become profit making rather than subsidised, meant that a lot of the more severally disabled people were generally eased out because they weren't productive enough.*

Detailing the development of Remploy, the Ministry of Labour (Edwards, 1958) had noted emerging concerns about the financial sustainability of the operation, which was already making a loss. Despite a steady post-war decline in clients judged as 'unlikely to obtain employment except in sheltered conditions', it was decided that Remploy could not be expected to accommodate all of them. Many workshops were closed as policy shifted towards a greater focus on integration in the open labour market, although Kochan (1996) still described the business as 'thriving'. However, Remploy is now moving further towards a role as publicly funded brokers of services rather than direct providers (Roulstone and Morgan, 2009).

From the mid-1980s there was also a move to encourage a new employment policy model, through the Sheltered Placement Scheme, offering work in mainstream settings, subsidised to the employer by the state (this later became the Supported Placement Scheme). Since the subsidised placement scheme was also seen as cheaper than traditional workshops change appeared inevitable (see Hyde, 1998).

A life without work

For Worton (born in the 1940s) the cumulative legacy of low expectations at a residential special school (discussed in Chapter Five) meant that she entered adulthood with little optimism or prospects of finding work. There was also no evidence that she was guided towards the segregated options described earlier.

> *When I left school I was classified as of average intelligence, perhaps, but given my multiple impairments I was unemployable. So when I left school I went home and I spent the next 11 years just basically sitting around at home in my mum's front room.*

Judy (also from the oldest generation) recalled her encounter with a similar lack of career expectation when she visited a special school later as an adult in the mid-1980s.

> *I was going round with a teacher and I was saying, 'Well now, what exams do they do, what's your career structure?' and she said, 'Well, we don't educate them to work'. And that really hit me, I thought my god! ... I think it was a feeling of justice or injustice, seeing people in these special schools that just weren't going anywhere ...*

It was this kind of prospect that had drawn attention from Warnock's Committee of Enquiry into the Education of Handicapped Children and Young People in 1978, referring to the need to prepare some young disabled young people for transition to 'significant living without work'. Despite their often progressive concerns with educational inclusion there was a rather stoical acceptance of the fact that many young people with physical impairments stood little chance of fulfilling their potential after leaving education in the 1970s:

> The problem of how to accept the prospect of a life without employment and how to prepare for it faces people with a variety of disabilities, including some who are of the highest intelligence but very severely physically handicapped. (Warnock Report, 1978, pp 202–3)

Apart from acknowledging that reciprocal peer support among disabled people would be beneficial, and advocating towards participation in voluntary work, the Report offered little idea of what might be best done or prepared for. In this situation, the prevailing policy framework in the early 1980s offered little beyond the expanding provision of 'day centres'. Barnes (1990) made a thorough investigation of the context and social situation of such centres at the end of the decade, characterising the lack of aspiration and challenge they inspired as leading to a kind of 'cabbage syndrome' amongst their users.

Matt's recollection of this period echoed the experiences reported in Barnes' study. He had initially resisted his social worker's suggestion of a day centre but was later persuaded, by a friend, to try it out. It was not long before attendance at the centre provided the main activity structure for his week.

> *I was getting bored and they came out with this bloody day centre and I told this guy at football and he said 'Oh, well I go there' ... I said 'Well, don't they make, you know, don't you make baskets and stuff?'. He said 'Well no, you don't have to do that; it's more like a youth club'. It was a brand new day centre, they had a pool table, they had a table tennis table. There was a joinery workshop. Interestingly, once I started going I was there Monday to Friday.*

Although Matt saw this as a temporary placement at the time, where he could reflect and prepare for employment, he felt this aspiration was not met with much enthusiasm by either the staff or the other centre users.

> *All the time I was there I was applying for jobs and there was a lot of resistance to the disabled person, 'You don't want to apply for a job, Matt. It's too hard. You want to stay here, it's much safer, much more secure.' Not necessarily in those words but that's what was coming out.*

Looking at it from the other side, Poppy (also born in the 1960s) found herself working in a local authority day centre as an activity coordinator.

> *At that time it was Bingo, Bingo or Bingo, and you got a cup of tea with that. It was very low key and I wasn't into that at all, and I thought, these people can do better, but it was a struggle to get them out of that Bingo culture.*

Bob (from the oldest generation) remembers how the Disablement Resettlement Officers offered him little hope as a young man new to the labour market in the 1970s.

> *They tried to place me in a day centre and I said 'No way, I'm not going there'.*

Bob spent two years unemployed after that but many years later (in the early 1990s) he went on to achieve a post of some strategic responsibility in the local authority, which brought him back into contact with similar institutions and similar preconceptions.

> *I was quite senior in social services, yet many people treated me like a client because they saw my impairment rather than who I was and what I was doing. So much so that one day I had a meeting at an adult training centre with the manager, and I walked in and said to reception, 'Good morning, I've come to …' and that's as far as I got. She was up, ran to the door and shouting up the corridor, 'Bill, or whoever, come quickly I've got a client in here', and Bill comes in, grabs me by the arm and started dragging me out and me going, 'No, no, no, no, listen'.*

As discussed in the previous chapter, there have also been increasing concerns that some further education institutions have been subtly transformed into a new generation of day care centres and segregated residential homes, in which young disabled people are maintained outside the mainstream in a cycle of 'training' that does not necessarily lead to progression into the labour market.

In a survey of 274 young disabled people in the 1980s, Hirst (1987, pp 64–7) found that two thirds 'moved directly from school to training centres or day centres', and even after attending further education 'a substantial proportion had nowhere to go particularly following employment training'. Moreover:

> Young people with physical impairment only … were more likely to have been wholly unoccupied at some time during the past-school period … . And at the age of 21 almost half (14) of the 29 young people who were wholly unoccupied were physically impaired only ($p<0.0001$). These findings suggest that young people with physical impairment experienced a more difficult transition to adult occupational life than other young people in the sample. (p 70)

In a follow-up, with 25- to 30-year-olds, Clark and Hirst (1989) showed again that this group were much less likely to have found a job or established significant markers of adult independence. With or without 'meaningful' activity outside employment, claims for long-term, non-working benefits like Severe Disablement Allowance continued to rise. As a consequence, government attention turned to welfare-to-work reform aimed at reducing the use of benefits to sustain disabled people who might otherwise be employed.

Jayne's experience of entering the labour market as a young adult in the 1980s provided traces of these changes. Her story suggested little support in making the initial transition from education, and the establishment of a life-without-work trajectory on long-term disability benefits. Despite her identification as capable of work, and two different skills-based courses, the outcome was voluntary rather than paid labour.

> *I was getting Incapacity Benefit of something of that sort then. SDA for so much allowance and then they found out I could work so I had to sign on the dole like everybody else. So I had to go and sign on every fortnight. Then I had to go on this employment training course and look for a job. Nothing came of that. I did a computer course on this employment training course through the Job Centre. Didn't find a job so it was back on the dole. Then I did my NVQ Level 1 in Business Administration on another training course. Then in 1992 after I'd just finished that course, it was suggested that I do voluntary work ...*

The replacement of SDA with Incapacity Benefit in 1995, and subsequent introduction of New Labour's 'New Deal for Disabled People' have been much debated. The new arrangements, introduced in the 1999 Welfare Reform and Pensions Act targeted people on disability benefits with a combination of obligation and support to enter employment. Roulstone (2000) and Barnes (2000), among others, queried both the policy rhetoric of inclusion and the assumption that all disabled people should be considered for employment in a structurally unequal labour market.

An evaluation of the New Deal by Stafford et al (2007) showed that there were 260,330 registrations up to 2006 and 43% had found jobs. In general, the recipients' experiences and outcomes were positive but concerns persisted about lack of awareness and fears that involvement might lead to financial disadvantage.

There were certainly aspirations to find work among those of the youngest generation not yet in employment. For example, as noted in

Chapter Two, Holly (born in the 1980s) was set on finding a paid job to escape what she saw as an unnecessary reliance on benefits.

> *At the moment I'm trying to get off, I'm trying to get a job so I can get off benefits, so I can stop doing voluntary work and actually, you know, be financially independent rather than having to – you know, rely on benefits all the time.*

There was no evidence, however, that such young people were particularly conscious of pressure from public agencies to make this shift, or that they were receiving much public help to do so.

Conclusions

Employment is an important issue in transition to adult life, both as a personal and a public issue. The stories exemplified how young disabled people's systematic marginalisation from the mainstream labour market has often been perpetuated, rather than challenged, by public policies and institutions. They also revealed a focused development of employment support policies, coupled with significant changes in protection from discrimination at work. Yet, it was more often agency, chance and circumstance that seemed to shape people's careers in the open labour market. By comparison, where public institutions were strongly implicated in life trajectories they were more often associated with movement away from the labour market, or towards under-employment and low-quality work.

While personal agency is important, the stories illustrate how social capital and labour market opportunity influence life chances. Micro-level interactions between structure and agency, and the anomalies they throw up, need to be read in the light of macro-economic developments. Young people of different generational cohorts entered the world of adult work under different labour market conditions. This affected the type of jobs available at different points in their working lives.

There was evidence of changing attitudes, with few recent examples blatant direct discrimination. There was evidence of support for more flexible work adjustments but these did not necessarily differ, in essence, from some of the informal arrangements negotiated by previous generations. New technologies did make a difference, however, for young people with physical impairments. The policy turn towards personal responsibility in employment, in the vaunting of legal rights and welfare-to-work policies, has been significant. There is some macro-level evidence that employment rates are increasing and that targeted support does work for some but there was little evidence in the stories that such policies were having much impact in the everyday lives of these individual people.

Questions for discussion

- How effective were early policy interventions to secure employment for disabled people in the immediate post-war period compared to the kinds of rights-based policies we have today?
- To what extent have developments in technology, particularly information and communication technologies, created new life chances and choices for people with significant physical impairments?

SEVEN

Living with 'disability'

Throughout this book the main focus has been to show how interactions with changing public policies and institutions affected people's private lives, and how individuals and their families navigated life choices in policy contexts. The two preceding chapters illustrated specific developments with reference to education and employment. This final chapter takes a step back to review, more holistically, how disability revealed itself in people's lives over time and how this impacted on the negotiation of personal identity. It shows how public policies and institutions play an important part in structuring the social spaces, relationships and life course expectations that come to define who is seen as 'disabled'. The discussion considers the extent to which opportunities to 'come out' as disabled have changed over time.

The examples show how encounters with public policies contributed to processes of making disability known in public spaces (for example, where disability status was marked out by labelling, differential treatment or physical segregation). They also show how public spaces framed a sense of disability in private worlds. It is equally important to appreciate changes over time in the kinds of cultural resources and role models available to young people as they seek to make sense of tensions between the public and private. Looking at the work of identity construction in this way helps to demonstrate some of the significant social changes that have taken place since the 1940s (not least in the development of a new disability culture and politics within civil society). The chapter deals first with the kinds of identity scripts and resources that were available to people, and then with the ways in which public and private spaces framed the construction of disability identities.

Intergenerational learning

It is generally assumed within cohort studies that different generations find themselves exposed to 'different rights, duties, statuses, roles, privileges, disenfranchisments' (Foner, 1988, p 176). However, it is also acknowledged that successive generations co-exist alongside each other and that cultural ideas and norms are transmitted from one to the next (Manheim, 1952). This assumption raises some questions in the case of young disabled people, the majority of whom are born to non–disabled parents and some of whom have been socially segregated by public institutions. Access to intergenerational learning, in terms of culture and identity, may therefore be limited in two ways – through a lack of opportunity to learn from older disabled people and lack of access to intergenerational learning within the family home.

The past and the present

Tom compared his own experience of growing up in the early 1950s with that of Gilbert (from the middle generation). He described a time when:

> ... *if you were disabled what you did was you become as normal as possible. You got on with stuff ... I had no concept of being kind of glad that I was disabled or anything like that. I mean that's a much later, sophisticated approach to disability. It certainly didn't exist when I was a kid ... I never had any disabled friends. My perceptions were all from an able-bodied perspective ... I used to find it difficult to be with disabled people, to talk to disabled people, to be in their company.*

> *I hated my body. I hated my legs, the way they were, and always have done, and I think that was symptomatic of maybe the two different eras that we'd grown up in. Gilbert grew up in an era sort of more steeped in disability rights, etc., and I'd grown up with the notion that the last thing you accepted was you were disabled. Whatever you did, you strived to be as normal as possible. So that was the big difference and I think it took me a while to make that leap.*

Conversely, Terry (born in the 1980s) offered a comparison with the experiences of older generations, indicating how he thought expectations and access for young people with physical impairments must have changed. He reflected on an encounter with an older disabled man who had attended his special school half a century before.

> *I know a man that went to my school in the early fifties, like the same school that I went to ... and he was told that, you know, he was told that he was just an object really ... he was just saying it's changed a lot ... we've got a lot more chances now, you know ... you're not as stuck at home. When he was growing up, he was*

basically just stuck at home ... I wouldn't have liked to have grown up in the forties.

Steve imagined how life might have been if he had been born in the 1940s by conjuring an image of the 'the mad woman in the attic' (Mrs Rochester) in Charlotte Bronte's *Jane Eyre*.

Sixty years ago, if I'd have been born 60 years ago, I imagine that I would be in a closet right now ... it'd be one of those where I'd be sat in a room. My family would keep me but it would be like I'd be in a room and they'd lock it and every so often they'd throw food in. Whereas the public life would go on downstairs and I wouldn't be part of it.

Holly drew on similar imagery of an unnurtured life, lived behind closed doors.

I suspect that disabled people were just left behind closed doors and weren't even bothered to educate, and the thought of them actually living alone independently would be completely out of the question ... Though my standard of education was quite moderate, I was still educated. I still accessed college, I still live alone. You know, I think if I lived in the 1940s it would have been extremely, extremely different. So in that way I think there has been a lot of social change ...

Harvey also felt there must have been big improvements and pointed particularly to changes in public law and policy, while being careful to acknowledge the extent of exclusion that still exists today.

There have been many, many Acts that have improved the position of disabled people; the DDA ... For example in higher education over the past 20 years, there is greater access for disabled people; not enough you know, but for example me and you [Sonali] have been to university. Twenty or 30 or 40 years ago that very rarely happened. We now live in an extremely affluent society and disabled people are still in the bottom quartile in society, still less likely to go into further education, still less likely to have a job and still more likely to be living in poverty.

Such comparisons of past and present say much about private perceptions of social change. Yet, it is noticeable that the youngest generation drew mainly on imaginings and metaphors to convey what life might have been like in the 'foreign country' of the past (Lowenthal, 1985). Such accounts belied a certain lack of access to transmitted knowledge about the lived realities and social conditions experienced by previous generations of disabled people. Indeed, this is one of the reasons why disability histories, including oral histories and social histories, are so important. They can help to provide some of the missing links in the intergenerational inheritance of disability culture. In the absence of such histories it is important to ask where young disabled people looked for knowledge to negotiate the 'unfinished business' of constructing sustainable identities for adult life (Priestley et al, 1999).

The availability of cultural scripts

Giddens (1991) argues that the narratives we tell about ourselves are an essential part of negotiating and maintaining identity, but underlines how these narratives may both accept or contest the discursive identities bestowed by mainstream culture. A great deal has been written about the representation of impairment and disability in popular culture, particularly in relation to television, film and English literature (for example, Barnes, 1992; Garland-Thompson, 1997; Mitchell and Snyder, 2000). In the historical context of this book it is relevant to note that there were very considerable social and technological developments in these media during the time between the childhoods of the oldest and youngest generations (that is, between the 1950s and the 1990s). For example, while most households had a radio, only one and a half million had a television set in the early 1950s, rising to more than 15 million by end of the 1960s. The BBC had begun limited public broadcasting in the early 1930s but television was not widespread as a cultural medium during the childhoods of the oldest generation. Commercial broadcasting only began after the 1954 Television Act but by the end of the 1950s programmes like *Armchair Theatre*, *Emergency Ward 10* and *Coronation Street* were starting to draw popular audiences with contemporary representations of 'real life'. Likewise, although an infrastructure for the internet had existed, the World Wide Web and its associated search engines did not become available until the mid-1990s (and only a minority of households in Britain had access to the internet even at the end of the 20th century).

These socio-technological factors are important because they framed the kinds of representational resources that were available to children and young people in making sense of disability and identity. The repertoire of cultural scripts about disability available to the families of the oldest generation was more limited. However, the established canon of classic theatre and fiction available at school and at home was by no means short of reference to physical impairment.

Davidson et al's (1994, p 33) review of the portrayal of impairment in 19th-century children's literature suggests that it was widely regarded as 'a fixed, divinely ordained state of being' which set people apart from the rest of society. Keith (2001) draws particular attention to the imagery of physical impairment in the repertoire of classic fiction for girls, where gendered messages reinforced compliance with male and medical authority in seeking cure. Focusing more on male characters, Hevey (1993) points to metaphors of helplessness, while Kriegel's (1987, p 33) reading of fictional characters suggested (also in gendered terms) that, 'the cripple is the creature who has been deprived of his ability to create a self ... He must accept definition from outside the boundaries of his own existence'. Crow (1990, p 1) argues that the misrepresentation of disabled people in children's literature has real implications for young people's identity formation, both in terms of how they see themselves and others:

> Disabled people in books are almost never real – never whole people with varied lifestyles and personalities ... Books rarely represent disabled people constructively. Restrictive portrayals of disability go beyond the printed page to restrict real-life opportunities for disabled people. Children frequently have only this misinformation to call upon in their contacts with disabled people or in their own experiences of disability.

This discourse of passivity, fatalism and compliance, highlighted by literary critics, has a resonance with some of the accounts of medicalised or institutionalised childhoods in the stories. However, as shown in earlier chapters, there was also much agency and resistance to such discourse.

A second source of popular cultural imagery, also identified in the disability studies literature, was that of charity fundraising (Shakespeare 1996; Drake 1996; Thomas 2004). Daisy (born in the 1940s) remembers how her impairment carried negative associations with charity, made all the more salient for a generation whose parents had grown up with family memories of parish relief and the 'workhouse' prior to the post-war welfare state.

It doesn't seem now like such a stigma to be disabled but when I grew up as a child. I think the history of charity in this country hasn't helped at all, because I grew up with these images of little blind boys standing there holding out a box, you know little statues, begging statues outside shops.

There were encounters with religious discourses of disability in everyday lives too. For example, Poppy recalled her first conscious encounter with the idea that she was not 'normal', just before she went to school:

When I got my wheelchair, going up X Street in [the city] and there's the big church at the end…this woman came out of the church… and she kissed me and she said, 'Go to church, God will heal you and make you better'.

Akeelah, born in Pakistan in the 1940s, was confronted with different (but related) messages as a child, arising from her family's religious culture in the 1940s and 1950s.

One thing is very clear, that I was treated differently. The extended family, they accepted that this is kind of God's way, maybe of punishment. Maybe you've done something bad …

Experiencing ridicule and name-calling from her peers when she went to mainstream school, and believing her impairment to be the will of God, Akeelah then began to question what she might have done to deserve this (before turning to question her faith instead). Such experiences underlined the particular challenge of negotiating social worlds in which class, gender and ethnicity were just as important as 'disability' in establishing a sense of self.

Attention has been drawn in the academic literature to the ways in which impairment or disability becomes a kind of 'master status', especially when public policies and institutions compartmentalise people's life course transitions based on this status alone (Goffman, 1968; Charmaz, 1983; 1994; 1995; Priestley, 1998c; Barnes and Mercer, 2010). This, in turn, has often made it difficult for people to sustain other important dimensions of their multiple, intersectional or situational identities (Vernon, 1999).

For Harvey (whose story was summarised in Chapter Two) the relevant identity discourses were of gender and class. It was his exclusion and estrangement from male peer culture, rather than barriers to educational achievement, that marked him out as different at school.

> *I'm from a background that is around manual work … so there isn't a massive emphasis on succeeding academically. So I kind of found it very difficult socially and emotionally as well because I didn't get a girlfriend, you know, I couldn't go out and drink on street corners and, you know, I was always focused on my academic work.*

During his time in segregated special education, Anton had construed his self-identity primarily in terms of disability status, more so than gender, class or ethnicity, as this was the primary category through which he received his education, services and peer contacts. Going to university brought exposure to the mainstream, sometimes heightening that sense of difference, but it also offered new and multiple identity scripts that had been obscured in the special school environment – particularly in relation to his ethnic identity.

> *With the ethnic background I was accepted by the Indian Societies [at university] and all that … you didn't feel left out or cut out or anything because they sort of absorbed you straight away.*

In this context, the commonality he found in ethnicity suppressed the difference he was experiencing in terms of disability. Similarly, Flora recalled how living in a predominantly 'white middle–class' residential special school made it difficult to develop a positive identity incorporating her ethnicity.

> *In my boarding school I was only one of five black or Indian children. All the other children were white, all the staff were white, so I felt disconnected from my Caribbean identity. At one time I didn't like being black, I resented being black because when I was young, they couldn't comb my hair and you know when you are a teenager, you want to look glamorous and because I didn't feel glamorous I felt ugly, I didn't like being black.*

Like Anton, the transition to further education gave Flora access to black cultural role models and opportunities to explore the identity significance of everyday practices (like braiding her hair) that made her feel good about her body, but had been unavailable to her in special school.

The troubles of 'passing'

Numerous authors have drawn attention to Goffman's (1959; 1963) portrayal of the stigma associated with 'spoiled identity' and its avoidance through the tactic of 'passing' as 'normal' (for example, Coleman, 1997; Thomas, 2007; Barnes and Mercer, 2010). Some of the accounts, particularly from those in the oldest generation, portrayed this social pressure to 'pass' and to obscure the presence of impairment in order to avoid any identification with disability. For Florence, Bella and Daisy the concealment of physical impairment was part and parcel of negotiating even very private relationships.

> *My fiancé was in the Navy and we'd never really discussed my disability. And so I had to have this calliper on while I was waiting for this [operation] ... and I wrote to him and decided I was going to end it. So I was thinking, oh, if he comes back and I've got the calliper on that's going to be it ... I don't think that relationship would have ever lasted as long as it did if it hadn't been the fact that he was away.* (Bella)

> *I couldn't bring myself to say I was disabled so I just said 'I've got a bad foot', so he sat down and as teenagers do we sat and snogged all evening and he went and got me drinks and things like that ... then, you know, the dreaded time came when we had to leave and I stood up and he saw that I'd got this limp, and he was so obviously and clearly shocked by it ... and I said 'Look, if you don't want to meet me on Saturday you don't have to'. And I expected him to say, 'No, its okay, I'd love to meet you'. Actually he turned to me and said 'Well, I expect lots of boys have said this to you in the past but I'd really rather not', and he said, 'I'll go now', and he just walked off. And he got about a hundred metres up the road and turned round and shouted back 'But I do feel sorry for you'.* (Daisy)

French (1994) argues that 'passing' is often more stressful than revelation since it involves constantly thinking of new excuses or avoiding situations where impairment will become apparent. Thomas (1998) argues that concealment strategies in childhood can have both empowering and disempowering impacts on later life but that they serve to hinder the development of a positive self-identification as 'disabled'. The negotiation of concealment, Thomas argues, has not only psycho-emotional but also very practical consequences (for example, the consequences of not asking for help from public services to which one is entitled). Thus, for Florence, a lifetime of passing and concealment made it hard to 'come out' and claim public support.

> *I was working in social work. I could see that people were getting mobility allowance and I thought I should be getting this. And it took me five attempts over three years before I got it, because people could not believe that I had a disability ... So I even went to my own department and said to the Welfare Rights Officer: 'Will you take my appeal up because I'm really struggling?'. And she said, 'But you don't have a disability, Florence'.*

The experience of coming out was no less daunting for Holly who, although born in the 1980s, had been in segregated residential education. She recalled the pressure of expectation on her first day at a mainstream college.

> *I completely realised that actually I'm the only one in a wheelchair, this is a little bit odd. I kind of knew that I would be but the realisation of that only happened on my first day ... I was trying to stand up and be like everybody else and mix in, but we were standing outside for ages and ages and ages and I started to feel quite faint because I needed to sit down ... I thought, I don't really want to make a point of being disabled, but I don't feel very well!*

It was noticeable that there was actually much less evidence of 'passing' or concealment strategies amongst those in the youngest generation. It is possible that some of this resulted quite simply from differences in the visibility of certain impairment characteristics linked to the historical times in which different cohorts were born (discussed in Chapter Four). For example, the post-war polio epidemics, the Thalidomide episode at the beginning of the 1960s, the increase in cerebral palsy at birth from the 1970s, and the increased survival rates of babies with 'severe' and 'complex' impairments marked different embodied experiences of 'physical impairment' among those who contributed their stories. Such traces are also reflected in, for example, Kalekin-Fishman's (2001) account of growing up with 'the hidden injuries' of a 'slight limp' in the 1940s, the stories of disabled women collected by Campling (1981) or the experiences of teenagers explored by Shah (2008).

In this sense, some authors have argued that the phenomenology of physical characteristics and the 'carnal politics of everyday life' should not be ignored in social explanations of disability (for example, Hughes and Paterson, 1997; Paterson and Hughes, 1999). However, the stories pointed to a more social explanation. The narratives of social segregation and inclusion of those who 'limped' were not easily distinguishable from those who used 'wheelchairs', for example. Changes in public perceptions of normality and difference certainly seemed more significant than associations with any particular embodied characteristic. Confidence in identifying with disability depended much more on changes in the definition of disability itself.

Becoming disabled through the social model

In her biographical work with activists in the US, Kasnitz (2001) shows how the realisation of a politicised disability identity can be a powerful and empowering 'Aha!' moment in people's lives. This is perhaps epitomised in Crow's (1992) account of her own encounter with the social model of disability.

> The social model was the explanation I had sought for years. Suddenly what I had always known, deep down, was confirmed. It wasn't my body that was responsible for all my difficulties, it was external factors. I was being Dis-abled – my capabilities and opportunities were being restricted – by poor social organisation. Even more important, if all the problems had been created by society, then surely society could un-create them. Revolutionary!

Daisy (born in the 1940s) recalled how the International Year of Disabled People (in 1981) offered new kinds of representations and a turning point in her own identity formation. She recalled seeing other disabled people in the media, experiencing similar problems to herself but with a focus on shared oppression caused by social relations, as opposed to personal troubles resulting from an impaired body:

> *When they had the first year of the disabled, I think it was, that changed a lot for people. There were a lot of things on TV that highlighted conditions and made people, started to make people more aware and it's been gradually growing since then.*

Around the same time, Matt had started to become aware of the opportunities for political activism presented by his encounters with disabling environments and stifling professional practices. He gave an example.

> *I'd been involved in campaigning access groups [locally]. I wanted to go and see [this pop band] and got some very negative experiences from the staff when we tried to apply for going. Said I couldn't go, said it'd be really loud and everything ... And so we complained, went on the front page of the papers and there was a great picture of the manager.*

The mobilisation and politicisation of organisations 'of' disabled people has been extensively documented in previous studies (Pagel, 1988; Campbell and Oliver, 1996; Barnes and Mercer, 2006). The development of such organisations in the 1980s was characterised by a shift from 'single-issue' and impairment-specific groupings to broader coalitions of common interests framed within the social model paradigm. For those who were exposed to such developments in the 1980s and 1990s the social and cultural capital they provided proved significant as a resource for alternative identity construction. For example, after going to college, Bob remembers coming into contact with one of the founders of UPIAS.

> *He actually confirmed what I already felt anyway, but for another disabled person who saw disability in political terms, was actually quite rare. So that changed my life forever meeting [him].*

Judy (from the oldest generation) 'really got involved' with the disability movement during this period, already in middle age by this time. Traces of the historical politicisation of disability identity were also evident in the identity narratives of some of those from the youngest generation, despite having no direct contact with political organisations or political activity. For example, the discourse of 'activism', 'rights' and 'equality' was an integral part of the positive way in which Holly had come to make sense of life as a young disabled person.

> *I accept my disability far more now than I ever did. I'm far more into disability rights and disability equality than I ever was, because for a long, long time I was very, very angry about it. And it was like well, my disability takes everything away from me. Whereas now that's kind of turned on its head and you know, I'm very much a disability activist.*

The historical clues in life stories of the three generations point to evidence of real change in the kinds of cultural resources and identity scripts available to young people developing their self-identity. They also suggest that these changes had significant impacts on older adults, who encountered them as catalysts to seeing the world, and themselves, in new ways. The emergence of the disability movement was particularly significant in providing new forms of social and cultural capital on which people could draw. Parallel developments in public policies for educational integration, equal opportunities and rights-based legislation also had an effect. To understand this more clearly the discussion now turns to the situations in which young people encountered the kinds of discourses outlined so far.

Belonging in public and private spaces

Watson (2002) explores narrative accounts of self-identity, distinguishing why people do or do not identify as 'disabled'. He draws attention to Oliver's (1996) contention that identification as a disabled person involves both acknowledgement of impairment and a conscious experience of 'externally imposed restrictions'. Indeed, sharing experiences of segregated schooling or inaccessible public transport with other young people may have a stronger influence on disability identity than a shared diagnosis of, say, polio or cerebral palsy (for example, Finkelstein, 1993; Priestley, 1998d). However, Swain and Cameron (1999) note that it is equally possible to encounter disabling barriers and discrimination without 'coming out' as disabled, while Watson notes that people often want to narrate a sense of self that minimises the significance of both impairment and disability in their lives.

Somers (1994, p 606) argues that 'it is through narrativity that we come to know, understand and make sense of the social world, and it is through narratives and narrativity that we constitute our social identity' (an assertion also cited by Watson). It is useful then to consider some of the ways in which people from the three generations articulated their own sense of self in relation to disability, and how these narratives were influenced by public policies and private relationships. The extent to which people were included or marginalised from full participation affected their childhood perceptions of disability and identity. However, the ability to make sense of this experience in positive and resilient ways was greatly influenced by the kind of cultural scripts that were available at the time (including those provided by new social and cultural capital emanating from the politicisation of the disabled people's movement).

Between hospital and home

As shown in Chapters Three and Four, the childhood accounts of those in the oldest generation drew attention to hospital treatment and family life as key influences on early identity negotiations (while those in the middle generation appeared to place more emphasis on educational experiences, for example). Those narratives pointed to the imposition of a rather medicalised identity discourse in public hospitals and schools, starkly contrasted with discourses of acceptance or denial in the private sphere at home. In this context, the stories suggested a dichotomous confrontation with identity and difference in public and private spaces.

The idea that impairment or disability carried less significance in family life was a recurrent one, identified also in previous studies (such as Watson et al, 1999). However, this could be interpreted in two ways, either as acceptance or as denial (something 'swept under the carpet'). Sometimes the two narratives sat, uncomfortably, alongside one another. For example, Daisy (born in the 1940s) remembered how:

> I've always had to feel, or felt, that I was normal. She [my mother] was always in denial of my disability really. She didn't want to acknowledge really that there was anything wrong with me.

Daisy's uncertainty as a child about whether she 'felt' or whether she 'had to feel' that she was 'normal' marks the kind of difficult confusion that many young people sought to make sense of as they grew up. In doing so, it was necessary to look for cues and role models in the social environment, cues that came from parents, professionals, peers and popular culture.

The intrusive and highly medicalised treatment regimes experienced in early childhood by those like Florence (whose story was summarised in Chapter Two) marked out a feeling of stark difference when staying away from home. For Florence, tied to her cot in the hospital ward for months on end, physical confinement in a medicalised environment contributed much to her growing understanding of disability as something negative and undesirable in her life. These powerful feelings of segregation and imperfection contrasted with her experience at home, where her adopted family made no acknowledgement of impairment and placed a strong emphasis on passing as 'normal'.

> I suppose you start with, 'Do I think I've got a disability?', and the answer to that is no, 99 per cent of the time. But, that's not to

> say that I don't think tha~~t~~ ~~_.__nowledge_~~ it,
> but with the family I grew u~~p~~ ~~_.__nowledged_~~ at all ...

Her mother's rejection of any stigmatised forms of public assistance hinted at attempts to avoid the kinds of 'courtesy stigma' that Birenbaum (1970) suggests attached to families and close associates of people with visible impairments. As Woods and Watson (2004) point out, the public signs and trappings of physical impairment (such as the design of NHS wheelchairs or callipers) have often lacked aesthetic appeal and, therefore, heightened perceptions of stigma. The stigma attached to 'welfare' was also considerable amongst parents who had grown up before the war. As Florence continued:

> *There was not DLA [Disability Living Allowance] in those days, my mother would never have applied for it anyway. My mother got offered an invalid kind of buggy and immediately turned it down and said, 'I'm not taking her in that'.*

Bella's understanding of disability in childhood was also shaped by the paradox of her parents' conspicuous pursuit of medical cure, combined with their concealment at home.

> *I think my mum and dad to a certain extent sort of perpetuated this, that with the next lot of surgery, that I would be cured, if you like. And so I was very compliant on the whole because I just thought ... I really believed, probably because of how it was sort of presented to me, I really believed if I had all this surgery then I would be able to walk, which I did eventually,, and that I would be totally okay sort of in the end. And it was a long time before I suddenly thought this is for life sort of thing ...*

Bella's recollection of 'compliance' in this scenario hints at the kind of role expectations portrayed by Parsons (1951) in his analysis of the 'sick role' as functional to social organisation (discussed by Barnes et al, 2003). There were few alternative identity scripts available to young disabled people at this time, from which to make sense of their place in the world. Indeed, the stories conveyed a sense that it was often long into adulthood before some people were able to resolve an identity that they were comfortable with. As Bella noted:

> *I don't think I really, really totally accepted I was disabled until I was … oh, I don't know, until I really started in social work, and I started doing all these personal development courses [in the 1980s].*

It is equally important to note that it was not just age and wisdom that helped people to see disability differently. Rather, it was the availability of new ways of thinking about disability in the public domain, stimulated by the emergence of the social model of disability, disability activism and equal opportunities policies. So, while children like Florence and Bella were encouraged to get on with the business of childhood at home, they were provided with no alternative narrative of disability with which to make sense of the, often painful, personal investment in normalising therapies and treatments. The fact that there was little explanation, consultation or consent attached to these treatment regimes (see Chapter Four) only added to the uncertainty.

Difference and sameness at school

Early identity confrontations at school focused on public practices that marked out children labelled with impairments as different from their peers, subjecting them to differential forms of adult surveillance and control. This in turn made it harder to establish peer friendships and networks. For example, Daisy felt that her earliest experiences of discrimination in public spaces had a psycho-emotional impact on her longer-term life trajectory. She recalled, in particular, how she was made to feel 'different' from the very beginning of her school career:

> *When it was playtime I was told I couldn't go out and play with the other children because I might get knocked over. So again, what sort of message does that give a little girl, first day of school, five years old? You know, you can't play with the others! And here I am at the age of 58, living on my own, no family, no children, you know, it's almost as if it pre-determined the rest of your life when that happens … I mean you remember that, you learn that you are different. I didn't learn that I was different until I went to school.*

Describing experiences some half a century later, it was clear that some of those in the youngest generation also felt marked out as different by public practices in schools (in mainstream schools as well as special schools). For example, Helen illustrated how the provision of formalised support and surveillance in mainstream school (via a learning support assistant) raised barriers to her participation in peer relationships.

> *I wasn't allowed to do anything on my own. They even had
> someone in the playground making sure I didn't hurt myself or
> anything. In my middle school it got even worse because they
> insisted that I had a member of staff with me 24/7 kind of thing.
> So actually the interesting thing is that until I went to high school
> I found it very difficult to make proper friends because the friends
> that I tended to make were those with the caring complex, or those
> who were quite odd themselves.*

Such experiences have been widely reported in previous research
involving children from Helen's age cohort in the 1990s (discussed
in detail by Priestley, 1999). For example, Watson et al (1999, p 13)
concluded that disabled children born in the 1980s remained subject to
a kind of 'rite of institution' (Bourdieu, 1992) in which the social space
and practices of schools marked them out as different and altered the
way others represented them. The important point to underline is that
public practices and institutional regimes affect people in both intended
and unintended ways. Thus, public policies for the organisation of
schooling have implications not only for academic performance but
also for personal relationships, self-confidence and self-identity in
children's private lives.

The case of physical segregation in special schools was perhaps
the most clearly marked in discussions of identity. For example, Dan
recalled the kind of help he received at special school and its psycho-
emotional impact.

> *You knew you was different, your disability whatever it was, was
> why you were there, and you had this all the time. You knew that
> you were different from anybody else, those outside, your friends
> at ordinary school. You needed this particular facility because you
> had a disability.*

As noted in Chapter Five, the institutional regime of residential
special schools framed the childhood worlds and relationships of many
who shared their stories of growing up in the 1970s. Attention was
drawn there to low academic expectations that established a sense
of future life trajectories towards lack of participation in meaningful
employment (see Chapter Six). There was evidence of a limiting
trajectory of expectation in relation to social relationships in adult life
too. For example, Poppy (born in the 1960s) recalled how:

... that was brought home by this woman, who came into our classroom at school one day and said to me, what did we want to do when we left school? And I said to her I wanted to have a house, and a job, and a family, and she said you can't have all that ...

Similarly, Matt felt that the limitations on his career expectations in special school carried a deeper meaning in terms of social identity and life trajectory.

I remember being asked what I wanted to do and for some sad reason I wanted to be an accountant and the teacher said, 'Well, don't you think you're aiming a bit high?' And I don't think that was about intellect. I think it was about 'You're disabled' ...

Without extensive exposure to the mainstream, and under the influence of low institutional expectations, leaving the closely defined world of special school presented quite a challenge. As Poppy put it:

[My school] was quite small you got to know people and you got used to disabled people ... but once I left it I felt so lost, I felt completely like I was nothing, I had no identity. I was a teenager, I had all these hormones and questions, 'Who am I? What am I going to do for the rest of my life? Am I going to be stuck in this bungalow with my parents?'. It was really depressing, I really missed my friends ...

The closed social environment of residential schools, in particular, lent itself to intimate bonds of friendship and peer interaction, which had both positive and negative implications for personal development (see also Shah, 2007). Holly (born in the 1980s) conveyed these contradictions from her own very recent experience.

I went to a special needs nursery and then started a special needs school at the age of five. So a lot of the people I went to nursery school with that I actually went to my main school with. So I've actually been with the same bunch of people from the age of two to the age of 18 ... found that quite hard because, although it's quite nice having the same, same group of people all the time, I found that there was no chance to grow. There's no chance to evolve into another person and learn from the mistakes.

Holly's view was that the special school environment was over-protected and failed to prepare her for adulthood but mixing with other wheelchair users in a mainly barrier-free environment was also liberating at the time.

> *Instead of seeing the disability you just saw a person ... you became 'blind', if I can use that term, to the fact that these, your friends, these people that you saw every day, were disabled. And within my family, you know, my disability was never referred to so it kind of just didn't register at all.*

It is then interesting, at first surprising, to note that many of those who later chose to 'come out' or 'be proud' as disabled people in adulthood had spent their childhoods under considerable institutional confinement, surveillance and marginalisation from participation in society. Indeed, Carter (2009) draws attention to the number of 'special school survivors' who have gone on to become high profile disability activists (see also Campbell and Oliver, 1996; Barnes and Mercer, 2006). Thus, while special schools were narrated as disempowering institutions in the stories they also provided fertile grounds for some people to develop shared identities within a new and resistant counter-culture.

Some of those in the youngest generation who went to mainstream schools (like Helen or Steve) also drew positive experiences and reference points from their encounters with other disabled children in other settings, such as activity or therapy-based groups. As Steve put it:

> *It was good 'cos, I mean, in mainstream school if you were the only one with a disability then you, eventually, you go to clubs like that and you realise that you're not the only one, so I mean you become like less isolated.*

Helen described the implications of participating, for the first time, in activities targeted specifically at disabled children (organised by a national charity) when she was 12 years old.

> *... constantly throughout my life I'd been defined as a disabled person first, been expected to be more adult than someone equivalent of my age would have been. I was surrounded by adults all the time, it was very difficult for me to misbehave at school ... I was always expected to be a mini adult ... And [the charity] suddenly had this opportunity to be with other young disabled people that were doing interesting and fun things that able-bodied kids would kill*

*to do. But to do it you had to identify with the fact that you were
disabled, but the thing that was more important was that you were
young and disabled, so it got me into it and I absolutely loved it.
It was such a revelation to come across other young disabled people
who were like me ... before [the charity] if you'd said 'disability',
I wouldn't be sitting doing this conversation with you. I was in
disability denial, not that I wasn't disabled but I didn't want to
be seen as a disabled person.*

Sharing experiences with other young people with physical
impairments (whether in service settings, political organisations or
arts and leisure groups) provided access to forms of social and cultural
capital that young disabled people valued, although they did not wish
to be segregated from the mainstream. However, these experiences
did not necessarily lead to the kind of politicised sense of identity
that had been developing through networks and groups directed by
disabled people themselves (Campbell and Oliver, 1996; Barnes and
Mercer, 2006). Pilot projects in peer mentoring run by disabled people's
organisations (within a social model context) have been shown to
have 'profound effects' on disabled children's outlook on life (Bethell,
2003). However, providing children with access to appropriate peer
networks that are sensitive to disability as culture, without re-creating
segregation, is as much a challenge for advocacy organisations as it is
for service providers.

The significance of further education

Many of the stories from the middle and youngest generations pointed
to transitions from school to college as key turning point in negotiating
identity and social belonging. There were several accounts in the stories
of the liberating consequences of transition into colleges of further or
higher education, which appeared, unlike other public institutions, to
offer rather more opportunities than limitations in identity negotiation.

*It was like a rite of passage. It was where I learnt to become who
I am now ... I learnt to become an independent adult ... to have
the choices that I wanted, and to be able to make those choices
... (Poppy)*

Tan (also born in the 1960s) went to a residential college of special
education but, for her too, the experience was qualitatively different
from being at special school. It was at college, she feels, that the

commonalities of experience with other young disabled people began to have a more positive impact on her awareness and identity.

> *College was just an experience of being let loose on the world. It was a growth experience, you know, it was a life growing experience rather than an educational experience ... it was a great experience, it was about growing as a human being, and finding, finding a place for yourself to just explore the world, you know. We just went out to the pubs and got really drunk all the time, and had parties and, do you know what I mean, it was about relationships and about sex ... and it was a time for becoming politicised without knowing that you were becoming politicised, because you were sharing experiences with one another ...*

Matt's experience of the transition to further education was narrated in a similar way.

> *... the first six weeks were just a complete shock to be honest ... You were left to fend for yourself much more. I grew up very quickly. My family were shocked because I went there as this very nice, sweet probably, 16-year-old and I came home three months later into heavy metal, politics, fighting, anything I could, and suddenly disagreed with everything ...*

On one level these kinds of accounts are not in the least surprising and would be expected in any study of young people growing up but it is the influence of public policy and institutions in the context of disability that is particularly relevant here. It is worth reiterating that the stories included experiences of both mainstream and segregated colleges. There were obvious differences but there were also similarities, mainly associated with gaining the basic activity freedoms of leaving compulsory schooling. For example, Anton attended a residential post-16 education college, having previously lived with his parents while attending a local special school as a day pupil. His initial excitement at new-found independence gradually gave way to a growing awareness of the restrictions associated with the institutional segregation.

> *I went on to college, stayed there for three years and that was a bit of a culture shock as well. When you're with your family and you've got your parents doing everything for you, the first year you feel like your completely free you've got no one telling you anything! Also you've got money, you can go to the post office and get the*

attendance allowance and various other things, and go to the pub and all that. It's quite a change. Well, the second year I started noticing the restrictions on us there. You start noticing that, hang on, this ain't as free as you think it is! And by the third year you begin to see really big restrictions.

The experience of then entering university opened up another world, and his first opportunity to make sense of identity in the mainstream.

You're meeting new people, different people, some very clever people as well, and most of those are able-bodied compared to the other places I was in … when you're with disabled people you tend to feel on the same level, you don't feel left out of things or having to prove yourself any more or things like that. But when you're surrounded by able-bodied people, for the first time especially, you do feel left out of things. Because they're talking above you, you feel sort of out of it, it takes a little while to change the way you think.

For Harvey, who experienced considerable peer exclusion in the community where he grew up, university was a revelation.

When you're trying to deal with the fact that, you know, this disability thing is a problem socially and stuff, you start to have like a self doubt and you start to question who you are and what you're about … It wasn't really until I got to university that I finally became comfortable with who I was. I started to gain a real close group of friends … I was going out and meeting people and going out drinking and doing, doing everything that everybody else did. So then I realised that, you know, this disability thing wasn't a problem, you know, I was socially adept.

While many barriers remain, inclusive schooling, non-discrimination legislation and the public Equality Duty have increased accessibility to mainstream higher education for students with physical impairments in particular (and they have increased the opportunities to gain the necessary academic entry qualifications at school).

Although there had been a small fixed allowance for disabled students since the mid-1970s it was not until the beginning of the 1990s that a more realistic and flexible Disabled Students Allowance (DSA) was introduced (covering assistive equipment, personal assistance, travel and other costs). The establishment of new support units within institutions, core funding to universities for disability access, and the introduction

of DSA have made a considerable difference to students in England since the 1990s (Holloway, 2001; Fuller et al, 2004; Riddell et al, 2005b; Harrison et al, 2009). There has, however, been concern that access to mainstream further education colleges has lagged behind (for example, Sanderson, 2001). There remains much to do but it would be fair to say that the liberating opportunities of participating in mainstream higher education have become more accessible to those of the youngest generation than their predecessors.

New identities through 'disability' work

In Chapter Six access to paid employment and meaningful career development was identified as a significant marker of adult identity construction (see also Shah, 2005a; 2005b). The world of work created social spaces in which disability identities needed to be negotiated (for example, because of direct discrimination, encounters with barriers or relationships with work colleagues). In this context, the stories provided traces of the ways in which more positive disability identities were forged through experiences of working in disability-related organisations. This included both paid and unpaid work in traditional organisations 'for', and new organisations 'of', disabled people (Barnes and Mercer, 2006), and the emergence of a new kind of rights-based 'disability' work.

Jayne was eventually offered a paid part-time job with the organisation where she had volunteered (a mental health charity). She was not the only person to have sought voluntary work as a way into paid employment, nor the only one to find it in a disability-related organisation. For example, Holly currently works voluntarily for a disability organisation in the city where she lives. She sees it as a stepping stone, to 'prove myself'. She had been looking for paid employment for a year without success and felt that her limited educational qualifications had been a real barrier to getting a job that would allow to her escape the benefits trap. Volunteering in a disability organisation provided her with a way in.

As discussed in relation to special schools (in Chapter Five), operating in a disability organisation may give rise to some ambivalence. Amy (born in the 1960s) became involved with an impairment-based charity, where she felt she was accepted and experienced a sense of shared identity. The work also gave her opportunities for career advancement.

> *... this professionalised me ... I became the [charity's] Publications*
> *Officer, for three years, and that was an empowering experience,*
> *because I'd got to work in an office environment.*

Some of the individual stories summarised in Chapter Two drew attention to the life course implications of participating in new kinds of 'disability work' that emerged during the 1980s and 1990s. Such opportunities, albeit for a minority of disabled people and not always paid, arose from the mobilisation of social claims by disabled people's organisations, a growing awareness of the social model, and a new identity politics. The chance to participate in raising disability awareness or to work within a disability-friendly organisation had a considerable impact on those who experienced it.

Some of the stories from the middle generation (born in the 1960s) were particularly marked by working with new organisations controlled by disabled people. For example, after graduating from university in the early 1990s, Poppy became involved in disability politics and the creation of disability work:

> *Three of us created a disability awareness company ... and we*
> *became directors, and we became trainers, and we were making*
> *quite good money as well.*

Changes in public policy towards a more rights-based framework also provided new kinds of jobs in public institutions, for example as 'access officers' in local authorities, as disabled students' advisors in universities, and in policy development or enforcement roles. For example, Kay (born in the 1980s) had experienced work in a residential institution and this led her to take a postgraduate course in disability studies. After a temporary placement she heard about a post at the Disability Rights Commission. For Kay, this represented her 'dream job' as it involved direct engagement with disability policy and being part of an organisation which, she believed, could make a difference to disabled people's lives:

> *The DRC is there a) to support the people and b) now especially*
> *to enforce things like the equality duties and stuff ... when you*
> *work in an organisation and you read about the cases that they've*
> *won and the settlements and stuff that have happened, and the*
> *things that have gone on, you begin to realise.*

Such opportunities have, however, not always proved secure. The winding up of the DRC and its merger into the Equality and Human Rights Commission in 2008 (described in Chapter One) gave rise to concern about the future representation of disabled employees in the rights industry. The intense financial sustainability pressures on local user-led organisations have also given rise to similar concerns (Barnes and Mercer, 2006) although some encouragement has been drawn from the establishment of a User-Led Organisations Development Fund by the Department of Health (Morris, 2007).

For the preceding generation (born in the 1960s) there were few paid opportunities to enter work through public advocacy or rights work but there were several examples of careers initiated by experiences of social care work with other disabled people, in social services or disability charities. For example, Bob had held various jobs in both generic and disability sectors that began when he started in an office job with the Spastics Society. He later went on to work with peer information and campaigning organisations in the 1980s.

At the same time, the emergent disability arts movement provided life-changing opportunities to some. For example, Gilbert's role as an actor in a television film in the early 1990s generated an invitation for him to work with a disabled people's theatre company. He began running workshops for young disabled people and has since developed a freelance career including acting, directing and writing. There were also experiences of engagement with the visual arts through mainstream art education.

Richardson (2007) highlights a lack of critical attention of the cultural and political significance of art schools during the 1960s and 1970s, noting that one in ten of all full-time students of further education in 1969 were studying art or design. The incubation of creative and artistic innovation in these environments (such as the 'pop art' movement) has often been linked with political consciousness-raising and unrest. Yet for Tan, as a disabled art student, it was hard to find artistic expression for the kind of disability issues she wanted to explore at this time.

> *I'm in a world of non-disabled people who have no knowledge and understanding of disability art and the politics of disability. They steered me away from doing work which was disability orientated … they said don't put wheelchairs in there, you know people don't wanna see wheelchairs, crutches. They don't wanna see that. So, I was steered away from it … I wasn't making any art work which was politicised at that point.*

The turning point for Tan, as it was for some others of her generation, was an encounter with the emergent disability arts movement that offered new and exciting possibilities. She wrote to the newly-founded Disability Arts In London (*DAIL*) magazine in search of research opportunities for her student dissertation. Through these contacts she gained inroads to exhibit her work alongside other disabled artists and, later, to produce more politically challenging pieces.

Reviewing the historical connections between disability arts and disability identity, Cameron (2007, p 501) argues that this movement enables not only a politicised identity but also the possibility of an 'affirmative model': 'Through the development of the culture of resistance that is disability arts, disabled people have developed a discourse that rejects personal tragedy narratives and that identifies impairment as part of human experience to be celebrated.' Disability activists and arts practitioners had pointed to the identity significance of the emergent disability arts movement and 'crip culture' since the 1980s, providing alternative spaces to resist and challenge cultural stereotypes (Vasey, 1992). Building an expressive culture from these spaces was also seen as enlivening the capacity for more politicised identity claims on public policy. For example, Finkelstein (1992, p 6) had asserted that:

> ... it is essential for us to create our own public image, based on free acceptance of our distinctive group identity before we can participate in the multicultural world. Such a cultural identity will play a vital role in helping us develop the confidence necessary for us to create the organisations which we need to promote the social change we all want.

Gill (1997) argues that the emergence of disability culture has fostered an alternative repertoire of identities, informed by a politicised movement, that provide opportunities to 'try on' new narratives towards the adoption of a rather different 'signature identity'. At the same time those like Cribb (1993) pointed to the tensions of a creating artistic ghettos in which disabled artists might become 'cotton wooled' from the establishment of more mainstream careers. For example, disability arts played a part in Amy's life too but she feels it is necessary to move on with the benefit of that experience.

> *It's a wonderful starting point, it's been a wonderful grounding, but you can't stay there forever, being patted on the back by your colleagues and peers, because what's the point?*

As these various experiences illustrate, the opportunity to engage in 'disability work' was a significant influence in the identity projects of some of those who shared their stories. It is important to reiterate, however, that such opportunities have only been available to a small minority, that many young disabled people have not come into contact with user-led organisations and that many disabled adults would choose to distance themselves from such association (Watson, 2002). However, as the examples show, it is equally important to affirm how the new kinds of 'disability work' that emerged from disability activism, disability arts and the implementation of rights-based disability policies provided radically new ways of being or becoming 'disabled'.

Conclusions

The stories suggested considerable change over time in the availability of different discourses of disability. The range of cultural scripts available to those growing up with physical impairment in the 1940s and 1950s was more limited than for those growing up in the 1980s and 1990s. The emergence of disabled people's political activism, increased community presence, the availability of disabled role models and the development of the social model of disability, all provided resources for changing lives. The examples showed how public policies and institutions, for example in health, education and employment, created social spaces and practices that marked impairment in very negative ways. But they also showed how those same institutions sometimes acted as catalysts for resistance and consciousness-raising about the commonality of disability as oppression.

It is important to emphasise that young people with perceived impairments are not only 'made known' by public practices but that they also 'make themselves known' (Priestley, 1999). The discussion in this chapter conveys something of the complex, often confusing, emotional labour involved in negotiating disability between public and private spaces but it suggests that there have been some very significant changes. There was less evidence of social obligations to 'pass' as 'normal' today and a greater opportunity to assert, even celebrate, physical difference. Moreover, there was a transformation of opportunity in the emergence of social and political discourses of disability that allowed those who were exposed to such ideas to make sense of contradictions that challenged young people in earlier times.

Questions for discussion

- What differences are there in the kinds of cultural images and identity role models available to young disabled people today compared to those that were available in the 1950s and 1960s?
- To what extent has the development of social model concepts and disabled people's organisations, during the 1980s and 1990s, provided new forms of social and cultural capital on which young disabled people can draw in constructing their self-identity and goals for life?

EIGHT

Conclusion

The preceding seven chapters have covered a wide-ranging exploration of the ways in which changes in public policies and institutions, coupled with changes in civil society, have impacted on the private lives of young people with physical impairments since the 1940s. This exploration was intimately informed by a critical engagement with biographical narratives generated from life history interviews with people from three generational cohorts, who experienced childhood and the transition to adulthood in different historical times. The method of analysis sought to engage with these narratives as a stimulus to pose questions about parallel developments in public policies and institutions. This final part of the book reviews these developments, drawing on key findings from the substantive chapters, and returns to the questions outlined at the beginning. It also reflects on the utility of using biographical evidence to tell histories of disability.

Reflections on biography

Activist and academic discourse within the social model paradigm has emphasised the commonality of disability as oppression and institutionalised discrimination. This is fundamental to a social understanding of disability in contemporary societies and to the mobilisation of a cohesive social movement. Disability, like patriarchy and racism, is also something that affects people in their private lives, both materially and psycho-emotionally. The personal experience so evident in biographical accounts conveys the diversity of individual lives. It is not surprising then that the 'biographical turn' in social science (see Rustin, 2000) has drawn much inspiration from post-structural critiques of grand theory but, as feminist thought has long reminded us, the 'personal' is also 'political' and the boundaries between public and private are often fractured or blurred. Disability studies, like feminist studies, have shown repeatedly how public policies and institutions arising from unequal social relations can reach deep into people's private lives and relationships. The lives of young disabled people have been particularly marked by this kind of public reach – making intimate lives very public and constraining private life decisions.

Stories demonstrate the very real ways in which policies (for example, policies for the provision of public health and social care, education, housing or transport) impact on everyday life and close personal relationships. The most graphic examples were those where policy implementation separated young people almost entirely from their families (in residential institutions of different kinds). These were not uncommon experiences across all three generations but they stand out when recounted individually, and this is one of the key advantages of incorporating biographical experiences alongside broad statistical trends.

Biographical narratives offer a way through public/private boundaries, often contesting and challenging the presumed impacts of policies. For example, the biographical data suggested that the oldest generation did not necessarily lead the most segregated of childhoods. This led to a more detailed examination to the contextual evidence and to a more critical questioning of chronologies of institutional provision. The stories should not be read, as some might claim, as unquestionably 'authentic' accounts because they were selectively and reciprocally constructed in the telling. However, they revealed hidden aspects of negotiation, resistance and agency to contest top-down historical accounts and provide a means of getting closer to the 'whole story'.

Biographical evidence is often 'messy' and uncertain, even when it conveys a clear sense of purposeful life projects. Life experiences have been remembered, imagined, selected and interpreted. As Thomas (1999, p 7) points out in her presentation of stories told by disabled women: 'Narratives are representations, involving interpretation and selection in their construction (the "telling"), in their consumption (my "reading"), in their reproduction (my "re-presentation"), and in their further interpretation (your "reading")'. The same is true for this book. The summary stories presented in Chapter Two maintained some narrative coherence, and were validated with the people concerned, but they are selective and partial accounts that portray a linear narrative constructed after the events. The fragmentation of episodes from a range of stories in the subsequent chapters is still more subject to selection and re-presentation. Moreover, a core element of the method was to contextualise and contest these narrative extracts with reference to evidence of the 'bigger picture', generating interpretations that were not necessarily intended in the original telling.

As discussed in Chapter One, it is important to engage with personal narratives in ways that are not simply 'anecdotal' and that try to respect fears of 'voyeurism'. Narrative is certainly not 'everything' but responding to people's personal accounts offered an important way of maintaining a presence for the voice of disabled people in a critical and reflexive research practice. In this context, the principle that disabled people are not the 'subject matter' was essential to maintain. Critical analysis needs to value personal accounts as knowledge, no less valuable than scientific knowledge, but it needs to maintain its focus on the institutions and social relations of disabling societies – on the message rather than the messenger. Connecting biography with history, the core of the 'sociological imagination', means ensuring that accounts of disability are not read as accounts of 'personal troubles' but as evidence of 'public issues'. Read in this way they provide new insights and explanations beyond the possibilities of non-biographical or purely biographical methods.

Key findings

The evidence presented in Chapter Three reinforced how important the bonds and resources of family relationships are to children and young people. It also showed how public policies and institutions have often intervened to separate children from those relationships (for example, for the purposes of providing medical treatment or schooling). The personal consequences of segregation from community life have been much rehearsed in the literature but the stories underlined the very personal and private consequences of segregationist policies, and the psycho-emotional 'scars' that disabling institutions can leave on family life. It is important, however, to reiterate that many people who shared their life stories also had very ordinary experiences of family life in childhood and adulthood, in which impairment or disability was not seen to have much influence in private lives and relationships.

Concerns were raised about the reach of medical authority into everyday lives, and its influence on important life choices beyond the legitimate scope of medicine (for example, in decisions about school placements, discussed in Chapter Four). The impact of medical institutions arose from a combination of professional practice and public resources provision. For example, prolonged treatment in long-stay hospitals (with restricted visitation rights) was framed by a scant availability of locally-based paediatric hospital centres. Regionalisation and economies of scale accentuated the segregative impacts of isolation hospitals, 'open air' schools, specialist schools (for narrowly defined categories of impairment) and industrial rehabilitation units. Post-war reconstruction, the archaic quality of public transport and poor roads (serving local need rather than national travel) exacerbated the severing of attachments in distant, often rural, locations.

Segregationist policies that have denied people's basic human rights (like slavery, apartheid, male property rights and long-stay institutions) acquire a kind of hegemonic normalcy largely because they are viewed as rational responses by the majority, from a distance or in the abstract. When their impacts are exposed and challenged on a human level, for example through the narration of biographical experiences of oppression, the assumed normalcy is brought into sudden and sharp relief. Thus, separating a child from their family on grounds of disability may have been commonplace but it should never be viewed as 'normal'.

The stories often demonstrated the agency and resourcefulness of young people and their families in negotiating, contesting or subverting disabling policies and practices. In particular, the stories from all three generations pointed to the resilience and resistance of mothers as a vital resource at key turning points in the life course. The most commonly identified example was in decisions about school placement. Opportunities for 'resisting consumers' (Fox and Ward, 2006) to contest professional authority, in decisions about both medical treatment and school placements have changed with the rise of the 'expert patient', parental choice and tribunal processes (although such processes can often be obstructive or difficult to navigate for all but the most articulate and forceful of parents). At the same time, paternal abandonment featured in several of the stories, as it has done in other research. This raised concerns about the relatively high risk of parental divorce and breakdown amongst families with disabled children.

The evidence characterised a policy framework that began with two alternative life course trajectories. The first was based on a kind of makeshift inclusion within the family (where impairment and disability were sometimes accepted, sometimes denied). The second was based on the prospect of segregation in public institutions (individual life pathways and turning points also point to the scope to switch track from one trajectory to the other). It would be tempting to suggest that expansion of the welfare state, and an increasing awareness of the 'disabled family', led to progressively enlightened policy support for the first trajectory and a curtailment of the second. However, the stories contest this linear narrative of policy enlightenment.

In particular, the evidence in Chapter Four showed how segregated educational institutions began to fill the institutional spaces created by receding medical authority and shorter stays in hospital. Indeed, they expanded most rapidly at the very time when policy debates were turning to critiques of segregation (during the 1970s). Despite the enabling provisions of the 1970 Chronically Sick and Disabled Persons Act, increasing investment in social services day centres continued this segregation into young adulthood. It may be more than coincidence then that the childhood stories of those born in the 1940s sometimes appeared more 'ordinary' than those born in the 1960s (with the exception of experiences in hospital).

Chapter Four also illustrated the influence of medical opinion and prognosis on family expectations about future life for children born with physical impairments. As discussed in Chapter Seven, the availability of alternative life narratives and identity scripts with which to challenge such opinions changed considerably over the historical period. There has been a qualitative shift in new ways of thinking about and identifying with disability (primarily arising from the identity politics of the disabled people's movement, the disability arts movement and the independent living movement). However, there are continuing concerns that families still lack exposure to alternative lay knowledge about everyday life as a disabled child or about disabled adult role models. Young people today still lack access to these resources but, for the minority who do come into contact with them, they can have transformative effects on personal lives and aspirations.

The examples in Chapter Seven showed how change in the cultural scripts available to young people influenced how they became known to themselves and to others. The discussion pointed to developments in the reach of the mass media and the infiltration of new and challenging disability identities, forged within new cultural spaces created by disability activism and arts. The kinds of 'spoiled identity' or 'passing' experienced by many in the oldest generation were much less evident in the identity repertoires of those from the youngest generation. Those in the middle generation told more stories of direct encounters with the disabled people's movement but those in the youngest generation had often picked up these politicised discourses by other means to become 'disability activists' by association if not in practice.

There was some ambivalence in the stories about access to peer culture in segregated services and institutions. The forced intimacy of sharing childhood worlds with other young disabled people (for example, in hospitals or residential schools and colleges) created confusion and resentment but it also gave rise to friendships that were, eventually, empowering for some people. For some it was the very experience of institutional segregation that sparked 'survivor' identities that enabled them to 'come out' or 'be proud' as disabled people. Yet, there were concerns that identities imposed through public services turned disability into a 'master status' that obscured the significance of class, gender, ethnicity or sexuality in people's private lives.

Over time, many more children with 'severe' and 'complex' physical impairments have lived into adulthood and many more have been supported to attend mainstream schools. This had been achieved through advances in medical technologies, through investment in personalised classroom support, individualised assessment of learning needs, and the introduction of non-discrimination legislation. However, increased provision of public support in the mainstream has brought new negotiations of self-identity and personal relationships (for example, with increased one-to-one adult company and surveillance having unintended social consequences for peer interactions at school).

The discussion in Chapter Six crossed the boundaries of transition from education to work, and from childhood to adulthood. This raised a wide range of issues and questions about the relationship between private lives and public policies, and between agency and structure. There was little evidence in the stories that historic investments in public employment services and careers guidance had been of much tangible assistance to young people with physical impairments entering the adult labour market for the first time – in any of the three generations. Indeed, there was much evidence that public policies and institutions had often steered people's life pathways away from the open labour market (towards sheltered employment, social services day centres, long-term welfare benefits or a cycle of unresolved 'training' courses in further education). The evidence did show some significant changes in policy towards a more rights-based approach (not least in the implementation and enforcement of the 1995 Disability Discrimination Act). The stories illustrated much vulnerability to arbitrary and direct discrimination but also the introduction of new policy opportunities to contest or pre-empt this.

The case of employment underlined how important it is to read both biographical histories and policy histories within the context of socio-economic histories. Examples from the stories exemplified theoretical claims in the disability studies literature about the 'elastic' nature of disability as an administrative category in the control of labour supply, linked to structural and demographic factors. Thus, there was evidence of the personal implications of changes in labour supply and demand resulting from, for example: war-time industrial demand, the exploitation of migrant colonial labour, the 'never had it so good' post-war boom, the economic slump in the 1970s and sustained growth prior to the recent economic crisis. Fluctuations in employment opportunity (and the intensity of public interventions in work and welfare policies) have mirrored these structural cycles. However, it is also fair to say that there have been improvements in employment rates for disabled people and a historic closing of the employment gap on non-disabled people.

Learning lessons for a new generation

Like many other observers of the late 20th century, Furlong and Cartmel (1997, p 8) conclude that 'In the space of one generation there have been some radical changes to the typical experiences of young people' (see also Irwin, 1995), but how true is this for young disabled people in Britain? To what extent have their life transitions and experiences been transformed over the same period? There is little doubt that there was a remarkable acceleration of policy concern with the situation of disabled people in the period under review, perhaps more so than at any other time in British policy history. The evidence shows how young disabled people growing up in Britain today often have different life choices and chances to those of their parents' or grandparents' generations (but how some things also stay much the same). For instance, in the early post-war period large numbers of children with physical impairments spent extended periods of time separated from their families in the depriving conditions of long-stay hospitals. The challenges encountered by their families were considered largely as a private matter rather than a public concern, and disability was construed more as a personal trouble than a social issue (save perhaps in the case of employment).

The greater recognition of disability as a public issue today is well and good but the rapid development and increasing reach of public policies, under professional authority, created problems of its own and added substantially to the disabling consequences for many young people. It was, if anything, growing dissatisfaction and critique of new, rather than old, institutional arrangements that led to a heightened awareness of disability as a form of institutionalised discrimination (for example, in personal encounters with expanding special school and social care provision in the 1970s). The emergence of disabled people's organisations in this critique was an important catalyst in generating alternative policy futures towards greater rights, choice and control in everyday lives. Changes in social attitudes, environmental accessibility, new technologies, user-controlled support services and rights-based legislation have all impacted in various ways upon people's experience of family, education and work. They have also impacted on people's personal sense of identity and belonging in British society.

The turn of the 21st century has brought new hopes but also new challenges. The 2010 Equality Act promised new protection from discrimination by association, with the potential to acknowledge some of the barriers to family life and friendship for disabled children. Public commitments to the principles and obligations of the United Nations Convention on the Rights of Persons with Disabilities appeared to promise a great deal. Rhetorically, policy has come a long way but the realisation of far-reaching objectives remains intensely challenging within the 2025 timeframe proposed by the last Labour Government. To meet these challenges we need to learn from the lessons of history, and to learn from of the experiences of disabled people in particular. The 2010 General Election campaign held out the possibility of a more comprehensive national right to user-controlled social care, which could make a considerable difference to many people's life choices if it were implemented. The personalisation agenda in health and social care is expected to progress (and has been welcomed by some disability groups) with the prospect of personal budgets being expanded for children, including for use in special education. However, the pioneering Independent Living Fund has been effectively closed to new applicants not in work. There is substantial new investment of more than a billion pounds for social care (pending historic change to the system of funding in 2011), but half is taken from the health service budget, and there are concerns that extra money will simply be absorbed in cuts to local government (where all budget ring-fencing is removed).

With a Conservative–Liberal Democrat coalition Government committed to dramatically rein back public expenditure in an uncertain economic environment, the challenges appear very great. There is already evidence that disabled people are at considerable risk from new austerity policies (Wood and Grant, 2010). Major cutbacks in eligibility to disability-related welfare entitlements will affect many adults, although disabled children have retained certain exemptions (for example, in continuing entitlement to Child Trust Fund payments). There will be unprecedented public sector cuts (and an estimated half a million job losses), which will impact on the availability of social services, social housing, children's services, transport and peripatetic support services inclusive education (as well as impacting on the relative success of disabled people's employment in the public sector). Cuts/caps in housing support (mortgage support, rent subsidies and housing benefit) impact disproportionately on disabled families.

The Disability Employment Advisory Committee and the Disabled Passengers Transport Advisory Committee have been abolished and reservations have been expressed about the future of the Equality and Human Rights Commission. The budget for Disability Living

Allowance (DLA) has been cut and people living in residential care lose its mobility component altogether. From 2013, all DLA claimants will require a new medical assessment and it is expected that many will lose entitlement or have benefits reduced. There is already further tightening of eligibility for support to disabled people provided through Employment and Support Allowance. All claimants are being re-interviewed with tighter medical-functional 'work capability' testing. Those judged able to work will have their benefits reduced after 12 months, and with less public support to find work. Yet, for those seeking work, the budget for the Access to Work scheme has also been cut. No funding is available for public sector employees and, even for those in private sector employment, it will no longer be possible to apply for many of the items that were most helpful to those interviewed for this book (including adapted chairs and desks, specialist information and communication technology or adaptations to buildings).

A radical reformulation of financial autonomy in health services and schools raises real uncertainties about the future coordination of supports previously directed by local education authorities and primary care trusts (the latter have been abolished altogether). In addition to cuts in local authority funding, schools choosing to become independent will take with them budgets previously allocated to shared services (such as peripatetic advisory teachers). In September 2010 the Minister for Children and Families launched public consultation towards the new administration's first Green Paper on *Children and young people with special educational needs and disabilities*. Some of the guiding policy principles will be familiar from previous chapters of this book, particularly in seeking 'better educational outcomes and life chances for children and young people ... from the early years through to the transition into adult life and employment' and the need for 'joining up support from education, social care and health, particularly for those with the most severe and complex needs and at key transitions' (DfE, 2010, p 4). There were also calls for 'greater choice for parents in the schools their children attend and the support and services they receive, whether in a mainstream or special school setting'. A return to the 'parental choice' agenda, in terms of choosing mainstream or special schooling, raises real concerns about continuing progress towards full participation and equality. During the General Election campaign, the incoming Prime Minister made a much publicised personal commitment to a 'moratorium on the ideologically driven closure of special schools', with a pledge to 'end the bias towards the inclusion of children with special needs in mainstream schools' (Conservative Party, 2010, p 53). Given the scars of segregation revealed in this book, and the fact that the last government chose to 'reserve' its full commitment to the inclusive education requirements of the UN Convention, the future looks far from certain for the next generation of young disabled people.

References

Abel-Smith, B. (2005) 'The Welfare State: breaking the post-war consensus', *Political Quarterly*, vol 51, no 1, pp 17–23.

Adam, B. (1998) *Timescapes of modernity: The environment and invisible hazards*, London: Routledge.

Alderson P. (1993) *Children's consent to surgery*, Buckingham: Open University Press.

Alderson, P. (2006) 'Who should decide and how?', in E. Parens (ed) *Surgically shaping children: Technology, ethics, and the pursuit of normality*, Baltimore, MD: Johns Hopkins University Press, pp 157–75.

Alderson, P. and Goodey, D. (1998) 'Doctors, ethics and special education', *Journal of Medical Ethics*, vol 24, pp 49–55.

Alderson, P. and Montgomery, J. (1996) *Health care choices: Making decisions with children*, London: Institute of Public Policy Research.

Alderson, P. and Goodey, C. (1998) *Enabling education: Experiences in special and ordinary schools*, London: Tufnel Press.

Allsop, J. and Mulcahy, L. (1996) *Regulating medical work: Formal and informal controls*, Buckingham: Open University Press.

Ammerman, R. (1997) 'Physical abuse and childhood disability: risk and treatment factors', *Journal of Aggression, Maltreatment & Trauma*, vol 1, no 1, pp 207–24.

Anderson, O. and Lerner, M. (1960) *Measuring health levels in the United States 1900–1958*, Health Information Foundation Research Series no 11, New York: Foundation.

Armer, B. (2007) 'Eugenetics: a polemical view of social policy in the genetic age', *New Formations*, vol 60, pp 89–101.

Ashton, D. and Field, D. (1976) *Young workers: From school to work*, London: Hutchinson.

Atkinson, R. (1998) *The life story interview*, London: Sage.

Audit Commission (2003) *Services for disabled children: A review of services for disabled children and their families*, London: Audit Commission.

Avis, M. and Reardon, R. (2008) 'Understanding the views of parents of children with special needs about the nursing care their child receives when in hospital: a qualitative study', *Journal of Child Health Care*, vol 12, no 1, pp 7–17.

Bagley, C., Woods, P. and Woods, G. (2001) 'Implementation of School Choice Policy: interpretation and response by parents of students with special educational needs', *British Educational Research Journal*, vol 27, no 3, pp 287–311.

Baldwin, S. (1976) 'Families with handicapped children', in K. Jones and S. Baldwin (eds) *Year book of social policy in Britain, 1975*, London: Routledge and Kegan Paul, pp 171-191.

Baldwin, S.M. (1985) *The costs of caring: Families with disabled children*, London, Routledge & Kegan Paul.

Barker, P. (1974) 'Psychological effects on children of admission to hospital', *Update*, vol 7, pp 1019–24.

Barnes, C. (1990) *Cabbage syndrome: The social construction of dependence*, Lewes: Falmer.

Barnes, C. (1991) *Disabled people in Britain and discrimination: A case for anti-discrimination legislation*, London: Hurst/BCODP.

Barnes, C. (1992) *Disabling imagery: An exploration of media portrayals of disabled people*, Derby: BCODP.

Barnes, C. (2000) 'A working social model? Disability, work and disability politics in the 21st century', *Critical Social Policy*, vol 20, no 4, pp 441–57.

Barnes, C. and Mercer, G. (2005) 'Disability, work and welfare: challenging the social exclusion of disabled people', *Work, Employment & Society*, vol 19, no 3, pp 527–45.

Barnes, C. and Mercer, G. (2010) *Exploring disability* (2nd edn), Cambridge: Polity Press.

Barnes, C. and Mercer, G. (eds) (1996) *Exploring the divide: Illness and disability*, Leeds: Disability Press.

Barnes. C. and Mercer. G. (2006) *Independent futures: Creating user-led services in a disabling society*, Bristol: BASW/The Policy Press.

Barnes, C., Mercer, G. and Shakespeare, T. (2003) *Exploring disability: A sociological introduction*, Cambridge: Polity Press.

Barton, L. and Corbett, J. (1993) 'Special needs in further education: the challenge of inclusive provision', *European Journal of Special Needs Education*, vol 8, no 1, pp 14–23.

BCODP (British Council of Organisations of Disabled People) (1986) *Disabled young people living independently*, London: BCODP.

Beck, U. (1992) *Risk society: Towards a new modernity*, Newbury Park, CA: Sage.

Beckett, A. (2009) 'Challenging disabling attitudes, building an inclusive society: considering the role of education in encouraging non-disabled children to develop positive attitudes towards disabled people', *British Journal of Sociology of Education*, vol 30, no 3, pp 317–29.

Begum, N. (1996) 'General practitioners' role in shaping disabled women's lives', in C. Barnes and G. Mercer (eds) *Exploring the divide: Illness and disability*, Leeds: Disability Press, pp 157–72.

Bennett, P. (1998) 'Special educational needs tribunals: an overview for educational psychologists', *Educational Psychology in Practice*, vol 14, no 3, pp 203–8.

Beresford, B. (1994) *Positively parents: Caring for a severely disabled child*, London: HMSO/SPRU.

Beresford, B. (1995) *Expert opinions: A national survey of parents caring for a severely disabled child*, Bristol: The Policy Press, in association with the Joseph Rowntree Foundation and Community Care.

Berthoud, R., Lakey, J. and McKay, S. (1993) *The economic problems of disabled people*, London: Policy Studies Institute.

Bethell, J. (2003) *'Our life, our say': An evaluation of a young disabled people's peer mentoring/support project*, York: Joseph Rowntree Foundation.

Bevan, A. (1948) 'A message to the medical profession from the minister of health', *British Medical Journal*, July 3, pp 45-65.

Bhaskar, R. (1975) *A realist theory of science*, London: Verso.

Bhaskar, R. (1997) *A realist theory of science* (2nd edn), London: Verso.

Bhaskar, R. (1998) *The possibility of naturalism: A philosophical critique of the contemporary human sciences* (3rd edn), London: Routledge.

Birenbaum, A. (1970) 'On managing a courtesy stigma', *Journal of Health and Social Behaviour*, vol 2, pp 196–206.

Black, J. (1978) 'Families with handicapped children – who helps whom and how?', *Child: Care, Health and Development*, vol 4, no 4, pp 239–45.

Board of Education (1958) *The health of the school child*, London: Ministry of Education.

Booth, T. and Booth, W. (1998) *Growing up with parents with learning difficulties*, London: Routledge.

Borsay, A. (2005) *Disability and social policy in Britain since 1750: A history of exclusion*, Basingstoke: Palgrave Macmillan.

Bourdieu, P. (1992) 'Rites as acts of institution', in J. Peristiany and J. Pitt-Rivers (eds) *Honor and grace in anthropology*, Cambridge: CUP, pp 79–89.

Bowlby, J. (1951) *Maternal care and mental health*, Geneva: World Health Organisation.

Bradbury, E., Kay, S., Tighe, C. and Hewison, J. (1994) 'Decision making by parents and children in paediatric hand surgery', *British Journal of Plastic Surgery*, vol 47, pp 324–30.

Bradley, S. (1995) 'The Youth Training Scheme: a critical review of the evaluation literature', *International Journal of Manpower*, vol 16, no 4, pp 30–56.

British Medical Association (2001) *Consent, rights, choices in health care for children and young people*, London: BMJ Books.

Bruce, M. (1966) *The coming of the welfare state*, London: Batsford.

Buckle, J. (1971) *Work and housing of impaired persons in Great Britain (Handicapped and impaired in Great Britain, Part II)*, London: Office of Population Census and Surveys.

Cahill, H. (2008) 'Male appropriation and medicalization of childbirth: an historical analysis', *Journal of Advanced Nursing*, vol 33, no 3, pp 334–42.

Calvocoressi, P. and Wint, G. (1972) *Total war*, London: Penguin.

Cameron, C. (2007) 'Whose problem? Disability narratives and available identities', *Community Development Journal*, vol 42, no 4, pp 501–11.

Campbell, J. and Oliver, M. (1996) *Disability politics: Understanding our past, changing our future*, London: Routledge.

Campling, J. (ed.) (1981) *Images of ourselves: Women with disabilities talking*, London: Routledge

Caputo, J. and Yount, M. (1993) *Foucault and the critique of institutions*, Pennsylvania, PA: Pennsylvania State University Press.

Carter, M. (1962) *Home school and work*, London: Pergamon Press.

Carter, N. (2008) 'A probable epidemic of congenital hydrocephalus in 1940–1941', *Developmental Medicine & Child Neurology*, vol 7, no 1, pp 61–4.

Carter, P. (2009) 'Fervour education', *Disability Now*, September, retrieved January 2010 from: www.disabilitynow.org.uk/living/features/fervour-education/.

Cavet, J. and Sloper, P. (2006) 'Participation of disabled children in individual decisions about their lives and in public decisions about service development', *Children & Society*, vol 18, no 4, pp 278–90.

Central Health Services Council (1959) *The welfare of children in hospital: Report of a committee of the CHSC (Chairman: Sir Harry Platt)*, London: Ministry of Health/HMSO.

Chamberlyne, P. and Rustin, M. (1999) 'From biography to social policy', *SOSTRIS Working Paper* 9, London: Centre for Biography in Social Policy, University of East London.

Charlton, J. (1998) *Nothing about us without us: Disability oppression and empowerment*, Berkeley, CA: University of California Press.

Charmaz, K. (1983) 'Loss of self: a fundamental form of suffering in the chronically sick', *Sociology of Health and Illness*, vol 5, pp 168–95.

Charmaz, K. (1994) 'Identity dilemmas of chronically ill men', *Sociological Quarterly*, vol 35, pp 269–88.

Charmaz, K. (1995) 'The body, identity, and self: adapting to impairment', *Sociological Quarterly*, vol 36, pp 657–80.

Chief Medical Officer (1958) *Health of the school child, 1956/57*, London: HMSO.

Chief Medical Officer (1962) *Health of the school child, 1960/61,* London: HMSO.

Clark, A. and Hirst, M. (1989) 'Disability in adulthood: ten-year follow-up of young people with disabilities', *Disability & Society,* vol 4, no 3, pp 271–83.

Clough, P. and Barton, L. (1999) *Articulating the difficulty: Research voices in inclusive education,* London: Paul Chapman.

Clough, P. and Corbett, J. (2004) *Theories of inclusive education: A students' guide,* London: Paul Chapman.

Cohen, D. (2001) *The war come home: Disabled veterans in Britain and Germany, 1914–1939,* Berkeley, CA: University of California Press

Cole, T. (1986) *Residential special education: Living and learning in a special school,* Milton Keynes: Open University Press.

Cole, T. (1989) *Apart or a part? Integration and the growth of British special education,* Milton Keynes: Open University Press.

Coleman, L. (1997) 'Stigma: an enigma demystified', in L. Davies (ed) *The disability studies reader,* New York: Routledge, pp 216–31.

Committee on the Child Health Services (1976) *Fit for the future* (Chairman: SDM Court), Cmnd 6684, London: HMSO.

Connors, C. and Stalker, K. (2003) *The views and experiences of disabled children and their siblings: A positive outlook,* London: Jessica Kingsley Publishers

Conservative Party (2010) *Invitation to join the government of Britain,* London: Alan Mabbutt on behalf of the Conservative Party.

Cowen, A. (1996) *Introducing the family fund trust for families with severely disabled children,* York: York Publishing Services.

Cribb, S. (1993) 'Are disabled artists cotton-wooled?', *Disability Arts Magazine,* vol 3, no 2, pp 10–11.

Croll, P. and Moses, D. (1998) 'Pragmatism, ideology and educational change: the case of special educational needs', *British Journal of Educational Studies,* vol 46, no 1, pp 11–25.

Cromwell, F. (1985) *Work-related programs in occupational therapy,* New York: Haworth Press.

Crow, L. (1990) *Disability in children's literature,* Transcript of a seminar by the Arts Council of Great Britain, Literature Department.

Crow, L. (1992) 'Renewing the social model of disability' in *Coalition,* July.

Daly, M. and Rake, K. (2003) *Gender and the welfare state: Care, work and welfare in Europe and the USA,* Cambridge: Polity.

Danieli, A. and Wheeler, P. (2006) 'Employment policy and disabled people, old wine in new glasses?', *Disability & Society,* vol 21, no 5, pp 485–98.

Daunton, M. (ed) (2000) *The Cambridge Urban History of Britain: 1840–1950*, Cambridge: Cambridge University Press.

Davidson, I., Woodill, G. and Bredberg, E. (1994) 'Images of disability in 19th century British children's literature', *Disability & Society*, vol 9, no 1, pp 33–46.

Davis, K. (1981) '28–38 Grove Road: accommodation and care in a community setting', in A. Brechin, P. Liddiard and J. Swain (eds) *Handicap in a social world*, London: Hodder and Stoughton, pp 322–7.

Davis, K. and Mullendar, A. (1993) *Ten turbulent years: A review of the work of the Derbyshire coalition of disabled people*, Nottingham: University of Nottingham Centre for Social Action.

DCLG (Department for Communities and Local Government) (2009) *Household projections to 2031, England: Housing statistical release, 11 March 2009*, London: DCLG.

DCSF (Department for Children, Schools and Families) (2010) *Breaking the link between special educational needs and low attainment: Everybody's business*, London: DCSF.

Department of Education and Science (1956) *Report of the committee on maladjusted children*, London: Stationery Office.

Department of Education and Science (1972) *The health of the school child: Report of the Chief Medical Officer of the Department of Education and Science for the years 1966–1969*, London: HMSO.

Dexter, M. and Harbert, W. (1983) *The home help service*, London: Tavistock.

DfE (Department for Employment) (1990) *Employment and training for people with disabilities: Consultative document*, London: HMSO.

DfE (Department for Education) (2010) *Green Paper: Children and young people with special educational needs and disabilities – call for views*, London: DfE.

DfES (Department for Education and Skills) (2003a) *Disabled children in residential placements*, London: DfES.

DfES (2003b) *Every child matters*, London: Stationery Office.

DfES (2007) *Special educational needs in England: January 2007*, London: DfES.

Disability Alliance (1987) *Poverty and disability: Breaking the link*, London: Disability Alliance.

Disney, R. and Webb, S. (1991) 'Why are there so many long term sick in Britain?', *The Economic Journal*, vol 101, no 405, pp 252–62.

Dobash, R. and Dobash, R. (1992) *Women, violence and social change*, London: Routledge.

DoH (Department of Health) (2001) *The expert patient: A new approach to chronic disease management in the 21st century*, London: The Stationery Office.

DoH (2002) *Residential special schools: National minimum standards inspection regulations*, London: The Stationery Office.

DoH/DfES (Department of Health/Department for Education and Skills) (2004a) *Disabled child standard, national service framework for children, young people and maternity services*, London: DoH.

DoH/DfES (2004b) *National service framework for children, young people and maternity services: Disabled children and young people and those with complex health needs*, London: Crown.

Dowling, M. and Dolan, L. (2001) 'Families with children with disabilities – inequalities and the social model', *Disability & Society*, vol 16, no 1, pp 21–35.

Drake, R.F. (1996) 'Charities, authority and disabled people: a qualitative study', *Disability & Society*, vol 11, no 1, pp 5–24.

Driedger, D. (1989) *The last civil rights movement*, London: Hurst & Co.

Edwards, J. (1958) 'Remploy: an experiment in sheltered employment for the severely disabled in Great Britain', *International Labour Review*, vol 77, pp 147–59.

Eisenstadt, S. (1956) *From generation to generation: Age groups and social structures*, Glencoe, IL: Free Press.

Elder, G. (1994) 'Time, human agency and social change; perspectives on the life course', *Social Psychology Quarterly*, vol 57, no 1, pp 4–15.

Field, F. (1977) 'Out for the count', *Low Pay Bulletin*, vol 13, pp 5–6.

Fiese, B., Hooker, K., Kotary, L., Scwagler, J. and Rimmer, M. (1995) 'Family stories in the early stages of parenthood', *Journal of Marriage and the Family*, vol 57, pp 763–70.

Finkelstein, V. (1993) 'The commonality of disability', in J. Swain, V. Finkelstein, S. French, and M. Oliver (eds) *Disabling barriers: Enabling environments*, London: Sage/Open University, pp 9–15.

Finkelstein, V. (1992) 'Disabled people and our culture development', *DAIL (Disability Art in London) magazine anthology: The first five years*, London: DAIL Magazine, pp 3–6.

Finkelstein, V. (2001) *The social model of disability repossessed*, retrieved January 2007, from http://www.leeds.ac.uk/disability-studies/archiveuk/finkelstein/soc%20mod%20repossessed.pdf

Finkelstein, V. (1999) 'A profession allied to the community: the disabled people's trade union', in E. Stone (ed) *Disability and Development: Learning from action and research on disability in the majority world*, Leeds: The Disability Press.

Foner, A. (1988) 'Age inequalities: are they epiphenomia of the class system?', in M.W. Riley (ed) *Social structures and human lives*, Newbury Park, CA: Sage, pp 176–91.

Fox, N. and Ward, K. (2006) 'Health identities: from expert patient to resisting consumer', *Health (London)*, vol 10, pp 461–79.

Fraser, D. (1973) *The evolution of the British welfare state: A history of social policy since the Industrial Revolution*, London: Macmillan.

Freidson, E. (1988) *Profession of medicine: A study of the sociology of applied knowledge*, Chicago: University of Chicago Press.

Frejka, T. and Sardon, J. (2005) *Childbearing trends and prospects in low-fertility countries: A cohort analysis*, Dordrecht: Kluwer Academic.

French, S. (ed) (1994) *On equal terms: Working with disabled people*, Oxford: Butterworth-Heinemann.

French, S. and Swain, J. (2000) 'Institutional abuse: memories of a 'special' school for visually impaired girls – a personal account', in J. Bornat, R. Perks, P. Thompson and J. Walmsley (eds) *Oral history, health and welfare*, London: Routledge, pp 159–79.

French, S. and Swain, J. (2006) 'Telling stories for a politics of hope', *Disability & Society*, vol 21, no 5, pp 383–96.

Fuller, M., Bradley, A. and Healey, M. (2004) 'Incorporating disabled students within an inclusive higher education environment', *Disability & Society*, vol 19, no 5, pp 455–68.

Furlong, A. and Biggart, A. (1999) 'Framing choices: a longitudinal study of occupational aspirations among 13 to 16 year-olds', *Journal of Education and Work*, vol 12, no 1, pp 21–36.

Furlong, A. and Cartmel, F. (1997) *Young people and social change: Individualisation and late modernity*, Buckingham: Open University Press.

Garland-Thomson, R. (1997) *Extraordinary bodies: Figuring physical disability in American culture and literature*, New York: Columbia University Press.

Giddens, A. (2008) *Sociology* (5th edn), Cambridge: Polity.

Giddens, A. (1984) *The constitution of society: Outline of the theory of structuration*, Berkeley, CA: University of California Press.

Giddens, A. (1991) *Modernity and self identity*, Cambridge: Polity.

Gill, C. (1997) 'Four types of integration in disability identity development', *Journal of Vocational Rehabilitation*, vol 9, pp 39–47.

Gillespie-Sells, K. and Campbell, J. (1991) *Disability equality training: Trainers guide*, London: CCETSW.

Gittens, D. (1982) *Fair sex: Family size and structure, 1900–39*, London: Hutchinson.

Goacher, B., Evans, J., Welton, J. and Wedell, K. (1988) *Policy and provision for special educational needs: Implementing the 1980 Education Act*, London: Cassell.

Goffman, E. (1959) *The presentation of self in everyday life*, Harmondsworth: Penguin.

Goffman, E. (1961) *Asylums: Essays on the social situation of mental patients and other inmates*, New York: Doubleday Anchor.

Goffman, E. (1968) *Stigma: Notes on the management of spoiled identity*, Harmondsworth: Pelican.

González, L. and Viitanen, T. (2009) 'The effect of divorce laws on divorce rates in Europe', *European Economic Review*, vol 53, no 2, pp 127–38.

Gooding, C. (2000) 'Disability Discrimination Act: from statute to practice', *Critical Social Policy*, vol 20, no 4, pp 533–49.

Goodley, D. (1996) 'Tales of hidden lives: a critical examination of life history research with people who have learning difficulties', *Disability & Society*, vol 11, no 3, pp 333–48.

Goodley D. and Tregaskis C. (2006) 'Storying disability and impairment: retrospective accounts of disabled family life', *Qualitative Health Research*, vol 16, no 5, pp 630–46.

Goodley, D., Lawthom, R., Clough, P. and Moore, M. (2004) *Researching life stories: Method, theory and analyses in a biographical age*, London: Routledge Falmer.

Gordon, C. and Longino, C. (2000) 'Age structure and social structure', *Contemporary Sociology*, vol 29, no 5, pp 699–703.

Gordon, D., Parker, R. and Loughran, F. with Heslop, P. (2000) *Disabled children in Britain: A re-analysis of the OPCS disability surveys*, London: Stationery Office.

Graham, H. (1985) 'Providers, negotiators and mediators: women as the hidden carers', in E. Lewin and V. Olesen (eds) *Women, health and healing: Towards a new perspective*, New York: Tavistock, pp 25–52.

Grant, I. (1961) 'Status of the general practitioner past, present and future', *British Medical Journal*, vol 2, no 5262, pp 1279–82.

Greenleigh Associates (1975) *The role of sheltered workshops in the rehabilitation of the severely handicapped*, New York: Greenleigh Associates, Inc.

Griffith, W. (1955) 'The first ten years of the Ministry of Education', *British Journal of Educational Studies*, vol 3, no 2, pp 101–14.

Griffiths, R. (1988) *Community care: Agenda for action: a report to the Secretary of State for Social Services*, London: HMSO.

Gruber, J. (2000) 'Disability employment benefits and labor supply', *Journal of Political Economy*, vol 208, no 6, pp 1162–83.

Habermas, T. and Bluck, S. (2000) 'Getting a life: the emergence of the life story in adolescence', *Psychological Bulletin*, vol 126, pp 748–69.

Halpin, D. (1999) 'Democracy, inclusive schooling and the politics of education', *International Journal of Inclusive Education*, vol 3, no 3, pp 225–38.

Halpin, D. and Lewis, A. (1996) 'The impact of the National Curriculum on twelve special schools in England', *European Journal of Special Needs Education*, vol 11, no 1, pp 95–105.

Hardiker, P. (1999) 'Children first: bringing disabled children within the child welfare fold', *Practice: Social Work in Action*, vol 11, no 4, pp 27–36.

Hareven, T. (2000) *Families, history and social change: Life course and cross cultural perspective*, Oxford: Westview Press.

Harris, A., Cox, E. and Smith, C. (1971) *Handicapped and impaired in Great Britain*, London: OPCS/HMSO.

Harris, N., Eden, K. and Blair, A. (2000) *Challenges to school exclusion: Exclusion, appeals, and the law*, London: Routledge Falmer.

Harrison, J., Henderson M. and Leonard, R. (2007) *Different dads: Fathers' stories of parenting disabled children*, London: Jessica Kingsley.

Harrison, M., Hemingway, L., Sheldon, A., Pawson, R. and Barnes, C. (2009) *Evaluation of provision and support for disabled students in higher education*, London: HEFCE.

Harrison, S. and Ahmad, W. (2000) 'Medical autonomy and the UK State 1975 to 2025', *Sociology*, vol 34, pp 129–46.

Harvey, D. and Greenway, A. (1984) 'The self-concept of physically handicapped children and their non-handicapped siblings: and empirical investigation', *Journal of Child Psychology and Psychiatry*, vol 25, no 2, pp 273–84.

Haskell, S. and Anderson, E. (1969) 'The education of physically handicapped children in ordinary schools', *The Irish Journal of Education*, vol 3, no 1, pp 41–54.

Hasler, F. (1993) 'Developments in the disabled people's movement', in J. Swain, V. Finkelstein, S. French, and M. Oliver (eds) *Disabling barriers: Enabling environments*, London: Sage/Open University, pp 278–84.

Healthcare Commission (2007) *Improving services for children in hospital*, London: Healthcare Commission.

Healthcare Commission (2009) *Improving services for children in hospital: Report of the follow-up to the 2005/06 review*, London: Healthcare Commission.

Heaton, J., Sloper, P. and Clarke, S. (2008) 'Access to and use of NHS Patient Advice and Liaison Service (PALS): the views of children, young people, parents and PALS staff', *Child: Care, Health & Development*, vol 34, no 2, pp 145–51.

Helfer, R. (1973) 'The etiology of child abuse', *Pediatrics*, vol 51, pp 777–9.

Herbert, E. and Carpenter, B. (1994) 'Fathers – the secondary partners; professional perceptions and fathers' reflections', *Children & Society*, vol 8, no 1, pp 31–41.

Hevey, D. (1993) 'The tragedy principle: strategies for change in the representation of disabled people', in J. Swain, V. Finkelstein, S. French and M. Oliver (eds) *Disabling barriers: Enabling environments*, London: Sage/Open University, pp 116–21.

Hirst, M. (1987) 'Careers of young people with disabilities between ages 15 and 21 years', *Disability & Society*, vol 2, no 1, pp 61–74.

HMSO (2004) *Social trends*, London: HMSO.

Hollomotz, A. (2009) 'Beyond 'vulnerability': an ecological model approach to conceptualizing risk of sexual violence against people with learning difficulties', *British Journal of Social Work*, vol 39, no 1, pp 99–12.

Holloway, S. (2001) 'The experience of higher education from the perspective of disabled students', *Disability & Society*, vol 16, no 4, pp 597–615.

Holmes, T. (1869) *The surgical treatment of the diseases of infancy and childhood*, London: Longman's.

Hornby, G. (1992) 'A review of fathers' accounts of their experiences of parenting children with disabilities', *Disability, Handicap & Society*, vol 7, no 4, pp 363–74.

House of Commons (1980) *Second report from the Social Services Committee: Session 1979–80: Perinatal and neonatal mortality* (Chairman: Mrs Renée Short), London: HMSO.

Hubbard, G. (2000) 'The usefulness of in-depth life history interviews for exploring the role of social structure and human agency in youth transitions', *Sociological Research Online*, vol 4, no 4, www.socresonline. org.uk/4/4/hubbard.html.

Hughes, B. (2007) 'Being disabled: towards a critical social ontology for disability studies', *Disability & Society*, vol 22, no 7, pp 673–84.

Hughes, B. and Paterson, K. (1997) 'The social model of disability and the disappearing body: towards a sociology of impairment', *Disability & Society*, vol 12, no 3, pp 325–40.

Humphries, S. and Gordon, P. (1992) *Out of sight: Experience of disability, 1900–50*, London: Channel Four.

Hunt, P. (1966) *Stigma: The experience of disability*, London: Geoffrey Chapman.

Hurt, J. (1988) *Outside the mainstream: A history of special education*, London: Routledge.

Hyde, M. (1998) 'Sheltered and supported employment in the 1990s: the experiences of disabled workers in the UK', *Disability & Society*, vol 13, no 2, pp 199–215.

Hyman, M. (1977) *The extra costs of disabled living*, London: National Fund for Research into Crippling Diseases.

Ignatieff, M. (1983) 'Total institutions and the working classes: a review essay', *History Workshop Journal*, vol 15, no 1, 167–73.

Illich, I. (1976) *Limits to medicine – medical nemesis: The expropriation of health*, London: Marian Boyars Publication.

Invalid Tricycle Association (1960) *Motor and electric invalid tricycles*, London: ITA.

Irwin, S. (1995) *Rights of passage: Social change and the transition from youth to adulthood*, ULC Press: London.

Irwin, S. (2000) 'Reproductive regimes: changing relations of inter-dependence and fertility change', *Sociological Research Online*, vol 5, no 1, www.socresonline.org.uk/5/1/irwin.html

Johnson, B. (1990) 'The changing role of families in healthcare', *Child Health Care*, vol 19, no 4, pp 234–41.

Johnson, M. and Sherman, S. (1990) 'Constructing and reconstructing the past and the future in the present', in E. Higgins and R. Sorrentino (eds) *Handbook of motivation and cognition: Foundations of social behavior*, New York: Guildford Press, pp 482–526.

Joint Committee on Mobility for the Disabled (1963) *The case for supplying suitably adapted small cars to the disabled*, London: Joint Committee on Mobility for the Disabled.

Joint Committee on Mobility for the Disabled (1968) *Conveyance of the disabled*, London: Spastics Society.

Jordan, D. (1979) *A new employment programme wanted for disabled people*, London: Disability Alliance.

Kalekin-Fishman, D. (2001) 'The hidden injuries of "a slight limp"', in M. Priestley (ed) *Disability and life course: Global perspectives*, Cambridge: CUP, pp 136–50.

Kanter, A. (2007) 'Promise and challenge of the United Nations Convention on the rights of persons with disabilities', *Syracuse Journal of International Law and Commerce*, vol 34, pp 287–318.

Kasnitz. D. (2001) 'Life event histories and the US independent living movement', in M. Priestley (ed) *Disability and life course: Global perspectives*, Cambridge: CUP, pp 67–78.

Keith, L. (2001) *Take up thy bed and walk: Death, disability and cure in classic fiction for girls*, London: The Women's Press.

Keller. H. (1905) *The story of my life,* New York: Doubleday, Page & Company.

Kelly, G., Lam, P., Thomas, A. and Turley, C. (2005) *Disability in the workplace: Small employers' awareness and responses to the Disability Discrimination Act (1995) and the October 2004 duties*, London: Department for Work and Pensions.

Kenworthy, J. and Whittaker, J. (2000) 'Anything to declare? The struggle for inclusive education and children's rights', *Disability & Society*, vol 15, no 2, pp 219–31.

Kerr, A. and Cunningham-Burley, S. (1998a) 'The new genetics and health: mobilizing lay expertise', *Public Understanding of Science*, vol 7, no 1, pp 41–60.

Kerr, A. and Cunningham-Burley, S. (1998b) 'Eugenics and the new genetics in Britain: examining contemporary professionals' accounts', *Science, Technology & Human Values*, vol 23, no 2, pp 175–98.

Kerr, A. and Shakespeare, T. (2002) *Genetic politics: From eugenics to genome*, Cheltenham: New Clarion Press.

Kew, S. (1975) *Handicap and family crisis: A study of the siblings of handicapped children*, London: Pitman.

Kochan, A. (1996) 'Remploy: disabled and thriving', *Assembly Automation*, vol 16, no 1, pp 40–1.

Kowalsky, M. (2007) '"This Honourable Obligation": The King's National Roll Scheme for Disabled Ex-Servicemen 1915–1944', *European Review of History: Revue européenne d'histoire*, vol 14, no 4, pp 567–84.

Kriegel, L. (1987) 'The cripple in literature', in A. Gartner and T. Joe (eds) *Images of the disabled: Disabling images*, New York: Praeger, pp 31–46.

Kuh, D., Lawrence, C., Tripp, J. and Creber, G. (1988) 'Work and work alternatives for disabled young people', *Disability & Society*, vol 3, no 1, pp 3–26.

Landsman, G. (1998) 'Reconstructing motherhood in the age of "perfect" babies: mothers of infants and toddlers with disabilities', *Signs: Journal of women in culture and society*, vol 24, pp 69–99.

Large, P. (1991) 'Paying for the additional costs of disability', in G. Dalley (ed) *Disability and social policy*, London: Policy Studies Institute, pp 101–5.

Laslett, P. (1977) *Family and illicit love in earlier generations*, Cambridge: University of Cambridge.

Law, B. and Watts, A. (1977) *Schools, careers and community*, London: Church Information Office.

Lawson, A. (2008) *Disability and equality law in Britain: The role of reasonable adjustment*, London: Hart Publishing.

Lawton, D. and Quine, L. (1990) 'Patterns of take-up of the Family Fund', *Child: Care, Health and Development*, vol 16, no 1, pp 35–53.

Levitas, R. (1996) 'The concept of social exclusion and the new Durkheimian hegemony', *Critical Social Policy*, vol 16, pp 5–20.

Lightfoot, J. and Sloper, P. (2003) 'Having a say in health: involving young people with a chronic illness or physical disability in local health services development', *Children & Society*, vol 17, pp 277–90.

Lomax, E. (1996) 'Small and special: the development of hospitals for children in Victorian Britain', *Medical History Supplement*, vol 16, pp 1–217.

Lonsdale, S. (1990) *Women and disability*, London: Macmillan.

Lowenthal, D. (1985) *The past is a foreign country*, Cambridge: Cambridge University Press.

McLaughlin, J., Goodley, D., Clavering, E. and Fisher, P. (2008) *Families raising disabled children: Enabling care and social justice*, Basingstoke: Palgrave.

McLean, K. and Pratt, M. (2006) 'Life's little (and big) lessons: identity statuses and meaning-making in the turning point narratives of emerging adults', *Developmental Psychology*, vol 42, pp 714–22.

McLean, K., Pasupathi, M. and Pals, J. (2007) 'Selves creating stories creating selves: a process model of self-development', *Personality and Social Psychology Review*, vol 11, pp 262–78.

Mallas, A. (1976) 'Current workshop practices: strengths and weaknesses', *Education and Training of the Mentally Retarded*, vol 11, pp 338–41.

Manheim, K. (1952) *Essays in the sociology of knowledge*, London: Routledge & Kegan Paul.

Martin, H. and Beezley, P. (1974) 'Prevention and the consequences of child abuse', *Journal of Operational Psychiatry*, vol 6, pp 68–77.

Martin, J. and White, A. (1988) *OPCS Report 2, the financial circumstances of disabled adults living in private households*, London: HMSO.

Martin, J., White, A. and Meltzer, H. (1989) *Disabled adults: Services, transport and employment*, London: HMSO.

Masefield, P. (2006) *Strength: Broadsides from disability on the arts*, London: Trentham Books Ltd.

Mattingley, S. (1965) 'Industrial rehabilitation', *British Medical Journal*, vol 1965, no 2, pp 930–2.

Mauldon, J. (1992) 'Children's risks of experiencing divorce and remarriage: do disabled children destabilize marriages?', *Population Studies*, vol 46, pp 349–62.

Meltzer, H., Smyth, M. and Robus, N. (1989) *Disabled children: Services, transport and education, OPCS surveys of disability in Great Britain, report 6*, London: HMSO.

Mental Deficiency Committee (1929) *Report of the Mental Deficiency Committee*, London: HMSO.

Michailakis, D. (2001) 'Information and communication technologies and the opportunities of disabled persons in the Swedish labour market', *Disability & Society*, vol 16, no 4, pp 477–500.

Middleton, L. (2003), *Disabled children: Challenging social exclusion,* Oxford: Blackwell Science Ltd.

Mills, C., (1959) *The sociological imagination*, Oxford: Oxford University Press.

Ministry of Education (1946) *Special educational treatment*, London: HMSO.

Ministry of Education (1959) *Handicapped pupils and special schools regulations*, London: Ministry of Education.

Ministry of Education (1961) *Special educational treatment for educationally subnormal pupils*, Circular 11/61, London: HMSO.

Ministry of Health (1948) *The development of specialist services*, Circular RHB(48)1, London: Ministry of Health.

Mitchell, D. and Snyder, S. (2000) *Narrative prosthesis: Disability and the dependencies of discourse (corporealities: discourses of disability)*, Michigan: University of Michigan Press.

Moncrieff, A. and Walton, A. (1952) 'Visiting children in hospital', *British Medical Journal*, vol 1952, no 1, pp 43–4.

More, C. (2007) *Britain in the twentieth century*, London: Pearson.

Morris, J. (1993) *Independent lives? Community care and disabled people*, Basingstoke: Macmillan.

Morris, J. (1998) *Still missing? Vol. 1: The experiences of disabled children and young people living away from their families*, London: The Who Cares? Trust.

Morris, J. (2007) *Centres for Independent Living/local user-led organisations: A discussion paper*, London: Department of Health/Crown.

Morris, J. (ed) (1989) *Able lives: Women's experience of paralysis*, London: The Women's Press.

Morris, J. Abbott, D. and Ward, L. (2002) 'At home or away? An exploration of policy and practice in the placement of disabled children at residential schools', *Children and Society*, vol 16, pp 3–16.

Morrison, E. and Finkelstein, V. (1993) 'Broken arts and cultural repair: the role of culture in the empowerment of disabled people', in J. Swain, V. Finkelstein, S. French and M. Oliver (eds) *Disabling barriers: Enabling environments*, London: Sage/Open University, pp 122–8.

Murphy, J. and Ashman, A. (1995) 'The education of children in hospital schools', *Australasian Journal of Special Education*, vol 19, no 1, pp 29–36.

Neale, B. and Flowerdew, J. (2003) 'Time, texture and childhood: the contours of longitudinal qualitative research', *International Journal of Social Research Methodology*, vol 6, no 3, pp 189–200.

Nixon, C. and Cummings, E. (1999) 'Sibling disability and children's reactivity to conflicts involving family members', *Journal of Family Psychology*, vol 13, no 2, pp 274–85.

Norwich, B. (1997) *Trend towards inclusion: Statistics on special school placements and pupils with statements in ordinary schools, England 1992–96*, Bristol: Centre for Studies on Inclusive Education.

Norwich, B. (2002) *Special school placement and Statements for English LEAs 1997–2001, Report for CSIE*, Exeter: University of Exeter.

Noyes, J. (2000) 'Enabling young "ventilator-dependent" people to express their views and experiences of their care in hospital', *Journal of Advanced Nursing*, vol 31, no 5, pp 1206–15.

ODI (Office for Disability Issues) (2009) *Factsheet – Employment*, retrieved January 2010 from: www.officefordisability.gov.uk/docs/res/factsheets/Factsheet_Employment.pdf

ODI (2010) *Disability equality indicators*, retrieved 30 April 2010 from: www.officefordisability.gov.uk/research/indicators.php

Office for National Statistics (2000) *School pupils: By type of school, 1970/71 – 1998/99*: Social Trends 30, London: Office for National Statistics.

Oliver, M. (1983) *Social work with disabled people*, Basingstoke: Macmillan.

Oliver, M. (1989) 'Conductive education: if it wasn't so sad it would be funny', *Disability & Society*, vol 4, no 2, pp 197–200.

Oliver, M. (1990) *The politics of disablement*, Basingstoke: Macmillan.

Oliver, M. (1996) *Understanding disability: From theory to practice*, Basingstoke: Macmillan.

Oswin, M. (1998) 'A historical perspective', in C. Robinson and K.Stalker (eds) *Growing up with disability*, London: Jessica Kingsley Publishers, pp 29–41

Pagel, M. (1988) *On our own behalf: An introduction to the self-organisation of disabled people*, Manchester: GMCDP.

Pahl, J. (1985) *Private violence and public policy: The needs of battered women and the response of the public services*, London: Routledge.

Parens, E. and Asch, A. (eds) (2000) *Prenatal testing and disability rights*. Washington, DC: Georgetown University Press.

Parfit, J. (1975) 'Siblings of handicapped children', *British Journal of Special Education*, vol 2, no 1, pp 19–21.

Parsons, T. (1951) *The social system*, London: Free Press/RKP.

Paterson, K. and Hughes, B. (1999) 'Disability studies and phenomenology: the carnal politics of everyday life', *Disability & Society*, vol 14, no 5, pp 597–610.

Pedersen, S. (1993) *Family, dependence, and the origins of the welfare state: Britain and France 1914–1945*, Cambridge: Cambridge University Press.

Pharoah, P., Platt, M. and Cooke, T. (1996) 'The changing epidemiology of cerebral palsy', *Archives of Disease in Childhood – Fetal and Neonatal Edition*, vol 75, no 3, pp F169–F173.

Piercy Report (1956) *Report of the Committee of Enquiry on the Rehabilitation, Training and Resettlement of Disabled Persons*, London: HMSO.

Pierson, P. (1994) *Dismantling the welfare state? Reagan, Thatcher and the politics of retrenchment*, Cambridge: Cambridge University Press.

Pinney, A. (2005) *Disabled children in residential placements*, London: Department for Education and Skills.

Pitt, V. and Curtin, M. (2004) 'Integration versus segregation: the experiences of a group of disabled students moving from mainstream school into special needs further education', *Disability & Society*, vol 19, no 4, pp 387–401.

Plowden Report (1967) *Children and their primary schools*, London: HMSO.

Plummer, K. (2001) *Documents of life*, London: SAGE.

Priestley, M. (1997) 'The origins of a legislative disability category in England: a speculative history', *Disability Studies Quarterly*, vol 17, no 2, pp 87–94.

Priestley, M. (1998a) *Disability politics and community care*, London: Jessica Kingsley.

Priestley, M. (1998b) 'Discourse and resistance in care assessment: integrated living and community care', *British Journal of Social Work*, vol 28, no 5, pp 659–73.

Priestley, M. (1998c) 'Childhood disability and disabled childhoods – agendas for research', *Childhood: A global journal of child research*, vol 5, no 2, pp 207–23.

Priestley, M. (1998d) 'Constructions and creations: idealism, materialism and disability theory', *Disability & Society*, vol 13, no 1, pp 75–94.

Priestley, M. (1999) 'Discourse and identity: disabled children in mainstream high schools', in S. French and M. Corker (eds) *Disability discourse*, Buckingham: Open University Press, pp. 92–102.

Priestley, M. (2000) 'Adults only: disability, social policy and the life course', *Journal of Social Policy*, vol 29, pp 421–39.

Priestley, M. (2003) *Disability: A life course approach*, Cambridge: Polity Press.

Priestley, M. (ed) (2001) *Disability and the life course: Global perspectives.* Cambridge: Cambridge University Press.

Priestley, M., Corker, M. and Watson, N. (1999) 'Unfinished business: disabled children and disability identities', *Disability Studies Quarterly*, vol 19, no 2, pp 87–98.

Priestley, M., Rabiee, P. and Harris, J. (2002) 'Young disabled people and the "New Arrangements" for leaving care in England and Wales', *Children and Youth Services Review*, vol 25, no 11, pp 863–90.

Prime Minister's Strategy Unit (2005) *Improving the life chances of disabled people: Final report*, London: PMSU.

Raz, A. (2005) 'Disability rights, prenatal diagnosis and eugenics: a cross-cultural view', *Journal of Genetic Counselling*, vol 14, no 3, pp 183–7.

Read, J. (1998) 'Conductive education and the politics of disablement', *Disability & Society*, vol 13, no 2, pp 279–93.

Read, J. (2000) *Disability, family and society: Listening to mothers*, Buckingham: Open University Press.

Record, R. and McKeown, T. (1949) 'Congenital malformations of the central nervous system: a survey of 930 cases', *British Journal of the Society of Medicine*, vol 4, pp 183–219.

Reed, J. and Harrison, C. (2002) 'Disabled children living away from home in the UK: recognizing hazards and promoting good practice', *Journal of Social Work*, vol 2, no 2, pp 211–32.

Reeve, D. (2002) 'Negotiating psycho-emotional dimensions of disability and their influence on identity constructions', *Disability & Society,* vol 17, no 5, pp 493–508.

Richardson, W. (2007) 'In search of the further education of young people in post-war England', *Journal of Vocational Education & Training*, vol 59, no 3, pp 385–418.

Rickman, J. (1939) 'Evacuation and the child's mind', Letter to the editor, *The Lancet*, 2 December, p 1192.

Riddell, S., Adler, M., Mordaunt, E. and Farmakopoulou, N. (2000) 'Special educational needs and competing policy frameworks in England and Scotland', *Journal of Education Policy*, vol 15, no 6, pp 621–35.

Riddell, S., Harris, N., Smith, E. and Weedon, E. (2010) 'Dispute resolution in additional and special educational needs: local authority perspectives', *Journal of Education Policy*, vol 25, no 1, pp 55–71.

Riddell, S., Pearson, C., Jolly, D., Barnes, C., Priestley, M. and Mercer, G. (2005a) 'The development of direct payments in the UK: implications for social justice', *Social Policy & Society*, vol 4, no 1, pp 75–85.

Riddell, S., Tinklin, T. and Wilson, A. (2005b) *Disabled students in higher education: Perspectives on widening access and changing policy*, London: Routledge.

Riley, J., Foner, A., Moore, M., Hess, B. and Roth, B. (1968) *Ageing and society, vol. 1: An inventory of research findings*, New York: Russell Sage Foundation.

Riley, M. and Riley, J. (1999) 'Sociological research on age: legacy and challenge', *Ageing and Society*, vol 19, pp 123–32.

Roberts, D. (1960) *Victorian origins of the British welfare state*, New Haven, CT: Yale University Press.

Roberts, E. (1984/1996) *Woman's place: An oral history of working class women, 1890–1940,* Oxford: Blackwell.

Roulstone, A. (1998) *Enabling technology: Disabled people, work and new technology*, Buckingham: Open University Press.

Roulstone, A. (2000) 'Disability, dependency and the New Deal for Disabled People', *Disability & Society*, vol 15, no 3, pp 427–43.

Roulstone, A. et al (2003) *Thriving and surviving at work: Disabled people's employments*, Bristol, The Policy Press.

Roulstone, A. and Morgan, H. (2009) 'Self directed support or neo-Liberalism: Are we speaking the same language on adult social care?', *Social Policy and Society*, vol 8, no 2, pp 333–45.

Rowe, J. and Lambert, L. (1973) *Children who wait*, London: ABAA.

Rowland-Crosby, N., Giraud-Saunders, A. and Swift, P. (2004) *Developing Connexions: Young people with disabilities, mental health needs or autistic spectrum disorders,* London: The Foundation for People with Learning Disabilities.

Runswick-Cole, K. (2007) '"The Tribunal was the most stressful thing: more stressful than my son's diagnosis or behaviour": the experiences of families who go to the Special Educational Needs and Disability Tribunal (SENDisT)', *Disability & Society*, vol 22, no 3, pp 315–28.

Russell, P. (1995) 'The importance of contact for children with disabilities', in H. Argent (ed) *See you soon: Contact with children who are looked after by local authorities*, London: BAAF, pp 100–19.

Rustin, M. (2000) 'Reflections on the biographical turn in social sciences', in P. Chamberlayne et al (eds) *The turn to biographical methods in social science*, London: Routledge, pp 33–52.

Rutter, M. (1972) *Maternal deprivation reassessed*, Harmondsworth: Penguin Press.

Ryder, N.B. (1965) 'The cohort as a concept in the study of social change', *American Sociological Review*, vol 30, no 6, pp 843–61.

Saldana, J. (2003) *Longitudinal qualitative research: Analyzing change through time*, Walnut Creek, CA: AltaMira Press.

Sanderson, A. (2001) 'Disabled students in transition: a tale of two sectors' failure to communicate', *Journal of Further and Higher Education*, vol 25, no 2, pp 227–40.

Sanghera, P. (2007) 'Abuse of children with disabilities in hospital: issues and implications', *Paediatric Nursing*, vol 19, no 6, pp 29–32.

Sass, E.J., Gottfried G. and Sorem, A. (1996) *Polio's legacy: An oral history*, Lunham, MD: University Press of America.

Scott, R.A. (1969) *The making of blind men: A study of adult socialization*, New York: Russell Sage Foundation.

Segal, S. (1961) 'Dull and backward children: post-war theory and practice', *Educational Research*, vol 3, no 3, pp 171–94.

Shah, R. (1995) *The silent minority: Children with disabilities in Asian families*, London, National Children's Bureau.

Shah, S. (2005a) *Career success of disabled high flyers*, London: Jessica Kingsley.

Shah, S. (2005b) 'Voices and choices: how education influences the career choices of young disabled people', *Journal of Research in Special Educational Needs*, vol 5, no 3, pp 112–17.

Shah, S. (2007) 'Special or mainstream? - the views of disabled students', *Research Papers in Education*, vol 22, no 4, pp 425–42.

Shah, S. (2008) *Young disabled people: Choices, aspirations and constraints*, Surrey: Ashgate.

Shah, S. and Priestley, M. (2009) 'Home and away: the impact of educational policies on disabled children's experiences of family and friendship', *Research Papers in Education*, vol 25, no 2, pp 155–74.

Shakespeare, T. (2006) *Disability rights and wrongs*, London: Routledge.

Shakespeare, T. (1996) 'Disability, identity and difference', in C. Barnes and G. Mercer (eds) *Exploring the divide*, Leeds: The Disability Press, pp 94–113.

Shakespeare, T. (1998) 'Choices and rights: eugenics, genetics and disability equality', *Disability & Society*, vol 13, no 5, pp 665–81.

Shaw, J. (2004) '"Expert patient" – dream or nightmare?', *British Medical Journal*, vol 328, pp 723–4.

Sheikh, K., Meade, T. and Mattingly, S. (1980) 'Unemployment and the disabled', *Rheumatology and Rehabilitation*, vol 19, pp 233–8.

Silver Jubilee Committee on Improving Access for Disabled People (1979) *Can disabled people go where you go?*, London: Department of Health and Social Security.

Smith, B. and Sparkes, A.C. (2008) 'Narrative and its potential contribution to disability studies', *Disability & Society*, vol 23, no 3, pp 17–28.

Social Exclusion Unit (1999) *Bridging the gap: New opportunities for 16–18 year olds not in education, employment or training*, London: HMSO.

Somers, R. (1994) 'The narrative construction of identity: a relational and network approach', *Theory and Society*, vol 23, pp 605–49.

Stacey, M., Dearden, R., Pill, R. and Robinson, D. (1970) *Hospitals, children and their families*, London: Routledge and Kegan Paul.

Stafford, B., Corden, A., Meah, A., Sainsbury, R. and Thornton, P. (2007) *New Deal for Disabled People: Third synthesis report – key findings from the evaluation*, Research Report No 430, London: Department for Work and Pensions.

Stone, D. (1984) *The disabled state*, London: Macmillan.

Strong, P. (1979) *The ceremonial order of the clinic, doctors and medical bureaucracies*, London: Routledge and Kegan Paul.

Sudbery, J. and Noyes, J. (1999) *The voices and choices of young people who use assisted ventilation: Bibliography and analysis of the literature*, York: Joseph Rowntree Foundation/University of Salford.

Sutherland, A. (1997) 'Disability arts, disability politics', in A. Pointon with C. Davies (eds) *Framed: Interrogating disability in the media*, London: British Film Institute, pp 182–3.

Swain, J. and French, S. (2001) 'The relationship between disabled people and health and well professionals', in G. Albrect, K. Seelman and M. Bury (eds) *Handbook of disability studies*, Thousand Oaks, CA: Sage, pp 734–53.

Swain, J. and Cameron, C. (1999) 'Unless otherwise stated: discourses of labeling and identity in coming out', in M. Corker and S. French (eds) *Disability discourse*, Buckingham: Open University Press, pp 68–78.

Szreter, S. (2009) 'History, policy and the social history of medicine', *Social History of Medicine*, vol 22, no 2, pp 235–44.

Tates, K. and Meeuwesen, L. (2001) 'Doctor-patient-child communication: a (re)view of the literature', *Social Science and Medicine*, vol 52, pp 839–51.

Thomas, C. (1998) 'Parents and family: disabled women's stories about their childhood experiences', in C. Robinson and K. Stalker (eds) *Growing up with disability*, London: JKP, pp 85–96.

Thomas, C. (1999) *Female forms: Experiencing and understanding disability*, Buckingham: Open University Press.

Thomas, C. (2001) 'Medicine, gender and disability: disabled women's health care encounters', *Health Care for Women International*, vol 22, no 3, pp 245–62.

Thomas, C. (2007) *Sociologies of disability and iIllness: Contested ideas in disability studies and medical sociology*, London: Palgrave Macmillan.

Thomas, P. (2004) 'Disablism and charity', *Coalition*, November.

Thompson, P., Lavery, M. and Curtice, J. (1990) *Short changed by disability*, London: Disability Income Group.

Thomson, R., Plumridge, L. and Holland, J. (2003) 'Longitudinal qualitative research: a developing methodology', *International Journal of Social Research Methodology*, vol 6, no 3, pp 185–7.

Thornton, P. and Corden, A. (2002) *Evaluating the impact of Access to Work: A case study approach*, Sheffield: DWP.

Thornton, P. and Lunt, N. (1995) *Employment for disabled people: Social obligation or individual responsibility?*, York: Social Policy Research Unit.

Tin, W., Wariyar, U. and Hey, E. (1997) 'Changing prognosis for babies of less than 28 weeks' gestation in the north of England between 1983 and 1994', *British Medical Journal*, vol 314, no 7074, pp 107–11.

Tomlinson, G. (1943) *Report of the Inter-departmental Committee on the Rehabilitation and Resettlement of Disabled Persons*, London: HMSO.

Tomlinson, S. (1982) *A sociology of special education*, London: Routledge.

Topliss, E. (1975) *Provision for the disabled*, Oxford: Blackwell/Martin Robertson.

Topliss, E. (1979) *Provision for the disabled* (2nd edn), Oxford, Blackwell/Martin Robertson.

Topliss, E. and Gould, B. (1981) *A charter for the disabled: The Chronically Sick and Disabled Persons Act 1970*, Oxford: Blackwell.

Tregaskis, C. (2006) 'Parents, professionals and disabled babies: personal reflections on disabled lives', in D. Goodley and R. Lawthon (eds) *Disability and psychology: Critical introductions and reflections*, Basingstoke: Palgrave Macmillan.

Ulrich, M. (2000) *Life course in the transformation of East Germany*, Madrid: Instituto Juan March de Estudios e Investigaciones.

United Nations Committee on the Rights of the Child (2008) *Consideration of reports submitted by states parties under Article 44 of the convention, Concluding observations: United Kingdom of Great Britain and Northern Ireland*, CRC/C/GBR/CO/4, New York: UN.

UPIAS (Union of Physically Impaired Against Segregation)/Disability Alliance (1976) *Fundamental principles of disability*, London: UPIAS/Disability Alliance.

Vasey, S. (1992) 'Disability arts and culture: an introduction to key issues and questions', in S. Lees (ed) *Disability arts and culture papers*, London: Shape, pp 7–13.

Vehkakoski, T. (2007) 'Newborns with an impairment: Discourses of hospital staff', *Qualitative Health Research*, vol 17, no 3, pp 288–99.

Vernon, A. (1999) 'The dialectics of multiple identities and the disabled people's movement', *Disability & Society*, vol 14, no 3, pp 385–98.

Vickerstaff, S. (2003) 'Apprenticeship in the "golden age": were youth transitions really smooth and unproblematic back then?', *Work, Employment & Society,* vol 17, no 2, pp 269–87.

Vierzigmann, G. and Kreher, S. (1998) '"Zwischen den Generationen": Familiendynamik und Familiendiskurse in biographischen Erzählungen' ['"Between generations": Family dynamics and family discourses in biographical accounts'], *Berliner Journal für Soziologie,* vol 8, no 1, pp 23–38.

Vincent, C., Evans, J., Lunt, I. and Young, P. (1996) 'Professionals under pressure: the administration of special education in a changing context', *British Journal of Educational Research,* vol 22, no 4, pp 475–90.

Walker, A. (1980) 'The handicapped school leaver and the transition to work', *British Journal of Guidance & Counselling,* vol 8, no 2, pp 212–23.

Warnock Report (1978) *Special educational needs: (Report of the Committee of Enquiry into the Education of Handicapped Children and Young People),* London: HMSO.

Warren, J. (2005) 'Disabled people, the state and employment: historical lessons for welfare policy', in A. Roulstone and C. Barnes (eds) *Working futures: Disabled people, employment policy and social inclusion,* Bristol: The Policy Press, pp 301–14.

Watson, N. (2002) 'Well, I know this is going to sound very strange to you, but I don't see myself as a disabled person: identity and disability', *Disability & Society,* vol 17, no 5, pp 509–27.

Watson, N. and Woods, B. (2005) 'No wheelchairs beyond this point: a historical examination of wheelchair access in the twentieth century in Britain and America', *Social Policy & Society,* vol 4, no 1, pp 97–105.

Watson, N., Shakespeare, T., Cunningham-Burley, S., Barnes, C., Corker, M., Davis, J. and Priestley, M. (1999) *Life as a disabled child: A qualitative study of young people's experiences and perspectives,* Edinburgh and Leeds: Universities of Edinburgh and Leeds.

Watts, A. (2001) 'Career guidance and social exclusion: a cautionary tale', *British Journal of Guidance & Counselling,* vol 29, no 2, pp 157–76.

Wendell, S. (1996) *The rejected body: Feminist philosophical reflections on disability,* New York: Routledge.

Westcott, H. (1994) 'Abuse of children and adults who are disabled', in S. French (ed) *On equal terms: Working with disabled people,* Oxford: Butterworth-Heinemann, pp 190–206.

Westcott, H. and Cross, M. (1996) *This far and no further: Tending the abuse of disabled children,* Birmingham: Venture Press.

Williams, B., Copestake, P., Eversley, J. and Stafford, B. (2008) *The experiences and expectations of disabled people,* London: Office for Disability Issues/DWP.

Williams, F. (1989) *Social policy: A critical introduction: issues of race, gender and class*, Cambridge: Polity Press.

Williams, P. (1965) 'The ascertainment of educationally subnormal children', *Educational Research*, vol 7, no 2, pp 136–46.

Wilson-Costello, D., Friedman, H., Minich, N., Fanaroff, A. and Hack, M. (2005) 'Improved survival rates with increased neurodevelopmental disability for extremely low birth weight infants in the 1990s', *Pediatrics,* vol 115, pp 997–1003.

Wood, C. and Grant, E. (2010) *Destination unknown*, London: Demos.

Woods, B. and Watson, N. (2004) 'A glimpse at the social/technological history of wheelchairs', *International Journal of Therapy and Rehabilitation*, vol 11, no 9, pp 407–10.

Woods, B. and Watson, N. (2005) 'When wheelchair innovation in Britain was under state control', *Technology and Disability*, vol 17, no 4, pp 237–50.

Young, M. and Willmott, P. (1957) *Family and kinship in East London,* London: Routledge.

Zola, I. (1972) 'Medicine as an institution of social control', *Sociological Review*, vol 20, no 4, pp 487–504.

Zola, I. (1977) 'Healthism and disabling medicalization', in I. Illich, I. Zola, J. McKnight, J. Caplan and H. Shaiken (eds) *Disabling professions*, London: Calder & Boyars, pp 41–68.

Index